Revenuers and

Moonshiners

. . . .

Revenuers &

Moonshiners

· · · · · · · · · · · · · ·

Enforcing
Federal
Liquor Law
in the
Mountain
South,
1865–1900
**Wilbur R.
Miller**

The University of

North Carolina Press

Chapel Hill & London

© 1991 The University of North Carolina Press

All rights reserved

Manufactured in the United States of America

The paper in this book meets the guidelines for permanence and durability of the Committee
on Production Guidelines for Book Longevity of the Council on Library Resources.

95   94   93   92   91   5   4   3   2   I

Library of Congress Cataloging-in-Publication Data

Miller, Wilbur R., 1944–

  Revenuers and moonshiners : enforcing federal liquor law in the mountain South, 1865–
1900 / by Wilbur R. Miller.

    p. cm.

  Including bibliographical references and index.

  ISBN 0-8078-1959-X (alk. paper).—ISBN 0-8078-4330-X (pbk.: alk. paper)

    1. Distilling, Illicit—Appalachian Region—History—19th century.   2. Liquor laws—Appa-
lachian Region—History—19th century.   3. Southern States—History—1865–1951.
I. Title.

HJ5021.M55   1991

364.1′33—dc20   90-49549

                                                                             CIP

Some material in this book was previously published in "The Revenue: Federal Law Enforcement and Popular Resistance in the Mountain South, 1865–1900," *Journal of Southern History*
55 (May 1989): 196–216. Copyright 1989 by the Southern Historical Association. Reprinted
by permission of the managing editor.

TO CAROLE

Contents

. . . .

A map will be found on page 2, and a section of illustrations

will be found beginning on page 82.

Preface

. . . .

This book began as something else, a study of federal civil rights law enforcement during the Reconstruction era of the 1870s. My previous work on urban policing and several years of teaching a course on the Civil War and Reconstruction led me to see Reconstruction as a novel federal policing effort in the face of determined southern resistance. Part of the explanation for its failure could be found in difficulties and dilemmas of balancing force and restraint experienced by ordinary policemen. Research in this area, though, soon convinced me that many other scholars have covered this ground and that I would add only a slight twist to familiar interpretations.

The apparent dead end led to this book. Amid the mountain of archival material on enforcement of Reconstruction civil rights and election laws were many references to internal revenue and moonshiners. In fact, most of the correspondence of several southern federal district attorneys was concerned with difficulties in collecting the whiskey tax and dealing with violent resistance. I had serendipitously found a new topic, one that not only addresses the police problem of federal authority in an area that has been scarcely explored, but adds a new element to historians' ongoing debates about whether the Civil War left a legacy of permanently expanded federal power.

In addition, the study of revenue enforcement offered a chance to compare it to Reconstruction, since many of the same officials were engaged in both tasks, though usually in different regions of their states. Contrasting the failure of Reconstruction with the relative success of revenue enforcement contributes to understanding a central question: What are the conditions under which unpopular laws can be enforced, and what are the limits of their enforcement? Policies and practices of government officials, political calculations and needs, and the nature of the people resisting authority all entered the picture.

The confrontation between revenuers and moonshiners who refused to pay the federal excise tax on their home-distilled whiskey was localized, mostly confined to the southern Appalachians. Local people, though, were challenging a fundamental aspect of national authority, the ability of the government to collect its taxes. A regional confrontation became a national issue, and its history is part of the nation's history.

This study is more about revenuers than moonshiners, adding to knowledge of federal policing, the nature of national authority, and the growth of a bureaucratic state in the late nineteenth century. Consequently, moonshining and its practitioners are seen from the perspective of the revenuers. I am not trying to make heroes of the revenuers, for it will be clear that there were corrupt and brutal men among them as well as some who were honest and brave. The ordinary revenuer had a job to do and usually tried to do it to the best of his ability.

Since this is an account of the interaction between federal officials and moonshiners, something about the moonshiners themselves and the southern Appalachian society in which they lived must be part of the story. Moonshiners have been traditional heroes, representatives of a stubborn individualism that appeals to Americans' resentment of government interference in their lives. Moonshiners have also been presented as simple country folk, victims of outside forces beyond their understanding or control. I have not sought to debunk or support either image but, in general, have come to understand moonshiners as men, and sometimes women, going about their business for a variety of reasons or motives. This discussion begins with chapter 2, and general readers may wish to begin there, since the first chapter addresses issues mostly of interest to specialists in late-nineteenth-century institutional history.

In describing mountain society, I have been able to rely primarily on the work of a group of historians, notably Ronald Eller, Gordon McKinney, Altina Waller, Durwood Dunn, and others acknowledged in my notes, who during the last ten or fifteen years reshaped our understanding of Appalachia. Reading their books, and the responses of McKinney, Waller, and an anonymous manuscript reader to my work, has enabled me to understand the moonshiner quite differently from the old, very widely disseminated image of the backward, quaint, squirrel-rifle-and-whiskey-jug-toting hillbilly. He and sometimes she were part of a changing society, a product of both the traditional aspects of mountain culture and the forces of industrialization that were reshaping Appalachian society after the Civil War. Revenuers were but one of the novelties many mountain people faced.

Thanks are due to Harold Hyman, who has followed this project as it took shape over the years and offered both encouragement and caution against trying to carry my arguments too far. If I am insufficiently cautious here, of course I cannot say that I did not have warning. William F. Holmes, the first academic historian to pay attention to moonshiners, also deserves thanks here for support in the early stages of this study.

Thanks to my wife, Carole Turbin, belong here rather than the usual place at the end. In the midst of writing her own book, she helped me figure out what mine was really about and contributed to formulating its argument. Her confidence was essential in seeing a very long and drawn-out project to its completion.

In addition to these intellectual debts is the practical help every researcher receives from archivists and librarians. I wish to thank especially Cynthia Fox and William Sherman, who seemed to take a personal interest in my hunt through Department of Justice and Bureau of Internal Revenue records in the National Archives. Likewise, Mary Ann Hawkins and Charles Reeves of the Atlanta Branch of the National Archives cheerfully helped in my efforts to mine at least the surface of their rich collection of federal court records. The staffs of the Southern Historical Collection and North Carolina Collection at the University of North Carolina at Chapel Hill were always courteous and efficient, as were those at the West Virginia University Library and the University of Georgia Library. Although my work there was more routine and less personal, the New York Public, Columbia University, New York University, and the SUNY Stony Brook libraries proved to be especially useful as well as convenient.

David Perry of the University of North Carolina Press kept faith in this book's sometimes rough progress toward publication. Ron Maner, project editor, and Stephanie Wenzel, copyeditor, people important in the publishing process who are not often acknowledged, deserve thanks for their contributions.

Finally, I wish to thank various funding agencies and hope that the book will justify their confidence in its author. The State University of New York's Research Foundation provided a grant that got this project started in its original form. The American Council of Learned Societies awarded me a fellowship which gave me the time and momentum to finish the book. The American Historical Association, the American Philosophical Society, and the National Endowment for the Humanities provided travel funds for trips to various collections.

I Reconstruction, Revenue, and the National State

. . . .

Amos Owens of Rutherford County, North Carolina, was one of many southerners who resisted the national government's intrusion into their way of life after the Civil War. He returned from the war to find his slave freed and a heavy tax imposed on the liquor he had been making for years. Owens responded to these two forms of Yankee oppression by joining the Ku Klux Klan and becoming a celebrated moonshiner. His double confrontation with federal authority landed him in prison three times, the first for violating the Reconstruction-era law against Klan activity, the other two for illicit distilling contrary to the revenue laws. There were others like Owens, Klansmen and moonshiners, who challenged the authority of the national state when it reached into their lives to punish activities they themselves did not consider crimes.[1]

Many contemporary observers believed that Union victory in the Civil War left the federal government a legacy of greatly increased power. This legacy included the constitutional amendments guaranteeing civil rights for emancipated blacks. These had to be enforced against southern whites' violence, fraud, and intimidation, mobilizing the federal judicial system and army against Owens and his fellow white supremacists. Taken more for granted by contemporaries and less well known to historians, the war also fostered another expansion of the state, a far-reaching system of internal revenue taxation. Wartime excise taxes on whiskey, tobacco, and other items were retained to pay the huge national debt and the cost of the government's

The Mountain South

expanded operations. Collection of these taxes required an army of new officials to insure that every drop of whiskey produced contributed its share of the revenue. These officials often confronted moonshiners like Owens who resisted taxation of traditional mountain dew. This book tells a largely untold story of how the revenue system developed into a permanent feature of the national government, and of its long struggle to assert and maintain its power to impose liquor taxes in the moonshiners' southern mountain domain. Operating within the limits of the nineteenth-century federal government, the bureau and its officials both embodied many of those limits and foreshadowed later development of a national state, an administrative apparatus capable of penetrating all parts of the nation's territory. [2]

Both contemporary commentators and historians analyzing the expansion of national authority after the Civil War have focused on the Reconstruction experience. James G. Blaine argued that the Republican party politicians who dominated the federal government after the war discovered that "every thing which may be done by either Nation or State may be better and more securely done by the Nation. The change of view . . . led to far-reaching consequences." Most historians, however, argue that Reconstruction's contributions to expanded federal power were not in fact very far-reaching. Emphasizing the failure of Reconstruction, they contend that efforts to protect civil rights did not lead to a permanent administrative state. They stress that centralization was narrowly confined by the nation's federal structure and American political traditions, which sharply restricted the institutional means of enforcing federal laws. The Civil War, according to Morton Keller, gave Americans a *sense* of profound social and political change more than it actually implanted permanent expansion of national authority.[3]

The collapse of civil rights enforcement in the face of southern resistance seems to have inhibited development of centralized power for many years. Reconstruction succumbed to traditional American racism, localism, and commitment to laissez-faire economics, revealing a lack of social underpinning for the novel assertion of national power. One historian, expanding on a turn-of-the-century commentator's phrase, described the federal government as a "weakened spring" in the later nineteenth century. Harold Hyman argues that the Civil War's impact on governmental power was far more important on the state than the national level. Stephen Skowronek minimizes the Reconstruction era's significance in the development of an

American administrative state and describes a patchwork slowly and un-evenly emerging into a coherent set of institutions only in the early twenti-eth century. The end of Reconstruction seemed to mark the close of a period of institutional change instead of paving the way for a new type of national authority.[4]

However, historians who have emphasized the restricted role of govern-ment after Reconstruction have overlooked the internal revenue system.[5] Students of administrative history and development of federal power are practically silent about the Bureau of Internal Revenue, looking instead to formation of a professional civil service, reform of the army, and economic regulation as sources of growing national authority. The revenue bureau deserves more than the passing nod it has received.

If a government is to be effective, able to extend its authority throughout its territory, then it must efficiently collect its taxes. The agency with that duty plays an important role in integrating the nation and in developing citizens' acceptance of an obligation to maintain their government. People pay taxes, not because they have a strong sense of patriotic duty, but because they fear the consequences of not paying. Even one person's resistance to taxation is a test of national authority that must be contained before it encourages other people to believe they can also get away with evasion. Individual moonshiners did not cost the government much in lost tax money, but collectively they did withhold substantial revenues. If moon-shiners believed that the authorities would leave them alone, more and more people in the southern Appalachian heartland of moonshining would take up "wildcat" distilling of corn whiskey or fruit brandy. Revenue officials could never eliminate moonshining, but they sought to make it clear that most illicit distillers would eventually face the consequences—fine and imprisonment—of their evasion.

Internal revenue or excise taxation had never been popular in America. The excise of 1791 prompted the famous whiskey rebellion two years later. Although the government suppressed the tax rebels, it retreated from its first attempt to collect excises. During the War of 1812 the liquor tax was only temporary and not burdensome on small distillers. The Civil War taxation, which extracted dollars and pennies from a vast number of prod-ucts and transactions, was also meant to be a temporary war measure. After the conflict, most of the excise taxes were lifted, but those on liquor and tobacco have remained to this day. Though levied on manufacturers, they appeared in higher prices paid only by individuals who chose to drink and smoke. To many supporters there was a moral component of the excises because they would raise the price of vice and reduce consumption. The tax did not discourage drinking or smoking, however, and the moral argument fell out of favor during the 1870s. The strongest argument for retention of the taxes, which temperance advocates began to view as an evil of the revenue system, was that the income from liquor and tobacco excises became a significant and necessary component of government revenues. The war's huge public debt had to be paid off, and as the years went by the government owed more to citizens in the form of veterans' pensions. During the 1880s, Treasury surpluses appeared as the national debt was liquidated, and some people advocated abolishing internal revenue taxation completely. Nevertheless, the whiskey and tobacco taxes came to be accepted by both political parties. Republicans had created the system and, while they dominated the executive branch, had a stake in its success, even though the party preferred increasing the protective tariff to meet the cost of government as well as to shelter American industry. Democrats, who furiously denounced the revenue system as oppressive centralization when they were out of power, discovered that if they wished to lower the tariff they had to maintain internal taxes. Like the Republicans, they also appreciated the hundreds of patronage appointments the tax collection apparatus provided. Although subject to partisan criticism of its administration by whichever party was on the "outs," the liquor excise and its collection bureaucracy had become an essential component of the state that neither party was ready to jettison.

During the later 1870s the revenue bureau established its ability to impose and collect taxes on liquor and tobacco. After several years of inefficiency and corruption, culminating in the notorious whiskey ring scandal of the mid-1870s, the bureau consolidated its regulatory aspect, the careful monitoring of distilleries to insure taxation of their entire product.

Bureau officials and distillers developed a close relationship that sometimes encouraged local corruption but usually reflected a sense of the mutual interests of the regulators and the regulated industry. Taxpaying distillers became important allies in the bureau's crusade against evasion. Revenuers and distillers also became allies against growing prohibition sentiment.

The heads of the bureau, called commissioners, were political appointees and presided over a vast patronage empire of hundreds of employees. Despite their essential partisan role, the commissioners developed a professional sense of their duty and responsibility that called for high standards of competence and honesty among their subordinates. Exceptions there were, but the bureau heads sought to weed them out when they learned of them. Commissioner Green B. Raum, who significantly improved the revenue service's honesty and efficiency between 1876 and 1883, used the success of his own bureau as an argument against the need for a civil service law. Under Raum, the revenue bureau also became an effective police agency, seeking out the moonshiners who distilled and sold their mountain dew without paying their share to Uncle Sam. Working with U.S. marshals who served warrants or arrested moonshiners caught in the act, and district attorneys who prosecuted all federal offenders, local revenue officials never abandoned their efforts despite continuing resistance and periods of discouragement and crisis.

Popular accounts of moonshining have generally pictured revenue enforcement as a futile effort against stubborn and determined individualists. Revenuers might be able to win battles, but never the war. In some regions they indeed confronted what seemed to be perpetual guerilla warfare, but the moonshiners could never feel permanently secure against arrest and seizure of their stills. Revenuers considered themselves successful when their informers came forward to reveal hidden stills and their raids discouraged violent resistance. The revenue bureau's simple goal was to bring in more tax money, both by discouraging widespread moonshining and encouraging mountain people to open small legal distilleries.

The bureau usually achieved its goals after the mid-1870s, except in two periods of protracted warfare. The first was in the late 1870s and early 1880s, when Commissioner Raum was making his determined effort to crack down on moonshiners. The outcome of his battle was uncertain at first, his efforts actually inspiring heavier resistance. At the end, though, he could point to increased tax revenues, decreased violence, and greater support from local citizens. His successors during the 1880s had to cope with localized resistance, but not the organized efforts of Raum's day. The second crisis came during the national depression of the 1890s, when farmers became desperate for cash that could be earned from mountain dew and Congress raised the liquor tax to compensate for a growing federal deficit. Revenue officials of both political parties had to cope with an outbreak of moonshining and increased resistance. They were able to contain, though not entirely eliminate, evasion and violence by the early 1900s.

The twentieth century introduced a complicating factor, the spread of local and state prohibition, which changed the nature of the conflict and undermined revenuers' gains during the late nineteenth century. The drying up of more and more areas of the South during the early 1900s eliminated all legal sale and local manufacture of liquor, encouraging moonshiners to become businessmen producing "white lightnin'" for a greatly expanded market. Prohibition laws encouraged moonshining in dry areas, but also in neighboring wet districts that exported their product to dry ones. This traffic made the federal task of tax collection more difficult even where prohibition was not in effect. Nevertheless, the revenuers kept up their fight and held their ground against growing numbers of opponents.

The arrival of national prohibition in 1920, a far greater expansion of the state than tax collection, led federal officials from a difficult task to an impossible one. Making drinkers pay higher prices for their liquor and punishing tax evaders were state powers most citizens recognized; denying drinkers the right to buy their liquor was state imposition of one group's morality upon another group. The revenue bureau had won increasing public support in its wars against moonshiners, but prohibition alienated thousands of people who had accepted the government's right to tax liquor but who exercised their own right to drink or not as they pleased.

In many ways national prohibition was a failure of state power comparable to Reconstruction: in both cases the federal government was attempting to enter citizens' lives by radically altering familiar institutions and behavior. Like prohibition, civil rights laws aroused growing opposition, and the government was unwilling to commit the resources necessary to overcome it. A closer look at the weaknesses of Reconstruction highlights the reasons why revenue enforcement was relatively successful before prohibition upset the delicate balance between authority and resistance.

Reconstruction, originally hailed by its champions as a bold assertion of federal authority to protect the rights of newly enfranchised black citizens, succumbed to growing resistance in the South and declining support in the North. Although southern violence had at first hardened northern determination to maintain Reconstruction, as the years went by its persistence, despite suppression of the original Ku Klux Klan, made many northerners believe that law and order were best preserved by abandoning Reconstruction enforcement and leaving white southerners alone. Over the years northerners became less committed to Reconstruction, and the effort to protect civil rights became more isolated as a partisan program of the Republican party.[6]

Many Americans, Republicans among them, believed that passage of constitutional amendments, civil rights laws, and force acts were sufficient demonstrations of national supremacy and protection of citizens' rights. Massachusetts senator Henry Wilson hoped that the strength of the national government, "going out from the capital into the lawless regions of the country, will awe and put down lawless men and strengthen the weak and timid, and give courage to men who would have law and order." Republicans spoke as if they supported a strong national state, but they never really faced the problem of how much force was needed to "awe and put down lawless men" in the South. They were unwilling to provide the financial and manpower resources for a sustained, permanent enforcement of Reconstruction. American cultural and political traditions effectively ruled out a national police force or a standing army that could provide the protection black citizens and their white allies needed.[7]

Northern Democrats and their southern allies appealed to traditional fear of standing armies and centralized government to undermine support for Reconstruction. They fostered a myth that the federal government had dangerously expanded its control over states and individuals. Some Republicans joined Democrats in their aversion to creating another Ireland, where repressive force had become permanent, increasing resentment and bitterness instead of increasing respect for law and order. Democrats attacked Republicans at a vulnerable point, their "insolence and arrogance" in claiming that their party "is the state."[8]

Republicans, who dominated national government for fifteen years, indeed acted as if their party were the state and did not develop a state independent of the party. Many people came to perceive Reconstruction simply as a partisan device to keep Republicans in power. As resistance to Reconstruction continued and southerners won sympathizers in the North, many Republicans themselves began to see civil rights enforcement as politically inexpedient. If retaining power meant abandoning principle, the choice was clear. Radicals who had blended a concern for power with principle faded from the scene during the 1870s, leaving party leadership to moderates and "stalwarts" who valued officeholding above all. Reconstruction would survive only as long as Republicans believed it politically useful and were powerful enough to implement it.

As Stephen Skowronek argues, none of the new national powers that Republicans exercised were "beyond the reach of party concerns." Although the Department of Justice and the United States Circuit Courts were direct outgrowths of Reconstruction, national power did not rest on a firm basis of permanent institutions. Supreme Court decisions gnawed away at the expansion of federal authority granted by Reconstruction legislation, and Democrats in Congress slashed appropriations and restricted the police role of the army. Unlike the revenue system when the Democrats inherited its administration in 1885, the national power that Reconstruction had created effectively disappeared with the end of Republican commitment and dominance. Republicans never developed a state that transcended their own political needs; they did not create a neutral or even bipartisan "administrative organization with imperatives of its own" in their efforts to define and protect national citizenship.[9]

This fundamental difference—Reconstruction's inability to rise above partisanship and the revenue system's usefulness to both parties—helps explain the revenue bureau's ability to function as an agent of national authority. Its necessity and utility allowed the bureau to develop its own administrative imperatives: taxing every drop of whiskey produced, and pursuing evaders into the most isolated hollows of the southern Appalachians when necessary. In confronting these resisters, the revenue officials often faced obstacles similar to those that undermined Reconstruction, but there were also important differences on the operational level.

Federal officials confronting resistance to revenue collection in the South were frequently the same men who had the duty of enforcing civil rights. District attorneys, marshals, and soldiers (until 1878) were responsible for upholding Reconstruction and worked with revenuers in the battle with moonshiners. In both areas of law enforcement these men struggled with insufficient resources and manpower, prosecution in state courts for alleged offenses committed while on duty, ostracism, and physical danger. Local juries were often hostile, and witnesses and informers were frequently silenced, driven away, or sometimes killed. In their enforcement of unpopular laws in a hostile community, the men on the "front lines" in the South experienced a dilemma familiar to policemen. Exercise of too much force would arouse resistance based on charges of tyranny and oppression. Too much restraint or leniency, on the other hand, would be interpreted as weakness and would also encourage resistance.[10] How officials coped with this dilemma marked a major difference between civil rights and revenue enforcement. Inability to balance force and restraint forever plagued and contributed to undermining the campaign against white supremacists, but officials were more successful in avoiding excessive force or weakness when they confronted moonshiners.

Ideally law enforcement should judiciously mix strength and restraint, but the effort to uphold Reconstruction was unable to do so. District attorneys, marshals, and other federal officials found it practically impossible to carry out the attorney general's repeated injunctions to enforce the laws "vigorously and impartially." Usually district attorneys were committed to their jobs and tried to be as vigorous as possible in carrying them out, but they were underpaid and overworked, rarely had an adequate staff of assistants, sometimes faced federal judges who were unsympathetic to Reconstruction, and endured attacks on their character and threats to their lives from white supremacists. Marshals faced similar obstacles and often lacked funds to pay witnesses or deputies, who were shot at and sometimes killed. Federal officials did not have a permanent force of detectives to gather evidence crucial to prosecution of Klansmen and other terrorists. The army, useful in preventing violence when it was mobilized, was steadily shrinking in size during the 1870s and never could act as a patrol force to maintain order. Law enforcement could rarely be "vigorous," but when brief crackdowns did occur, as in breaking the Klan in 1871–72, they evoked cries of oppression or "bayonet rule" that received increasing sympathy among northerners weary of Reconstruction. Concessions or leniency designed to win support from law-abiding southerners were taken advantage of as signs of federal weakness. "Impartiality" proved impossible because Reconstruction enforcement was inherently political despite the care that some officials took to deflect criticism.[11]

In dealing with moonshiners, Revenue Commissioner Green B. Raum was able to develop a strategy of selective leniency, in the form of suspended sentences, combined with sufficient force to establish his officers permanently in the southern mountains. The leniency began to win the support of law-abiding citizens and helped reduce complaints of excessive force. Raum and his successors were careful not to allow leniency to be seen as weakness or passivity. When too many moonshiners took advantage of suspended sentences to resume their activity, the revenuers swept through the mountains again, arresting offenders and seizing their stills. Moonshiners could evade and resist the revenuers for awhile, sometimes mounting formidable organized efforts, but the crackdown inevitably followed. Though too much force did evoke angry charges of arbitrary arrest and brutality, criticism never congealed into a systematic attack on the entire revenue system or a national movement to abolish the whiskey tax. Criticism sometimes led to reforms in the revenue bureaucracy, which helped reduce opposition. In contrast, the only reform acceptable to critics of Reconstruction was dropping the effort to protect black civil rights altogether.

Revenue officials' attempts to balance strength and restraint were more effective than in civil rights enforcement partly because moonshiners, however violent and determined many of them were, were collectively weaker than white supremacists. They were limited to the Appalachian region and embodied distinctly local attitudes and behavior. In contrast, white supremacist vigilantes represented almost universal feeling and were supported by the South's wealthiest and most powerful citizens. They could draw on a reservoir of sympathy throughout the South; even people who disapproved of their tactics endorsed their goals. The campaign for restoration of white supremacy united southerners more effectively than their war for independence.

Revenuers did not face a "solid South" determined to resist them. Although moonshiners were often effective locally because they had their neighbors' sympathy and support, they were hampered because some people were willing to aid revenue enforcement by informing against them or serving on posses. Assisting the revenuers was dangerous, and many informers or posse members paid a high price; but from a variety of motives, sometimes personal animosity to an individual moonshiner, they chose to side with the federal invaders. Only briefly, during the crackdown against the Ku Klux Klan of 1871–72, could federal officials rely on much aid from informers against white supremacist vigilantes.

Although local politicians courted the moonshiner vote, they were never able to organize politically as white supremacists most effectively did. Unlike white supremacists, moonshiners usually did not have the backing of the local elites. Increasingly during the later nineteenth century, the town-based middle class began to look down on rural mountaineers, and part of their efforts to bring order to their communities included opposition to moonshining. White supremacist violence was backed by a national political campaign to topple Reconstruction; the battle was on all fronts. In contrast, political efforts to repeal the revenue laws were unsuccessful even when the Democrats controlled Congress. Organizations like the Georgia whitecaps of the 1890s became powerful locally and did seem to have a political sense, but they were exceptions to the usual individualistic forms of moonshiner resistance. Some moonshiners like Amos Owens never gave up, but as Owens himself knew, neither did the revenuers. He won many of his own battles, largely by skillful evasion rather than violence, but as a group moonshiners were never strong enough to force the government to conclude that fighting them was not worth the effort.

Two essential components of an effective national state are the government's ability to monopolize violence and impose taxes. Reconstruction represented the failure of the federal government to monopolize violence; the ambitious program to protect national citizens succumbed to the violence of other citizens determined to overturn it. During the same period, though, the federal government was demonstrating its determination and ability to collect its liquor taxes. As long as the government confined itself to tax collection, it achieved a general consensus in support of its authority, except in the Appalachian South. Deadly conflict over the whiskey tax was mostly confined to that region, but whether the national government could collect its taxes there was an issue of national importance. Assertion of federal authority during Reconstruction had divided North and South; revenue was resisted in the South but also drew the sections together in a web of national taxation. The revenue system was a direct and permanent legacy of the Civil War, which survived the failure of Reconstruction.

The revenue bureau did have one foot firmly in the old style "limited state of courts and parties." Congress carefully scrutinized and itemized its appropriations for the bureau instead of relying on experts to formulate budget details; the bureau depended on federal courts, prosecutors, and marshals for most of its enforcement against tax evaders; and it was thoroughly an adjunct of party politics in its appointment practices. Nevertheless, it also had a foot in a newer bureaucratic order: both parties came to accept the excise tax and the need to collect it, making the bureau safe from partisan dismantling; revenue officials were paid salaries rather than fees (in contrast to Department of Justice subordinates); and the bureau was an early industrial regulator as well as law enforcer. The bureau fit part, though not all, of William Nelson's description of a modern bureaucracy: its power was brought to bear directly on individuals, and its goal of tax collection was backed by police (deputy U.S. marshals and deputy revenue collectors) and military units (soldiers joined revenue posses until 1878) capable of forcing obedience.[12] Most importantly, it was able to reach throughout a vast territory to collect the liquor taxes and pursue moonshiners.

2 The Political Economy of Mountain Dew

. . . .

As the southern black and the white supremacist began to fade
from national attention as Reconstruction wound down in the middle
1870s, a new southern figure moved toward center stage. This was the
Appalachian moonshiner, more often called a "blockader" by his neighbors
because he distilled corn whiskey or fruit brandy without paying the federal
tax and "ran the blockade" of revenue officers to sell his product. To the
local-color novelists and journalists who became popular after the Civil
War, the moonshiner seemed to typify all that made Appalachia different
from the rest of the nation. He became a standard literary character representing the outlaw as a rugged individualist or victim of historical processes
beyond his comprehension or control. In more modern terms, southern
moonshiners resembled Eric Hobsbawm's "primitive rebels" and "social
bandits" on American soil. They were rebels, supported by their neighbors
but not politically organized. They were outlaws but only because a distant
central government "criminalized" part of their way of life by imposing a
tax on home-distilled whiskey they had produced for generations. Novel
readers may have seen moonshiners as colorful, and modern scholars may
have perceived them as participants in "archaic" social movements, but to
the federal government they were less colorful than costly because of their
tax evasion and shooting at revenue officers attempting to suppress their
illegal activity. By 1876 most of the work of district attorneys and marshals
in Appalachia was revenue cases, in Georgia amounting to four-fifths of
federal prosecutions.[1]

Although illicit distillation occurred in regions as diverse as Utah Territory and Brooklyn,[2] moonshining was concentrated in the mountains and foothills of the southern Appalachians and neighboring Piedmont areas. One of the blockaders' strongholds was in the Blue Ridge border areas of eastern Tennessee, western North and South Carolina, and northern Georgia. Another concentration was in the Cumberlands of eastern Kentucky, West Virginia, and western Virginia. The Ozarks of Missouri and Arkansas contributed their share, along with the hills of northern Alabama and Mississippi. In 1891 the Appalachian region accounted for 68 percent of the nation's cases of selling liquor without a license and 77 percent of the cases of illicit distilling, better known as moonshining.[3]

According to the accounts of nineteenth-century journalists, travelers, and novelists, the people of the southern highlands lived in scattered, isolated settlements removed from the mainstream of national life. They were "our contemporary ancestors," "our own lost tribes" whose lives seemed locked in an archaic log-cabin frontier. Modern historians have discredited this stereotype, making clear that by the 1880s "progress," in the form of land speculation and extractive industries, was already invading mountain communities and changing their old patterns. The changes—arrival of railroads and lumbering and mining—created a much more diverse and complex society than portrayed in the older image. An even more recent development in the region's historiography is a closer look at the preindustrial era, generally considered as the period between original settlement and the Civil War. Even then the mountain communities were much less cut off from the outside than the stereotype suggests.[4]

Modern writers point out the stressful impact of social and economic change but also emphasize that these developments were rapid in some areas and slow and uneven in others. A valley penetrated by a railroad, denuded of its virgin forests and scarred by mineshafts, its creek bordered by a grim company town, might be over the mountain ridge from another where farmers continued familiar patterns of life. For example, Clay County, West Virginia, in the heart of the coal district, contrasted sharply with Monroe County, which lacked coal deposits and retained a stable agricultural way of life through the twentieth century.[5]

Even stable communities, though, were not entirely cut off from the larger world. As late as 1900 in the East Tennessee settlement of Cades Cove, women produced most clothing from homespun flax, made quilts in the traditional way, canned or dried most of the farm-raised food, and bought only a few staples from the local store. But they also bought sewing machines, and the community received regular mail deliveries including mail-order catalogues. During the nineties a telephone service was established, and the general store and some homes had phones. Ellen Semple, a geographer who traveled through the eastern Kentucky mountains during the 1890s, described a cabin in which "almost everything . . . was home-made," except "the iron stove with its few utensils, and some table knives," which "testified to any connection with the outside world." The stove was perhaps more eloquent testimony than Semple suggested: it may have been manufactured in the Northeast and bought through a mail-order catalogue by the mountain family. Shipped to the railroad terminus, the stove was then transported home by the farmer himself or a neighbor with a sturdy wagon and good team. The wife was probably quite pleased to be relieved of old-fashioned open-hearth cooking. Old and new were interwoven in the fabric of people's lives.[6]

Integration of old and new ways suggests that modernization modified but did not immediately or entirely supplant traditional attitudes and patterns of behavior in rural communities that only indirectly experienced industrialization. As much as possible, people retained what they valued in the old and adopted what was convenient in the new. Even in the new mining and lumber towns, or the piedmont textile mill villages, where change seemed to be occurring overnight, aspects of rural culture persisted to provide a sense of continuity and rootedness. This diversity and uneven development was the essence of mountain society and is important in understanding the moonshiner's place in it.[7]

A glimpse at the moonshiners' cultural and economic milieu reveals some of the factors that encouraged and sustained their activity. Most of the revenue raids occurred in rural mountain communities, although the moonshiners found customers in county seat towns, lumber and mining camps and company towns, and textile mill villages. Although many moonshiners were versatile entrepreneurs who kept pace with their changing society, their base of operations was usually a still site along one of the more inaccessible creeks, and most of them farmed when they were not at their stills during the fall to early spring distilling season. Consequently, our first look will be at the more traditional mountain communities where most moonshiners lived, followed by a view of the social and economic changes of the later nineteenth century that reached many of those communities and underlay the growth of moonshining. Blockaders thrived in both slowly changing and rapidly changing areas. One of their heartlands was eastern Kentucky and West Virginia, where lumbering and mining developed rapidly; another was northern Georgia and western South and North Carolina, where change was not strongly felt until after 1900.

Preindustrial or traditional communities were more diverse than the old image of isolated log-cabin settlements. Geography may have hemmed in some settlements by mountain barriers, but in other areas it contributed to contact with the wider world. Fertility of the soil, and ability to reach markets in Knoxville by an annual four-day round-trip wagon journey, made Cades Cove farmers more commercially oriented than in other areas. Nearness to a river down which logs could be floated, as in the case of West Virginia and Kentucky communities in the Tug Valley, was also a vital factor influencing local development. Historical events also could shape the community. The Civil War, in which Unionist Cades Cove was subject to constant guerilla raids from North Carolina, inflicted economic devastation that, followed by postwar depression throughout East Tennessee, retarded the community's development and made it more self-contained and isolated than it had been earlier. Each area was shaped by distinctive geographical and social conditions.[8]

Two neighboring districts known for their moonshining reveal both the diversity and the common elements of mountain communities. Whitewater Township, in northwestern Oconee County, South Carolina, was part of the territory of Lewis Redmond, a nationally famous moonshiner leader. It was one of the more isolated regions, with rugged mountain spurs reaching into its northern end. Whitewater had no roads, railroads, or towns in 1880. Every male was a farmer, except a dry goods dealer who seems to have operated his simple store while boarding in another man's home, and a "whiskey maker," licit or illicit not specified. Whitewater had three families of lower economic status than the others, in which a middle-aged male head was a farm laborer, probably a renter. Four black families added an element of heterogeneity. Compared to the remainder of Oconee County, Whitewater was an area of relatively recent settlement, with 20 percent of the men and 11 percent of the women born out of state, both higher than the county proportion of 7 percent.

The Tallulah district, along the southern border of Rabun County, Georgia, was noted for the quality of its mountain dew. The terrain was less rugged than in Whitewater. A road traversed the vicinity, and by 1891 a branch railroad terminated at the village of Tallulah Falls, just across the gorges of the Tallulah River. Most people were farmers, but there were a couple of blacksmiths, a sawyer, a house carpenter, a huckster, and a chairmaker. A widow worked at home as a weaver. Together the sawyer and the carpenter undoubtedly provided frame houses for local people instead of the traditional log cabin. There were some miners, who were remnants of gold-mining operations that had been more extensive before the Civil War. There were two black families. Lack of resident schoolteachers meant little opportunity to reduce the community's illiteracy, affecting about one of every three men and over half of the women. A larger proportion of the people were migrants from other states, mostly North Carolina, than in Whitewater. Forty-one percent of the men and 26 percent of the women, the male proportion higher than Rabun County's general 29 percent, were born in other states. This migration to Tallulah contributed to Rabun County's growth between 1870 and 1880, which was the greatest of any decade before 1940. Although Rabun County was isolated, with no railroad reaching Clayton, the county seat, until 1905, the Tallulah district was somewhat closer to the currents of nineteenth-century life than more mountainous Whitewater.[9]

Tallulah and Whitewater had distinctive social identities, but they also shared important elements of rural mountain culture. Preindustrial rural mountain communities were based on the small family farm, which though never entirely divorced from the market economy, was mainly devoted to raising corn, vegetables, cattle for milk, and poultry and hogs for the family. Commercial raising of cattle, sheep, hogs, or turkeys; lumbering; or gathering of wild plants with market value, such as sumac or ginseng, were also important elements of the mountain economy. Some farmers became primarily market oriented, but most considered these sources of income largely supplemental to provide cash for buying manufactured products from the local store. One aspect of agriculture that people skilled in the art had pursued for generations was the production of whiskey from corn or brandy from apples or peaches. Sometimes local distillers gained a wide reputation, but most sold to their neighbors or traded the liquor for the corn or fruit they supplied. Some efficient farmers combined distilling with hog raising, for they could fatten their hogs on the "still slops" or used corn mash after the alcohol had been extracted from it by distillation. For a farmer with a small still, there was actually more profit in the hogs than in the whiskey. As with commercial activity in general, some people made distilling their primary occupation, but others used it to supplement subsistence agriculture.[10]

Like most American country folk, southern mountain farmers did not live in compact villages. Most commonly their houses were strung out along the bottom and sides of the hollow formed by the stream bed or cove at the base of hills. People's houses were surrounded by forest, which made neighbors' homes a half mile away visible only when smoke was rising from the chimney. In one community of eighty-three families surveyed in 1908, the average distance from the school was about two miles; from a doctor, four miles; from a store, about three miles; and from a church, about two miles. Such distances were not much different from those of many midwestern farmers, but they seemed farther because people had to follow twisting, climbing mountain roads or paths instead of midwestern roads running straight to the horizon.[11]

Nevertheless, mountaineers were not necessarily cut off from each other. People often invited passing neighbors in for a chat, and both men and women walked or rode long distances to country stores or to visit friends and kin. Men worked together in planting and harvesting and building fences or houses. Where roads existed, they labored at an annual stint of county road maintenance. Women gathered in canning or sewing and quilting bees. Whole families attended corn shuckings, yearly election day festivities, and church meetings. The trip to market crops was also communal, with better-off farmers lending wagons and teams to poor relations. Traditional "hoe-downs" brought the young people together in a lively social life. Distance did not necessarily sever contact: the settlers along the Nantahala River in Macon County, North Carolina, considered all the people within a ten-mile radius to be neighbors. Despite physical separation, the people shared the work, culture, and attitudes of the mountains.[12]

The heart of this culture was the family and extended kinship network, sometimes broadened to include unrelated people who were obligated to the patriarch in various ways (perhaps as employees or members of a Civil War military unit he commanded). People often lived within walking distance of kinfolk, but the network of kin could reach outside the settlement or even the county. This web of kinship was tightly woven in the Tallulah district, where 103 of 149 families listed in the 1880 census shared their surname with other members of the community. Of Whitewater Township's 133 families, 83 shared surnames with other residents. Two families, the Whitmires and Chastains, had representatives in both Tallulah and Whitewater.[13]

Mountain families were usually nuclear, with only a few containing adult members of more than one generation. Single men and women only occasionally lived alone. The Tallulah and Whitewater families were not as large as the usual image, both averaging between three and four children, in contrast to Cades Cove, where six to eight was the average. In 1900, about one in five families in both Tallulah and Whitewater had seven or more children. Most women over forty-five had borne (including those who died) fewer than ten children, in contrast to Cades Cove, where most had borne between ten and twelve. Many women in both areas married as teenagers, but not enough to make very large families usual in these settlements. In Tallulah in 1900 nearly one in four (24 percent) had married at age sixteen or younger; four women were only thirteen; three, fourteen. In Whitewater, 15 percent married this young, with only one thirteen-year-old, but four at fourteen. Early marriages occurred, but were not typical in these communities.[14]

In both districts people sometimes lived close to their relatives in groups of as many as four or five households, a common pattern elsewhere as well. In Whitewater several Nickles family members lived in a small enclave in 1880: James, age forty-five, and his (presumably second) wife Mary Jane, thirty, and their young children lived near James, Jr., age twenty-one, and his wife and infant, and two Nickles widows, Charity and Martha, ages fifty and seventy, respectively. Although entire kin networks migrated out of both areas, others expanded over the years as sons settled down in the community of their birth, like Whitewater's Cantrells, Alexanders, and Nicholsons between 1880 and 1900. In Tallulah the Lovells grew from eight households in 1880 to eleven in 1900; the Chastains, from two to nine. Moonshining, often a family operation like the ordinary small farm, fit into the pattern of kinship networks. Blockaders frequently lived in areas surrounded by kinfolk who worked with them and protected them from revenue raids or who punished informers.[15]

Although mountaineers shared their strong sense of family with other rural Americans and many urban immigrant groups,[16] the small size of their

settlements often made the extended family and the community cotermi-
nous. Cades Cove by 1900 was "actually one large extended family," and
according to Ronald Eller, in most communities the nuclear and extended
families were not only the most significant economic unit but set the "matrix
within which politics and government, as well as organizations for religion,
education and sociability developed." Family ties "served to a marked degree as the essence of the community itself."[17]

Family and local friendships were the heart of the preindustrial social
class structure. The earliest settlers usually occupied the best lands, and
later arrivals settled further into the mountains. The first residents often
became the community elite, living and working in a valley or cove or the
county seat towns that were government and economic hubs of the region.
More prosperous farmers, who sometimes rented land to neighbors, also
served as doctors, teachers, merchants, justices of the peace, or lawyers
handling the litigation in which mountaineers, like other Americans, frequently engaged. They were most connected to the outside world and
most oriented toward nineteenth-century values of progress and mobility.
This elite enjoyed status based on length of residence and family connections. They became politically powerful, as did western North Carolina's
slaveholders, but they fought for regional interests in state politics and did
not look down upon ordinary farmers or seek to change their culture or
attitudes.[18]

Nevertheless, those who held even a small number of slaves were tied to
the dominant groups throughout the South and usually allied with the
Confederacy when the Civil War broke out. Cades Cove farmers were
shocked and angered when the local squires actively assisted Confederate
guerrillas raiding from North Carolina. In the Shelton Laurel valley of
North Carolina, the small farmers were also Unionists. Several of them
became victims of a massacre led by two prominent citizens of the county
seat town, Marshall. According to Phillip Paludan, historian of the incident,
there was "no real sense of community between . . . the more metropolitan
towns and the traditional communities." Latent conflicts became open
during the bloody guerrilla fighting in the mountains, and at war's end the
local elite was discredited, some individuals fleeing the community to escape vengeance. The vacuum would later be filled, in some areas by younger, locally oriented leaders, but in others by a new elite, both residents and

outsiders, eager to develop natural resources utilizing their own or outside capital.[19]

Some groups were also of lower social and economic status than the majority of the residents. Their position was not defined by poverty, since families often aided their poor kin, but by behavior. Such was the case in Cades Cove, where Chestnut Flats was an enclave of outlaws, moonshiners, and prostitutes who often stole food and livestock rather than bothering to raise it themselves. They were ostracized by respectable farmers. In other areas, some moonshiners lived in similar enclaves under a dominant leader or "king."[20] The preindustrial class structure was shaped by family ties and local standards of proper behavior.

Economic and political changes during the later nineteenth century began to reshape society in the mountains, separating many families from their land and emphasizing social class based on ties to outside institutions rather than on family connections or personal character. Despite these disruptions, the family proved a durable core of mountain culture, a mechanism for coping with new living patterns and surroundings. Decisions to migrate to mining or mill towns were family decisions, often influenced and aided by relatives, and some of the mill towns became "one big family" with a web of households united by marriage as in the rural communities. On the farm the family was integrated into daily life; in the new industrial settings it would help its members face the dangers and demands of a new economic order.[21]

The new order came to Appalachia in stages or "ever-building waves" over the thirty years between 1870 and 1900 and was most pervasive after the turn of the century. Major national depressions, from 1873 to 1879 and from 1893 through 1896, slowed the investment in and building of the railroad infrastructure necessary to exploit the mountains' timber and mineral resources, but industrialization was rapid in the prosperous interludes.

The first stage of development was the "selling of the mountains," buying up of farmers' timber and mineral lands by outside speculators. Capitalists discovered the value of the mountain resources after the Civil War, and promoters of the "new South" by the 1880s were advertising their states' potential for extractive industry. Farmers, who kept a large portion of their land uncultivated, met the speculators or their agents as pleasant strangers who stopped by for a chat and suggested buying the unused land they had already spotted as valuable. Thinking that there was plenty of land and trees for all, or unaware of the value of mineral resources, people usually sold for very little money or granted rights to the land below the surface without understanding how disruptive the use of it would be. Mountaineers were not long in discovering that they had been cheated, and in later years they were less hospitable to strangers when they inquired about land. Then the transactions sometimes became less pleasant, and speculators resorted to complicated legal maneuvers involving inheritance and dubious or manipulated titles. Occasionally they burned out a recalcitrant farmer. Mountaineers in their turn resisted the outsiders, sometimes attacking surveying parties in the same way moonshiners ambushed revenue posses. The result of increasing sales of farmland was absentee ownership, with families sometimes remaining as tenants on their old homestead.[22]

The earliest industrial development was logging. Farmers had long cut timber on their lands to provide supplemental income, and sawmills existed in many mountain communities to meet local needs. People near navigable rivers, and those willing to haul timber overland, developed cutting of huge virgin hardwoods into a substantial business. "Devil Anse," patriarch of the Hatfield clan, was a successful timber entrepreneur with some thirty employees during the 1870s. He earned his soubriquet "Devil" partly from his capitalistic drive. For smaller and less ambitious farmers, lumbering provided an opportunity for seasonal employment in sawmills or cutting trees for operators like Hatfield.[23]

After 1890, as railroads came closer to the great timber stands, lumber companies bought up huge tracts and began a wholesale stripping of the forest, leaving bare slopes subject to erosion. Logging became a full-time occupation as young men migrated to lumber camps in the woods and families settled in company towns surrounding sawmills. Intensive lumbering came first to eastern Kentucky, West Virginia, and southwestern Virginia; after 1900 the thud of axes and the scream of ripsaws was common in the forests of Tennessee, North Carolina, and Georgia.[24]

Paralleling the development of the timber industry, and often facilitated by the same railroads that carried the logs out of the mountains, was mining, most intensively for coal. The earliest operations were during the 1870s and 1880s as railroads reached into southeastern West Virginia and southwestern Virginia, but the 1890s depression delayed large-scale exploitation of coal beds. Beginning in the late nineties, mining expanded rapidly in West Virginia between 1900 and 1910 and in eastern Kentucky after 1910. Smaller-scale development occurred in southwestern Virginia and eastern Tennessee during the early twentieth century.

Mining brought many farmers off the land into full-time wage or "public" work, where they sometimes met blacks and European immigrants. These new groups were considered more "docile" or reliable because the mountain people often treated their jobs as supplemental or seasonal instead of submitting to the industrial discipline the bosses demanded. Those who did leave the land permanently usually migrated with their families to company towns, living in overcrowded frame houses lacking adequate sanitary facilities and cloaked in coal dust. Many miners developed black lung or were killed or injured on the job; their families were in danger of contracting the diseases of urban overcrowding, particularly tuberculosis. Mining, like lumbering, also left its impact on the land, gouging holes in hillsides and polluting mountain streams. Despite the harshness of their environment, people of all groups were able to maintain many of their traditions. In Stonega, Wise County, Virginia, immigrants, blacks, and mountain whites lived in separate sections. Within each group, "older cultural patterns were drawn upon to help in the adjustment to newer patterns. Tradition informed and guided innovation." Patterns of family life, retention of rural ways, attitudes toward work, and for some, drinking moonshine whiskey were all ways of coping with a new way of life.[25]

Both lumbering and mining were located in the mountains, and the work was men's work. The piedmont textile mills, which recruited entire families of mountaineers after 1900, drew people out of their familiar land and dramatically affected the lives of rural women and children as well as men. Each family member old enough, and some children were working by eight or nine, had distinctive jobs in the clanging, lint-filled factories. As in the mines, families usually lived in company towns in plain, monotonous houses and had to cope with new occupational diseases or injuries as well as illness fostered by poor sanitation and overcrowding. Also like miners, millhands resisted factory regimentation by retaining some of their rural ways: growing garden plots or keeping a hog, quitting work to go fishing or make a crop on the old farm. Since blacks were excluded and very few immigrants found the southern mills appealing, bosses hoped to reduce the constant migration of workers in search of better jobs by recruiting mountaineers, but they too brought their independence and much of the traditional culture with them to the new environment.[26]

Economic and social change in the mountains, which was rapid and traumatic in some areas, slow to arrive or indirect in others, affected mountaineers in diverse ways. Industrialization offered opportunities for a broader life and provided scarce cash, but it also undermined farmers' self-sufficiency and weakened their tie to the land. People indirectly as well as directly affected by industrialization experienced declining self-sufficiency. In some areas, traditional inheritance practices or purchase of land by speculators left families with farms too small to support them. Dividing the patriarchal lands among the sons, who built houses and broke the soil in uncultivated sections of the old farm, gave each new farmer less room to start afresh and forced more people to cultivate less-fertile hillside land. In Cades Cove, despite a population decrease, the size of an average farm shrank from about 84 acres to about 31 acres between 1850 and 1880 (a loss of 53 acres). In northern Georgia, mountain farmers' landholdings were considerably larger than in Cades Cove, and while some counties witnessed larger acreage losses, others did not decrease as much. Between 1880 and 1900, farms in Fannin County diminished on the average by 62 acres (from 175 to 113 acres), but in Union the holdings shrank by only 43 acres (162 to 119). Farmers of Logan County, West Virginia, and Pike County, Kentucky, who owned their land at the turn of the century had to make do with an average of about one-third of their 1880 holdings (from over 300 acres to 110 acres). Such shrinkage meant less for the family itself and a smaller crop to take to market.[27]

In some regions the decline of subsistence farming was dramatic, leaving growing numbers of young men landless as tenants or farm laborers. Logan and Pike counties witnessed an increase of landless families from 30 to 50 percent between 1850 and 1870, reaching 70 percent in 1900. In Whitewater over half (56 percent) of the families were renters in 1900, while in 1880 only a few people had been recorded as "farm laborers." Northwestern Georgia's Gordon, Murray, and Whitfield counties, the domain of the organized whitecap vigilante movement that defended moonshiners in the 1890s, had the largest proportion of tenants in the state's mountain and neighboring piedmont areas: 50 percent for Gordon and 43 percent for Murray and Whitfield. Rabun County and the Tallulah district were better off, but about a third of its families rented their farms, similar to Cades Cove, Tennessee. As in the Cove, most of Tallulah's tenants were age thirty-nine or younger (62 percent compared to 70 percent in the Cove). The relative youth of the tenants suggests the possibility of land ownership later in life, by inheritance or purchase. Whitewater's larger proportion of tenants was more evenly divided, with 55 percent thirty-nine or younger, implying a somewhat higher level of permanent tenancy. A contemporary observer described Kentucky mountaineers by 1890 facing the prospect of becoming tenants, often on their own land that they sold to lumber or mining companies; of emigration; or of adaptation to the new economic order by becoming storekeepers or wage laborers. Those who rejected these alternatives retreated farther into the mountains, asking only to be left alone.[28]

Living on smaller farms or landless, many mountain people became poorer and less able to rely on their own resources. Cash was scarce; farmers in Macon County, North Carolina, rarely saw $50 in cash from one year to the next. During the later nineteenth century, mountain people's need for cash increased because manufactured goods began to supplement and then to supplant homemade products. Although they often could revert to old ways in an emergency, people began buying such things as matches, commercial dyes and printed cloth, and kerosene lamps (without chimneys, which broke in transit over the rough trails). Sometimes they even purchased cornmeal if they had a bad crop or if their farm was too small to supply the family. As early as 1888 Charles Dudley Warner described the mountaineers of Harlan County, Kentucky, as "*until recently* a self-sustaining people." Local property taxes, low but rising in areas where outsiders were buying land for timber or minerals or where railroads were being built, also required cash payment, and many people had trouble raising the money.[29]

For mountain families who wished to remain on their land, marketing farm products was increasingly necessary to acquire cash. In some areas, though, marketing was restricted by the geographical barriers that hampered many highlanders' economic opportunities. In Union County, Georgia, the people "raise a few hogs, a little wheat, and make the bulk of their crop in corn. There is no market near them, and when the years accounts are cast up they find themselves with enough bread and meat but without a cent of money." Mountaineers sometimes did not fare well when they could reach the markets. In Burke County, North Carolina, farmers living ten miles from the railroad saw half the price of their corn eaten up by shipping costs, making them "poorer every year." After traveling two days to town, highlanders encountered worldly derision of their "quaint costumes and grotesque teams" and purchasers' demands that they " 'take in trade' something they do not want." Some mountaineers raised turkeys and hogs, which they drove to market, but they did not always get good prices because the animals lost weight on the trek. One agricultural product, though, always commanded a ready market and could be easily transported on a mule— mountain dew.[30]

Whiskey or brandy could indeed bring in more cash than most farmers ever saw, particularly if the tax bite were avoided. A mule able to carry only 4 bushels of corn could pack whiskey equivalent to 24 bushels. If the mountaineer had a team and wagon with access to a road, he could haul about 20 bushels of corn on a long journey to market, where he could get $10 for his load. If he converted his corn into liquor, he could carry the equivalent of 40 bushels, 120 gallons of whiskey. In the 1890s his whiskey without a revenue stamp would bring at least $150. Those who could not afford the investment in distillation equipment could barter their corn for whiskey made by their more industrious neighbors, who would accept 3 bushels of cornmeal as the price of a gallon of their whiskey ($1.10) in 1881.[31]

Contemporaries disagreed about the profitability of moonshining. A. H. Brooks, a veteran revenuer, argued that only a few men made money as blockaders. He thought that the typical moonshiner was "a very poor miserable man, who drinks up a good deal of the profits." Another experienced revenue officer, though, asserted that moonshining was highly profitable: the blockader "can make money by running an illicit distillery, and *money* and *fun* are above all, the articles he is seeking for in this life." A journalist was more precise about the economics of illicit distilling. Giving the figure of $1.10 to $1.20 per gallon of moonshine in a good market in 1901, he also concluded that wildcatting could be profitable. The average size still could produce 80 gallons a week, giving a seasonal income of $90 per week in cash or barter. Deducting $20 for materials such as the corn, the moonshiner could earn $70 a week during the distilling season. As in any risky business, success in moonshining probably depended on the distiller's skill, ambition, and ability to market his product. For those willing to take the risks, there was money in corn juice.[32]

Lack of markets for other farm products was the most common contemporary explanation for moonshining, and modern writers repeat it as part of the image of blockaders as victims of mountain isolation. Durwood Dunn, however, argues that other ways to supplement farm income were available, at least in Cades Cove, that would help sustain a family. He says that making whiskey was "an easy way out," implying agreement with the revenuer's view that moonshiners sought the most money for the least work. It is clear that mountaineers turned to wildcat distilling for diverse reasons, more complex than either simple need for cash or entrepreneurial quest for profits.[33]

Some moonshiners were not seeking an alternative marketable product or looking toward the profits of blockading. A few were most interested in the whiskey itself. Daniel A. Tompkins, North Carolina's textile industry pioneer, met an old wildcatter on the road who said he made money, but "I drinked up the profit and more too and had to quit." Other people seem to have taken a turn at the still for short-term, specific purposes. According to a mountaineer, some farmers made brush whiskey to pay local property taxes, meeting one obligation by evading another. One moonshiner, Samson, told a sympathetic reporter that he was not "making this whiskey to speculate on." Instead he was only making enough to buy books and shoes so his three children could attend school and "get a little taste of education." A mountain woman told visitors that "thar's some things you rally want money fur," but "how kin we kerry the corn to barter when thar is no road?" "Thar is a way—" she hinted, and predicted that next time the visitors came she would have a chair and frock for the baby. These people were not really "moonshiners," but individuals who borrowed somebody else's apparatus or used their own still only occasionally to do a little stilling to raise money for specific purposes.[34]

Some blockaders may have been "just a simple-minded countryman, who makes whisky instead of selling eggs and butter," like Tallulah's John Crawford, a thirty-eight-year-old farmer with seven children who signed with an *x* when he was tried for distilling, working at an illicit still, and illegally selling liquor at both wholesale and retail in 1881. Samuel Cantrell, tried in 1890, appears in the 1900 census of Tallulah as a tenant farmer aged forty-four with six children. Other Tallulah moonshiners were fairly substantial members of their communities. James Tilley, a farmer aged forty-three with six children, was able to pay the expenses of travel from Atlanta, where he was tried, to serve his term in the Hall County jail at Gainesville, closer to home in Tallulah. In 1881 Cicero Blalock, a young man of thirty-three, pled guilty to moonshining and served three months in the Hall County jail. Although he declared himself too poor to pay the $200 fine, a few years later he was serving as Rabun County tax collector, and in 1900 he was living in Tallulah as a fifty-two-year-old farmer who owned his land and headed a family of seven children. Just as it is difficult to delineate a typical mountaineer, it is hard to describe a typical moonshiner: he could be a simple farmer; he might be a social outcast like the distillers of Chestnut Flats, Cades Cove; but he could also be a solid, respected citizen.[35]

General circumstances or specific needs of mountaineers' lives pushed some people toward illicit distilling. Others, in true entrepreneurial fashion, saw the opportunities in selling blockade whiskey to thirsty lumberjacks, miners, and millhands. Industrialization was a "pull" factor for many moonshiners. Some regions in the mountains witnessed the sudden growth of company towns or new cities like Middlesborough, Kentucky, which increased from sixty valley farmers to five thousand people between 1883 and 1889. Older communities also expanded, like Asheville, North Carolina, a tourist center and rail hub that grew from two thousand residents in 1880 to ten thousand in 1890. Whether rude camps in the woods or cities with all the modern amenities, these towns attracted whiskey drinkers who both patronized legal saloons and drank moonshine white lightning. Some company bosses outlawed saloons. The closed company towns, supplied by a single store, did not provide markets for local farmers' produce. They did, though, unintentionally provide customers for blockaders. The new elite of managers and professionals whose careers were tied to industrial development looked down upon the mountaineers and strove to improve the quality of life and moral tone of the towns. They often championed local option prohibition to suppress the rowdiness for which some places became notorious. In doing so, they helped reduce public tolerance of drinking and moonshiners, but if successful in drying up the towns, they also opened a wider market for blockaders.[36]

The blockader, rooted in the rural culture of the mountains, often made a successful and profitable transition to the modern world. Moonshiners entered their trade for different reasons, some choosing it for lack of alternatives, others seeing opportunities in making mountain dew. However diverse their motivations, most had to be risk takers skilled in a complex art.

Illicit distillation was by no means easy work, especially when carried on in secret at risk of arrest and destruction or confiscation of moonshiners' stills. "Blockadin' is the hardest work a man ever done," a mountaineer recalled, "And hit's wearin' on a feller's narves. Fust chance I git, I'm a goin' ter quit!" Illicit distillers had to haul bushels of corn up mountainsides and whiskey down, spending long nights in unheated still-houses always alert for betrayal. Moonshiners usually located their stills in crude log shelters near the heads of the coves or hollows formed by swift mountain streams that provided the cold water necessary for their operations. Hidden by trees or almost impenetrable mountain laurel and reached by paths known to only a few people, stills were usually safe from prying eyes. As the government accelerated its enforcement of the revenue laws in the later seventies, blockaders installed their stills so they could be easily carried off on the first warning of an impending raid. Many a posse reached a still-house to find everything but the valuable still itself.[37]

Some ingenious moonshiners developed unusual hiding places for their operations. Caves under riverbanks were favorites. One old North Carolina distiller, Charles Folias, often seemed to disappear into the ground just as revenue officers were about to apprehend him. He in fact ran into a tunnel leading to the cave where his still was hidden. One day, however, he encountered a nest of rattlesnakes in his tunnel: if he went forward he would be bitten; if he backed out he would be arrested. He gave up, telling the revenuers that he "was forced to surrender on account of the infernal snakes inside, and you deserve no credit for it." Another cave operation was more elaborate. It could be reached only by an underwater entrance beneath the riverbank and was accidentally discovered by a revenuer searching the island where he suspected a still was located. The cave had originally been a hideout for deserters from the Confederate army during the Civil War. One of the most complex hiding places, beyond the means of most moonshiners, was disguised as a blacksmith's shop. The bellows were used to fan the flames under the still, and water was brought in through underground pipes. Urban illicit distillers could operate disguised as legitimate businesses, but this elaborate arrangement was unique in the mountains. Finally, the Reverend Baylus Hamrick, a Baptist minister, operated a still hidden in the basement of his own house. Such arrangements evaded detection for many years.[38]

Mountain dew required several weeks of processing from harvested corn to final product, the work usually of two or three persons who shared the $15 to $30 investment in a copper still and worm. Sometimes a single person would work a crude still consisting of half a barrel turned upside down over a soap kettle; the copper tubing for the worm was the only purchase necessary. Distillation began with sprouting the unground corn: warm water was poured over the ears for about three days, draining out through a hole in the bottom of the barrel. When two-inch sprouts appeared, converting the starch into sugar, the corn was ready to be dried and ground into meal. The blockader or a friend who owned a small "tub mill," producing one-half to two bushels of meal per day, carried on this operation. Pouring boiling water over the meal converted it into "sweet mash," which was allowed to stand for two or three days. If rye was available, rye malt, prepared like the cornmeal, was added to hasten fermentation, which took eight to ten days and required maintenance of a constant temperature without a thermometer. A skilled distiller could tell the proper degree of fermentation by the sound in the barrel; it was at perfection when the bubbling resembled rain drumming on a roof or a slice of pork frying in the pan. The result was "sour mash," the liquid portion of which was called "beer," alcoholic and "sour enough to make a pig squeal." This beer was then poured into the still, which had an enclosed copper cap and spiral tube, the worm. This worm was surrounded by a watertight barrel or box through which cold water was kept running. Stills consequently had to be located near flowing streams. The moonshiner built a fire under the still, often within a stone furnace surrounding the pot to prevent heat loss. The heat caused the alcohol in the beer to vaporize and then condense into a liquid again while passing through the cold worm. The spirits, at this stage impure "singlings," drained into a receiving tub or barrel.

A second distillation was necessary to remove the water and oils remaining in the singlings. With a fire at lower temperature, the process of boiling, vaporizing, and condensing was repeated to produce "doublings." This stage was delicate and required skill and experience: if distillation were too brief, the liquor would be sour and weak; if too long, pure alcohol. The final result was a clear whiskey, ready for immediate consumption without aging.[39]

Mountain dew varied in strength and taste according to the distiller's skill. A Kentucky revenuer "heard it estimated" that three-fourths of the whiskey consumed in his district was moonshine "considered much better" than legal whiskey. A newspaper reporter who tasted the Tallulah district's product described it as "somewhat thicker than the regular article, and is less firey. It tastes fairly well, although it has a flavor suggestive of fallen leaves." Another writer considered moonshine "raw and fiery to the civilized palate, with a faint smoky aroma." Though harsh, it was pure, since "its makers know none of the arts of adulteration." Not all outsiders agreed about the quality of brush whiskey. An 1867 writer condemned moonshine whiskey as "nearly all *very bad*," because of mountaineers' adulteration of the liquor with buckeye tree pods to give a "bead," or bubbles that appeared when the whiskey was shaken, an indication of proof. Twenty years later another writer described moonshine as "a vile production, repulsive in taste and smell," resembling diluted pure alcohol. Finally, a reporter's personal experience of the effects of Rabun County, Georgia, moonshine in 1885: "The instant he has swallowed the stuff he feels as if he were sunburned all over, his head begins to buzz as if a hive of bees had swarmed there, when he closes his eyes, he sees six hundred million torch-light processions all charging at him, ten abreast, and when he opens his eyes the light blinds him and everything seems dancing about." After passing out, this particular novice took forty-eight hours to sober up. Some of these descriptions fit a beverage called "mountain dew," but others are more appropriate to concoctions denominated "white lightnin'," "bust-head," "pop-skull," "white mule" (because of the kick), "red eye," "forty-rod" (the distance the stuff makes one run before passing out), or "bumblings" (from the noise in a drinker's head, as described above).[40]

Mountain people were not necessarily heavy drinkers, as many were too poor to afford regular consumption of even locally made whiskey: "In drinking, as in everything else, this is the Land of Do Without," the early-twentieth-century chronicler of mountain life Horace Kephart declared. "Comparatively few highlanders see liquor oftener than once or twice a month." Charles Dudley Warner said that travelers who had read about moonshining would be disappointed in the sobriety of mountain people near Boone, North Carolina. Nineteenth-century writers pictured mountaineers as drinkers but rarely drunkards. In some communities like Cades Cove, churchgoing farmers condemned drinking, especially public or social drinking.

Alcohol became a problem at home when drunken men abused wives and children. More conspicuously, drinking led to violence when men got drunk at large public gatherings outside of their own communities. "Corn squeezins" were an essential element in gatherings of men at barbecues, political rallies, court sessions (after adjournment of the grand jury), dances, or parties. Whiskey contributed to the fights that sometimes marred such occasions. Young men, often landless and footloose, made up a volatile group in some mountain communities. Their sense of honor could be a chip on their shoulders, and they routinely carried pistols or knives. They were sensitive to personal slights, and whiskey dissolved their inhibitions. They sometimes released them, as at Christmas, in shooting up the settlement with little harm, but at other times in deadly fights with rivals. The danger- ous effects of whiskey were very apparent to people near Morganton, North Carolina. In 1885 drunken young men disrupted services in Mountain Grove Church; Charles York stabbed his brother John to death in a drunken rage; and at Glen Alpine Station a crowd from the country with "new apple-jack holding sway" became rowdy, "shooting, cursing and cut- ting up generally" with a homicide as a result. In Dahlonega, Georgia, the election for constable of the Yahoola district in 1873 was accompanied by "a considerable quantity of spirits . . . which, of course, caused some rowing" climaxed by a stabbing. Next year three drunken young men "conducted themselves so badly" at a church meeting that it was broken up. The local editor denounced whiskey drinking and carrying of concealed weapons as "two curses which should be put down, and that speedily." In Kentucky's Harlan County a man attempting to kill his son-in-law in a drunken fight over a card game shot and killed his own wife and brother when they tried to interfere. A local jury held that the killing was an accident. In some areas, people seem to have tolerated drinking sprees as a release of energy, despite sometimes unfortunate results. Rising temperance sentiment in the later nineteenth century reduced this tolerance, but some mountaineers defied churchgoers and retained their old attitudes toward liquor.[41]

Blockaders developed clever ways of reaching their customers, often their immediate neighbors. Sometimes they hid a jug and cup in a brush heap; the customer would leave his money in the cup after taking his drink. Another method was use of "bell trees" or hollow trunks, known only to local regulars: after the customer left his money and rang the bell in the log, he could return a short time later to find a cup of mountain dew. Such marketing of course depended on local people's trust of each other. Less secretive moonshiners placed fresh-cut laurel branches in the road on Saturday afternoons. Local men knew that following the direction of the branches led to the distiller himself dispensing from his jug.

Some blockaders sought wider markets, hauling their ten-gallon kegs out of the mountains on mule-drawn sledges. One group of North Carolina moonshiners sold to bootleggers who filled jugs slung over the back of their horse and then dispensed the liquor into containers that tippling valley farmers left near the road along with the requisite cash. Other wildcatters marketed their product directly from their wagon, usually hiding the liquor under apples or other produce, to customers in valley towns or to drovers who passed by on the way to market.[42]

Some moonshiners took advantage of modernization, particularly the railroads, to expand their operations. A judge confidently predicted that "a railway through these wildernesses would cure illicit distilling" by bringing farmers closer to markets, but sometimes the cure helped spread the problem. Railway networks enlarged the market for enterprising distillers. In the early twentieth century the station platform at Traumfest, North Carolina, was often stacked with jugs of "vinegar" that exuded "a powerful alcoholic smell." An 1889 map of a moonshine district near Pruitton in Lauderdale County, Alabama, revealed a railroad and two long-distance roads not far from the still sites. Some moonshiners clearly had one foot in the mountains' traditional culture, but the other was in the modern world that was increasingly penetrating the Appalachians.[43]

Moonshining, like mountain farming, was often a family business. In lists of persons arrested during raids, the same surname frequently appears. Raiders in South Carolina in February and March 1877 netted two Taylors, two Turners, two Trammels, two Pittmans, two Quinns, and three different Turners. A Georgia sweep in 1875 brought in two Brandts, two Bennetts, two Greens, and three Scotts. An 1879 Kentucky raid landed four Johnsons and two Ferrells; North Carolina revenuers captured four Yorks in 1877. Four members of the Ramsey family, immigrants from Kentucky, were arrested in Arkansas in the 1890s. One party of raiders had warrants for ten members of the same family; they were thwarted by a seven-year-old girl, niece of the patriarch, who ran ahead to warn the distillers. Harrison Gibson of Kentucky and his five sons, along with two sons-in-law, became wealthy after stilling for several years around the turn of the century.[44]

Most moonshiners were white men. There were a few black blockaders: two were captured in an 1876 South Carolina raid; one was arrested in Virginia in 1879; and three in South Carolina in 1885. A black woman in Elbert County, Georgia, operated a still with a white partner. The white woman confessed that she had been moonshining for several years, but the revenuers let her go because she had a small baby with her. The black woman, though, "had to tramp the usual road paved for the violator of the revenue laws." Revenuers surprised another integrated still in Georgia in 1891. The white blockaders surrendered, but the blacks "were game" and "met the enemy with a volley of distillery refuse." The possemen, their clothes saturated and stinking, finally closed in and captured the resisters, except old Simon Turnipseed, who was caught only after an officer fired at him. Blacks were more likely to be hired as laborers by larger white operators than to have their own stills. However, by the turn of the century in North Carolina, blacks were becoming more important as blockaders, making up about one-fourth of the state's moonshiners. As among whites, a black preacher could sometimes preach at a service while his associates sold his own "wild cat" to the congregation. The most common black violation of the revenue laws was retailing without payment of special tax, which meant peddling half pints or pints of whiskey from jugs at "Negro frolics" or meetings.[45]

Since moonshining was a family business, women were often supporters of their menfolk. They sometimes met the revenuers at the door of their houses, pretending ignorance of their husband's, father's, or brother's whereabouts. When they did give information, a revenuer found it "wholly unreliable as regards the locality of the distilleries." Sometimes they had the important responsibility of delaying the officers while the men escaped, or they gave warning themselves of the revenuers' approach. In Georgia, women yelled, cursed, and blew horns as a raiding party rode through a valley. "*I never in my life,*" a deputy exclaimed, "*heard so much profanity and filthy language as was incessantly thrown in our faces by the women, wives and daughters of the distillers.*" South Carolina women "gave a peculiar shout or warning, which seemed to arouse the whole neighborhood," and raiders were soon under fire. An inexperienced deputy was forced to withdraw under the onslaught of a sturdy mountain woman, who gave him a thorough tongue-lashing and pummeled him with her fists. One moonshiner's wife, who was "caught and brought down from the hills" after her husband's death, was the "wildest thing" a Sunday-school teacher and her valley neighbors had ever seen. They discovered that she had brought her husband's still, undoubtedly her most valuable possession, hidden in the bedclothes.[46]

Some women went even farther for their men. Susan Van Meter, "a dashing young widow" from Kentucky, was arrested in 1881 for shooting at a deputy marshal trying to arrest her lover. The judge asked if she meant to kill him, perhaps chivalrously offering her an escape, but she replied: "Of course I tried to kill him, and am only sorry that I failed. He was after John . . . , and I knew he would catch him; and I love John well enough to die for him." A few months earlier she had jumped from a second-story window in her nightgown, running two miles to warn John that a posse was after him.[47]

A few women were moonshiners themselves. Lucy McClure, kin in spirit to Susan, had been sought for eight years "as one of the most persistent and daring of West Virginia's moonshiners." Twenty-four years old, she was "a young athletic woman of great nerve and presence of mind, she was a fine rifle and revolver shot, and rode a beautiful sorrel horse, which has many a time saved her." Mollie Miller of Tennessee may have been less dashing, but she was a deadly opponent of the revenuers. She was first noticed during a raid on her father's still, in which three revenuers were killed and the rest retreated under heavy fire. During a later raid, guided by a man who "had a grudge against" him, Sam Miller died. A few days later the marshal received a coffin with the informer's body. Mollie went on to become a leader of Polk County moonshiners, credited with the deaths of three revenuers and four or five informers. She was arrested only once but received a light sentence because of weak evidence. After construction of a railroad that reached Mollie's domain, the officers were able to break up her gang; Mollie retired, occasionally being summoned to Chattanooga to appear as a witness. After collecting her fees, she walked sixty miles to her home. She died in bed. Tennessee was also home to Betsy M., a "moonshineress" who allegedly weighed 600 pounds. Seated on a low bed, she dispensed mountain dew to whomever came her way. She was unmolested by revenuers, supposedly not only because she was determined to resist but because her great weight made it impossible to force her to travel against her will over the rugged three miles to the nearest wagon road. Near her house were the graves of several sons, some of whom had been killed in revenue raids, others in a local feud. Betsy was a Melungeon, "an olive-skinned people of corn-whiskey renown" who had lived in Hancock County, Tennessee, for generations. Mrs. Henderson of Habersham County, Georgia, distilled for twenty years. When she was arrested she explained that she had been accused of killing her husband and sold liquor to pay the lawyers working to exonerate her. Melinda Turner, a fifty-year-old widow, was colorful in a folksy way. Living in an isolated, one-room cabin high on a mountainside in White County, Georgia, she said that "I have made whisky since my old man died, . . . and I guess I'll make it till I go whar he is. . . . I'm as good a hand to make the corn-juice as you ever laid eyes on in your borned days." Taken to the Atlanta jail, she described the city, which she was seeing for the first time in her life, as so noisy that she "couldn't hear her ears." Nancy McCoy Hatfield Phillips, a McCoy who first married a Hatfield and, later, Frank Phillips, a bitter enemy of the family, joined her husband in helping support the family by selling moonshine. One woman, Bettie Smith of Fentress County, Tennessee, was allegedly the author of "that wild and stirring romance, 'The Blue-Headed Sapsucker, or the Rock Where the Juice Ran Out.'" Her trial was the occasion for probably apocryphal banter about Bettie's age and her explanation of how and to whom she sold her whiskey: "Some time ago a party of gentlemen came out into my neighborhood to hunt deer. The party got out of whiskey, but found it difficult to buy any. After a while I told a man if he would put his jug down on a dollar and go away, he might when he came back, find the jug full of whiskey." The judge asked, "Would you know the man?" "Oh yes, sir," the sprightly woman responded, "I recognized him in a moment. You are the man, judge." Some women in the mountain South aided and protected their men in the moonshine business, and occasionally they took a hand in producing wildcat whiskey themselves.[48]

Blockaders were always prepared to satisfy their neighbors' or more distant customers' thirst for something stronger than pure mountain water. Moonshiners were often in a better position than most mountaineers to experience benefits from industrialization. They were quick to take advantage of expanding markets in camps and company towns and gained new recruits from farmers needing cash for specific purchases or payments or tempted by the profits from mountain dew. They fit Gordon McKinney's general description of entrepreneurs: "The more enterprising secured capital and started their own businesses utilizing the resources of the mountains." Moonshiners' capital investment was their still; their re-sources, the corn and clear, cold water of mountain streams.[49]

Increasingly over the years, though, modernization cost them the support or tacit sympathy of solid citizens, especially in the towns, who were em-bracing the nineteenth century's moral attitudes toward liquor. Revenuers, of course, were another agent of modernization whom blockaders did not welcome. Change, as often, led to conflict.[50]

3 The Right to Make a Little Licker

Moonshiner Resistance

to Federal Authority

. . . .

Imposition of federal taxes amounting to 90 cents a gallon in the later 1870s, raised to $1.10 in 1894, threatened an important local industry among the highlanders. Rural distillers could not afford to absorb the tax themselves nor to compete with tax-paying distilleries by passing it on to their customers, who were perennially short of ready cash. After generations of producing home brew in peace, new laws "criminalized" farmers' means of making a little money. During the Civil War several southern states passed laws prohibiting use of grains and other products for anything but food. These measures outlawed home distillation, but hard-pressed Confederate authorities could do little to enforce them. Many moonshiners, including the Reverend Baylus Hamrick, began their careers in violation of these laws. Immediately after the war the federal revenue laws were loosely enforced, but later intensification of government efforts "caught many a man who honestly believed that he had a right to make 'a little licker.'"[1]

Distillers could not plead ignorance of the law for very long, but to the typical moonshiner, "tradition was more binding than law. His father made whisky on the same plantation and if it was right in his father's time, how could it ever be wrong?" He was "soundly convinced that the law is unjust, and that he is only exercising his natural rights." Mountain people "claimed that inasmuch as this is a free government—a Republic—every citizen should be allowed to make a living for himself and family as best he can; and if he does not steal, or trample upon the rights of his neighbors, the Government should not interfere with him." Georgia highlanders expressed a "spirit of mountain independence which believes that a man has a right to do pretty much what he pleases," agreeing with Alexander Stephens that "a farmer should have the same right to boil his corn into 'sweet mash' as to boil it into hominy." So long as they did no harm to their neighbors, these men considered whiskey-making a natural or inalienable right. A Georgia blockader told former attorney general Amos Akerman "he'd like to know what his grandfather 'fit' in the Revolution for if he was not to be allowed to make a little corn whiskey." A North Carolina newspaper articulated the revolutionary theme in more detail: "Taxation without representation caused a bloody and prolonged war, and resulted in the establishment of a Republic known as the United States of America. Taxation in these United States, without representation, is not carrying out in good faith, the policy inaugurated by the Revolutionists. The genius of our government has become wholly deformed." Another paper declared that enforcement of the law by "a lot of spies and smellers" was "repulsive to the sense of a free people" and even the subjects of monarchical governments resisted the "system of official espionage." This language of natural rights and republican virtue, a common currency among nineteenth-century groups expressing grievances, sought to create an image appealing to Americans generally and to win political support for blockaders.[2]

Moonshiners sought political sympathy, but mountaineers were divided in their partisan allegiance. During the Civil War the mountains had been the scene of bitter fights between Union and Confederate sympathizers, and these conflicts often carried bitterness into later years. In Fannin County, Georgia, the terrorization of the local deputy revenue collector and his son reopened "the old animosities of the War, when this county was in terrible commotion." The old conflicts were not the direct cause of the shooting at and burning of the barn and store of J. A. Stuart, the revenue man, but feelings aroused during the trial of the accused terrorists were "much more violent on both sides" because of the lingering hostilities. A writer from White County, Georgia, charged that a corrupt deputy marshal had been a Unionist guerilla during the war, "men who were brought up on still-slop . . . who deserted their homes and firesides, when their stricken country lay prostrated and mourning, and went far back into the mountains and stole hogs for an *amusement* and robbed the houses of soldiers who were bleeding on the fields of the Old Dominion." In light of such conflicts and attitudes, one might expect that political opinion on the revenue issue would divide along partisan lines, with former rebel Democrats opposing the tax and old Union men, many of whom remained loyal to the Republican party after the war, supporting it.[3]

In some regions moonshiners did express Democratic resentment of Yankee centralization. South Carolina wildcat distillers believed that "the revenue regulations are part of the yankee oppression resulting from the late war." Near Greenville, a town at the foot of the mountains, three "rifle clubs" organized to overthrow Reconstruction in 1876 were "composed largely of illicit distillers." Lewis Redmond, a famous moonshiner leader, and his band were Democrats. During a raid in 1870 blockaders surrounded a party of revenue men and soldiers, shouting that "they had been Confederate Soldiers for four years, had often fought and whipped Yankees." An assistant district attorney in Georgia speculated that local moonshiners had "perhaps a lurking sentiment that the United States is yet a foreign government, and that its officers and agents are intruders upon their reserved rights." Revenuer George W. Atkinson spoke of an "element, and it is by no means small, who insist that there is no such thing as a General Government; that it is a mere usurpation, and that to it they owe no allegiance whatsoever. . . . This spirit of intolerance is the natural outgrowth of the rebellion."[4] It is not surprising that former rebels objected to revenue collection, but mountain Unionists and Republicans also opposed it.

Highland Republicans often did not share the national Republican administration's views of the revenue issue. Commissioner of Internal Revenue Green B. Raum hoped that once mountain people realized that the government was "not undertaking to impair their rights as citizens, and they threw off the scales that were upon their eyes," they would vote Republican. In the mountains, though, people voted Republican even while complaining about the revenue system's violation of their rights. Of thirty-two East Tennessee counties that consistently voted Republican, ten figured in revenue reports as scenes of moonshiner resistance. Republicanism and moonshining were equally strong in Georgia's Habersham, Gilmer, and Murray counties. During the early 1880s Wilkes County, North Carolina, long famous for its blockaders, and the moonshiner enclave of the South Mountains, in Burke County, supported the Republicans. A South Carolina district attorney described mountaineer "original Union men" who "fought savagely against the conscription of the rebellion. The principles of the Republican faith, found there a natural entrenchment," but these men, responding to the lack of a market for their corn, found the revenue laws "passing strange." A bureau of labor statistics agent, captured by moonshiners who thought him a revenuer, received a lecture from their leader: "We uns hev got jist as much right to make our own licker outen our corn as we've got to make our own bread outen it; an' it nattally gits up our boys' dander to hev our liberties took away from us by our own Guvment what we fought to keep up agin the Secesh." In the nineties another mountaineer told a magazine writer, "We-uns fit for the gover'*ment* in wartimes, and hit thess natcherly look like hit ortn't be hard on we-uns atter that thar." The moonshiners of Hancock County, Tennessee, had been "entirely loyal" during the war, three-fourths of them having served in the Union army. To these mountaineers, fighting for the Union was not for the privilege of paying taxes on their mountain dew.[5]

Politicians acted on these viewpoints. In 1881 some Georgia Republican leaders joined independent Democrats in a platform that included a call for abolition of the revenue system "as soon as the reduction of the national debt will permit." Former governor Joseph Brown of Georgia, a U.S. senator in 1884, declared that the old Unionists were "so badly treated by the revenue officers that there is probably no place in the South now where there is less of real love for the Union and its laws." Two Democratic Georgia congressmen and a Virginia Republican also warned that the revenue laws would alienate mountaineers from the Republican party. Tennessee Republican congressmen constantly complained about revenue enforcement, and Representative L. C. Houk besieged the attorney general with requests for pardons of his moonshiner constituents.[6]

In North Carolina's Byzantine politics of liquor control, many Republicans were openly hostile to the revenue laws. The party's state platforms of 1884 and 1888 urged elimination of the revenue system. As early as 1870 a Republican newspaper warned that excise enforcement was causing mountain supporters to "become soured and stand still, while the new rebellion [by the Klan] gathers head like a rising storm." The editor pointedly thought it was "a shame that the most loyal portion of our state should be traversed by armed U.S. officers and soldiers, to 'smash up' a few copper stills" while "no armed force can be obtained to patrol disloyal sections, for the purpose of protecting life and property." O. H. Dockery, a leading North Carolina Republican, charged that revenue enforcement drove mountain Unionists into the Democratic ranks, arguing that western counties that voted solidly Republican in 1868 were Democratic by 1877. In Wilkes County, a Mr. Bryan ran for Congress as a Republican during the seventies, boasting that he had been a moonshiner, and "called upon the people to come up and look upon a 'he-blockader.' " How they voted after looking at him is not recorded, but it is clear that North Carolina Republicans shared their Democratic neighbors' objections to the revenue system.[7]

Revenue collectors appointed numerous subordinates, ranging from 24 in Arkansas to 237 in the fifth Kentucky district and 325 in the sixth North Carolina district. In several states, especially Georgia and North Carolina, the collector was head of a powerful patronage machine that struggled with a rival faction in the party for control of federal offices. During the Harrison administration, Revenue Commissioner John M. Mason worked to "harmonize" squabbling Republican factions in the South. Congressman J. M. Brower of North Carolina believed that Collector Eaves had not given Brower's supporters as many positions as they deserved. Anxious for party unity in the state, Mason assigned two deputies to Eaves to help during the fruit brandy season and "suggested" that the collector appoint two of Brower's friends. However, Eaves did not seem to have heeded his superior's advice, because Brower complained later that Eaves and his deputies were "using their official positions to bring him into disrepute" and prevent his reelection. Mason had to dispatch a revenue agent to investigate the quarrel privately. Some Tennessee Republicans were upset at the appointment of temporary special deputy collectors for raids against moonshiners, thinking that one congressman's district was being favored. Mason took pains to assure them that the deputies were only temporary. Generally, as he advised Kentucky revenuers, he wanted his subordinates to "keep the officers of your district out of all unnecessary quarrels and complications, collect the revenue, enforce the law, and keep in the middle of the road, and all will be well in the end." Mason was a conscientious overseer of an intricate but clashing patronage machinery; he complained that it was "very difficult to distribute the patronage in such a manner as to prevent it becoming a very great element of weakness." If he appointed no subordinates in a district, he was attacked for ignoring loyal supporters of the party; if he appointed people, the rejected office-seekers declared that he had "selected exactly the wrong men." Mountain Republican politicians denounced the revenue system to win highlanders' votes, but sometimes patronage quarrels also led some of them to condemn the system because it had not rewarded them with offices.[8]

Ordinary southern highlanders, whether Republicans or Democrats, usually shared opposition to taxation that disrupted their economy and way of life. A federal judge in North Carolina observed that "prominent political speakers of both political parties often address the people and for the purpose of winning popular favor, denounce in strong language the *injustice, wrong, oppression,* and *outrage* of the Internal Revenue Laws. These laws have but few defenders except the Courts and the officers of the Government." A military officer reporting on the North Carolina, Georgia, Tennessee, and Virginia border area asserted that "the hostility to the revenue laws is not confined to one political party but is general." He did "not think the charges that these violations of law result from determined hostility to the government are clearly established. They show no more determination in attempting to defraud the revenue than is exhibited in Brooklyn & other cities." Georgia provided a practical demonstration of this bipartisan opposition to revenue enforcement. Under the Hayes administration, Democrats urged replacement of the Republican marshal to reduce conflict over the revenue laws. Democratic marshal Fitzsimmons sought to conciliate moonshiners by rejecting large armed posses in favor of sending at most only two deputies on raids. He also urged blockaders to surrender rather than resist and encouraged them to come in for a hearing before a newly appointed U.S. commissioner (equivalent to a justice of the peace) in the mountain district. Fitzsimmons's supporters claimed his policy was successful, but apparently Democratic deputies were being shot at as often as their Republican predecessors, with what Commissioner Raum called "rigid impartiality."[9] It was the tax, not who collected it, to which mountaineers objected.

Politicians schemed and denounced, but the mountaineer had to guard his still with "his own wits and a well-worn Winchester or muzzle loader." If possible, he preferred to use his wits. Although gunfights with casualties on both sides became common as the government crackdown intensified in the late seventies, most moonshiners wanted to save themselves from arrest, with a possible prison term in the distant North, and their stills from being smashed up by the revenuers. Only the most confident or careless block-ader would leave his still-house unguarded, and many times moonshiners posted pickets to give ample warning of a posse's approach. As raiders neared the Snider Settlement in North Carolina they saw men on the mountain peaks running to spread the alarm; soon they heard "the blowing of horns and the peculiar hoots" that signaled danger to the moonshiners. "So complete is the system of signals that no stranger can be seen without instantaneous alarm being given all through the neighborhood." Similarly, raids in northern Alabama were "heralded in the hills and mountains of the distillers," and moonshiners were rarely taken by surprise; "the ringleaders *always* escape capture." Troops, used in raids during the seventies, were more conspicuous than civilian posses, and "as soon as a squad of soldiers start out it is heralded all through the country by the papers and the people," giving blockaders enough time to "run off their stills." When bluecoats stopped at the house of a mountaineer in the Rocky Bottom and Cain Creek district of South Carolina, one of his children ran out to spread the alarm, and soon the soldiers heard guns firing and horns blowing, the sounds being carried along for miles. Henry Tankersley, who made "the best illicit whiskey in Georgia," became famous as a moonshiner Paul Revere in the winter of 1893. Spotting the revenuers before they reached the mountains, he leaped on his "fast mule" and rode for thirty miles, shouting, "Look out! the revenoors is a-comin'." Occasionally members of the raiding party themselves would tip off the moonshiners. Once a mailman opened an informer's letter to a deputy revenue collector and wrote on the envelope that he would warn the blockaders. Citizens from whom revenue men and occasionally commanders of infantry detachments rented horses not only provided poor mounts but spread the news of an impending raid. A suc-cessful raid—in which blockaders were actually caught by surprise despite their precautions—required great secrecy and careful planning.[10]

Most moonshiners were ordinary people scattered among their neigh-bors. In some areas, though, there were settlements of extended family members who kept revenuers out for years. The Snider Settlement in Ashe County, North Carolina, was an enclave ruled by a band of outlaws who either won the sympathy of honest neighbors or paralyzed them with fear. The cabins of the settlement were scattered in a valley enclosed by moun-tain spurs. During the Civil War the area harbored a band of bushwhackers, including members of the Snider family, who "indiscriminately plundered and murdered Union men and rebels." After the war these men became moonshiners. Another area in the North Carolina Smokies, "one of the densest laurel fields that can be found in the whole mountain range," was the domain of two families, the Sheltons (thirteen of whose kin had been massacred by Confederates in 1863) and the Joneses. They had been stilling unmolested for years because one Shelton had threatened to kill any invading revenuers. The "Dark Corner" on the Carolina border, where it was allegedly impossible to drink clear water from the creeks polluted by distillery waste, was a similar enclave of outlaw moonshiners. The Howard clan and others successfully resisted revenue officers although many law-abiding citizens had urged the federal district attorney to do something about the band. An East Tennessee enclave was Chestnut Flats in Cades Cove, Blount County. Dominated by G. W. Powell and Jules Gregg, who ran a wildcat brandy distillery, the flats became "periodically inundated by outlaws of all descriptions who drank, gambled, whored, and shot each other to pass the time," as well as stealing farm animals from their neighbors. Much to the disgust of most of the farmers and their historian, the flats gave the whole cove area a distorted reputation.[11]

Some of these enclaves were dominated by moonshiner "kings" who attracted local young men by their courage and the opportunities they offered as blockaders. Hutsell Amarine, who lived with kinsmen and others in Blount County, Tennessee, was a notorious moonshiner who killed the revenue collector's son during a raid. Before Amarine's arrest in 1881, his group "established such a reign of terror that the people are literally afraid to do or say anything" against them.[12]

At the end of the century Young Graham was a powerful king of moonshiners in Nevada County, western Arkansas. He and his band "completely intimidated" their neighbors so witnesses would never testify before a grand jury. Since local supporters knew the deputy marshals, Graham received ample warning of their approach. He was also protected by numerous dogs who patrolled his property. The marshal sent two men, strangers to the locality, who actually got the drop on Graham with their rifles and arrested him. However, his wife stepped out of the house and leveled her Winchester at the possemen, who were forced to flee. Some of his kinspeople tried to persuade him to submit to the law, but he "steadfastly" refused.[13]

The most famous outlaw moonshiner king was Lewis Redmond of South

Carolina, who became a sort of Jesse James of the mountains. Redmond, born in Georgia, moved to North Carolina and carried on illicit distilling. His log cabin pierced with portholes and well stocked with weapons was perched on a bluff overlooking the Tennessee River. He could spot anybody approaching the house along a single narrow pathway at the edge of a cliff. Revenuers seem to have left him alone in this fortress, and when they did try to capture him, the mountain man escaped. One raiding party was close enough to hear Redmond carousing with a jug of his own moonshine. However, when they burst in, he had already escaped up the chimney. Deputy Marshal Duckworth tried to arrest him while he was carrying liquor in a wagon to sell in town, but Redmond killed the lawman. The blockader then thought it best to move to South Carolina, where he lived with his two sisters and "one of his concubines" in a cabin on the border of Oconee and Pickens counties. Other kinfolk lived nearby, including his young brother-in-law Amos Ladd, killed by revenuers in 1878. Redmond's courage and cleverness won the admiration of local young men, who looked upon him as their leader. He was "agile as a panther" and evaded arrest because of his intimate knowledge of the terrain. Local farmers seem to have feared him and his followers, some having received threats when they tried to recover animals stolen by him or his men.[14]

In 1877 Deputy Collector E. H. Barton had been after Redmond for several months, finally capturing him at a house he was visiting. The revenuers tied up one of his men but did not have enough rope for the outlaw. As soon as Barton went outside for more rope, Redmond jumped up and ran for safety through four-inch-deep snow. The revenuers fired at him but missed. Immediately giving chase, the officers were ambushed from the roadside, Barton and another deputy receiving wounds. Redmond then took the offensive, determined to recover the horses and wagon the revenuers had captured. He and "nine of his heavily armed mountain roughs" rode up to Barton's house, demanding Redmond's horses or Barton's life. The revenuer told him that the horses were in Greenville. Redmond made Barton's wife mount one of the officer's horses and lead another to accompany them to the nearby village of Easley. In town he made her cash a check for $105 to pay for the captured horses. He took the money and then ordered her to dismount, taking Barton's best horse and leaving the other, saying that he did not want to "take the last thing" the revenuer had. Local citizens who watched the proceedings cheered, "*Hurrah for Redmond*: he has done just right."[15]

During the next year, 1878, Redmond and thirty followers stormed the Pickens County jail, releasing three of their friends and relatives arrested on moonshining charges. A state grand jury indicted the outlaw leader, but only for stealing two overcoats from the jail! Judge Mackey, not particularly sympathetic to revenuers himself, had to argue with federal jurors to secure a later indictment for Redmond's role in the jailbreak. To pursue the overcoat thief, the sheriff organized a hundred-man posse, including members of a local militia company, who marched and galloped about in a perhaps deliberately clumsy pursuit. Despite a $500 reward on his head, Redmond was not arrested.[16]

Redmond's final capture in 1881 was appropriately dramatic. While squirrel hunting, he heard his dogs howling and thought they had found some game. Instead he found himself surrounded by a posse of revenuers. Raising his gun to fire, Redmond was not quite quick enough for the lawmen, who shot first, wounding him in several places. He was first taken to jail in Asheville, North Carolina, but rumors of an impending rescue caused his transfer to Greenville, South Carolina. There may have been no rescuers there, but there was no lack of supporters. A local newspaper urged people to "forget his faults in admiration of his undaunted courage and unmistakable dash." People visiting the jail while he was awaiting trial gave gifts of food, whiskey, and cigars; women admirers sent the illiterate mountaineer perfumed notes. "Disgusting as it must appear to sensible people," grumbled a disgusted but fascinated *New York Times*, "it is a fact that Redmond is at this time the most popular man in South Carolina." In an interview with the *Times* reporter, he said, "I know I done wrong, but it wasn't all my fault. There were some big men who led me on," including a state senator and a judge who were scathing critics of the revenue laws, "and I was a fool to listen to them." Redmond had killed two men, although he was not charged with murder; their deaths may have influenced the judge to throw the book at the blockader. Eight separate, consecutive illegal distilling charges netted him four years in the federal penitentiary at Auburn, New York, and a year for conspiracy in his attack on Barton brought his time to five years. His popularity was unabated: ladies of the Woman's Christian Temperance Union petitioned for his release in 1884. After two or three years in prison, he seemed to be dying of tuberculosis. At the behest of Senator Wade Hampton, he received a presidential pardon to spend his last days at peace in his own home. However, in 1900, "Major Redmond, hale and sound, is still making whisky in a licensed distillery in Walhalla, a little mountain town in South Carolina. A famous brand of 'mountain dew' is sold under his name, and his lithograph portrait adorns the heads of the barrels." Mountain folk were survivors.[17]

Amos Owens, who introduced this study, was a different type of monarch. As the "cherry bounce king" of Rutherford County, North Carolina, he was "greater than Redmond," according to his admiring biographer. He began his career as a perfectly legal distiller in 1846, developing a popular liquor compounded of corn whiskey, honey, and cherry juice that was known throughout the South. Every June he honored the cherry harvest with a "cherry bounce celebration" attended by people from far and wide. An ex-Confederate soldier who had done time in a Union prison camp, Owens returned to his home on Cherry Mountain to find his only slave freed and the Yankees demanding payment of a whiskey tax. He became a Ku Klux Klan leader, and his first sentence to federal prison in 1872 was for Klan activity. Equally opposed to taxes as to Reconstruction, he also became a blockader, serving his next prison term in 1876 for illicit distilling. He vowed never to yield, but when revenuers caught up with him, he neither fled nor resisted. He appeared in federal court many times between the 1870s and 1890; at first he was acquitted because his wit and repartee won over both judge and jury. Once Judge Dick told Owens that he had given the court "lots of trouble," to which the sprightly Irishman replied, "This hyar court's give *me* lots of trouble too." Three terms in the federal penitentiary seem to have been enough for Owens: at his last trial in 1890 he surprised judge, revenuers, and spectators with a tearful declaration that he would give up moonshining. Apparently he kept his word and became a deeply religious man in his old age.[18]

Whether notorious or ordinary, hard like Amarine or cheerful like Owens, moonshiners could often count on their neighbors for support and protection. Whether induced by sympathy or fear, this support frustrated revenuers. Whenever a raiding party along the Georgia-Alabama border encountered a local farmer, he "took to the woods." If they spoke to one, he claimed not to know the name of his next-door neighbor, and nobody would act as guides. While the posse had to search for moonshiners on its own, "these ignorant (?) [*sic*] people take advantage of our absence to take a short-cut to warn the distillers of our advance." Had local people helped a West Virginia posse, "We would have been spared many an hours hard toiling in deep hollows, on rocky hillsides & steep mountains" and would have found several large distilleries within a mile or less of where they were fruitlessly searching. Revenuers in Texas who knew the way to a still experimented with asking the way from local residents; even at houses a short distance from the still, no one knew anything about it. A wall of silence as well as of armed men protected the moonshiners.[19]

When moonshiners were arrested, sympathy continued to provide allies. It was very difficult to find men to serve on federal juries who were willing to indict or convict blockaders. Georgia moonshiners were supported by "a general feeling" that "no convictions can be obtained" in U.S. courts, "the boast being publicly made that the jurors are on the side of prisoners and against the Government." White South Carolina jurors suspended their normal prejudices when they refused to convict a group of blacks of illegal sale of small amounts of liquor, believing it was not "the intention of the law to punish this class of offenders." Although the judge denounced the verdict as "contrary to the law and the evidence and . . . monstrous and licentious," an hour later the same jury declared a man not guilty of illicit distillation who had confessed during preliminary examination. To secure an indictment of Lewis Redmond, Judge Mackey had to force the grand jury to return three times and to remove one of the jurors before they brought in a bill "on the plainest and most reliable evidence." Impartiality was an extremely rare virtue among jurymen in revenue cases.[20]

Fear of moonshiners as well as sympathy for them also frustrated efforts to arrest them. Local people knew well the consequences of even being suspected of informing or "reporting" on moonshiners. The "best citizens" of northern Georgia apparently opposed illicit distilling, having "*whispered*" this opinion in Marshal Smyth's ears "for several years," but no one dared provide information for the revenue men. "In the very few instances in which these citizens have assisted us, the 'worst citizens' have so harassed them in various ways that they have generally been obliged to leave their homes and go elsewhere." In South Carolina "the more intelligent citizens and men of property would prefer to see law enforced but they live in constant dread of the distillers and their friends and do not dare to give any information or even to furnish food and forage" to revenue posses. Al-

though some blacks were moonshiners, they were among the few supporters of federal authority in the South and were "very valuable" as informers
and guides, but only "if properly protected" from the harsh punishments
blockaders meted out to them. This protection was usually beyond officials'
capacity. Even the governor of Arkansas felt the pressure against cooperating with revenuers. The marshal requested him to supply breech-loading
rifles for a raiding party, but he refused. He said that if any blockaders were
killed or wounded with the state-issued weapons, "he would have to leave
the State." One of the most difficult tasks of revenue enforcement was
breaking through this fear to learn of the existence and location of illegal
stills.[21]

Informers who told revenue men the names of illicit distillers, guides who
conducted raiding parties personally or provided detailed directions to
stills, witnesses who testified against moonshiners, and jurymen who voted
for indictment or conviction were all "Judases" despised by many mountain
people and were targets for exemplary punishment. Since revenue enforcement depended heavily on information, blockaders often resorted to intimidation of potential informers or witnesses and punishment of people who
had betrayed their neighbors. Their methods were similar to those of white
supremacists.

Collector Andrew Clark of Georgia kept the most thorough records of
violence against people who helped the revenuers. Between January 1877
and February 1881 Clark reported the killing, wounding, or beating of
twenty-eight informers, suspected informers, or witnesses. In 1877 a black
suspected informer disappeared, presumed dead at the hands of moonshiners; another informer was killed by a relative of a blockader; and a man
accused of informing was shot and killed by moonshiners. A suspected
informer was attacked in his own home and wounded. Another informer,
who received many threats to his life, was killed while plowing his field.
Moonshiners burned the house of a suspected reporter. In the next year
there were fewer murders but more "outrages" in Georgia. Masked blockaders shot and killed an informer in his own home. A black guide who had
been shot and wounded during a raid was arrested by the state for carrying
concealed weapons and sentenced to the chain gang, "where he finally
disappeared, it being generally believed that he was murdered by those
against whom he would have testified in the U.S. Courts." A black informer
was abducted, tied to a tree, and shot at; an accidental intruder on a still was

beaten and left for dead. Two suspected informers were whipped by disguised moonshiners; a suspected informer's house was fired into and his hogs were killed. Lumpkin County blockaders burned an accused informer's barn, shed, and fences and killed his ox. Disguised moonshiners attacked a woman and her son suspected of betrayal: the boy was shot at, the woman "shamefully beaten." In 1879 a black man who was not in fact an informer was killed by masked men in Walton County; another black was mortally wounded in Campbell; and a white Judas was shot and badly wounded in Rabun. The Pool brothers were attacked at home, and one was killed. Moonshiners attacked an informer and his wife, seriously injuring both; another reporter and a guide were nearly killed by disguised blockaders who also burned their barn. In 1880 a witness was killed by a convicted moonshiner, and an informer was wounded in his own house. Another informer was shot and beaten at home, and moonshiners knocked down a suspected informer with a stick while he was attending church. In South Carolina three informers were killed in 1877 and eleven were shot at, beaten, or driven from their homes in 1877 and 1878.[22] Disguises, attacks on blacks, and the general treatment of informers and witnesses are familiar to students of the Ku Klux Klan and other white supremacist vigilante groups.

Many of the worst areas of Klan violence in the early 1870s were regions where moonshiners were also active. Klansmen, or members of groups who appropriated the name and methods of the Klan, attacked revenue officers and informers. In Polk, Yancey, Jackson, Cleveland, Rutherford, Transylvania, Clay, and Ashe counties, North Carolina, the revenue collector in 1871 described moonshiners as "under a kind of protectorship of that secret organization called 'Ku Klux Klan'." The Klan "filled many people with such terror" that they were afraid to "bring its vengeance upon them." A South Carolina revenue officer received a threatening letter headed "K.K.K."—"You are hereby notified that 15 days will be allowed you to wind up your affairs & leave this county for good, if you do not take heed, you must abide the consequences." In Missouri the collector "experienced a great deal of opposition and threats" after a raid, and one of his deputies was shot and wounded by three men disguised "in black dresses supposed to be calico." The collector often received warnings that "there were organizations who are going to attempt to murder me." Once thirty men set out from a moonshiner district to assassinate him but were prevented by rain and high water. "In every instance" witnesses against blockaders "were run off" by terrorists. Deputy Collector Guild of Georgia reported in 1874 that the Klan threatened to kill every white man who voted Republican and that his own buggy was destroyed during the night by twenty or thirty armed men who were "traveling around the house where I was staying nearly all night." Deputy Marshal Henry Martin of South Carolina, in camp with a squad of troops on a revenue raid, received a threatening letter less refined than the one sent to the revenuer earlier: "Theas few lines is to let you know that you must leave . . . by 10 O Clock to Morrow or the Kucluck will kill ever one af you[.] You hiv no busyness hear and you will do well to leave by the time allowed or the Kuclucks will go a for you." This missive was signed with seventeen names all in the same handwriting. In Owen County, Kentucky, Klansmen attacked all people associated with the federal government: revenue officers, the deputy marshal, blacks, and witnesses in cases against the Klan. For many Klansmen, like Amos Owens, the issues of Reconstruction and revenue were inseparable.[23]

The Klan name could still inspire terror long after Reconstruction. An informer received a note "adorned with a variety of KuKlux emblems" from the "Pickens Black Hawks" in 1878 telling him to leave or "we will git you sure when we burn powder at you we git you." A Virginian who provided meals to revenuers received a note from "a clan of kuklux," who later came to his house in disguise looking for the deputies. Moonshiners of Stanly County, North Carolina, reminded a revenuer of "the famous 'Ku-klux' of the South . . . or the banditti of Italy" with their "secret lodges, with passwords, grips, &c." These men "arrested" a salesman who fortunately was a smooth enough talker to convince them he was not a revenuer. They drove from their homes local people who had given lodging to revenuers, and they ambushed any deputies who invaded their territory. "Die at home" was their watchword. In Virginia in 1881, Revenue Agent Tracie described moonshiners' beating and whipping of black informers as a "revival of KuKluxism." The Georgia whitecaps of the 1890s were routinely called Ku Klux, though their critics distinguished them from the "good" Klan of Reconstruction days. Most groups who attacked officers or informers were ad hoc vigilance committees, but the Klan and the whitecaps defended moonshiners as part of their general mission of protecting the local community against outsiders or traitors within, white or black.[24]

Georgia whitecaps were particularly well organized: between 1891 and 1893 they whipped witnesses and informers and attacked revenue officials in Gilmer, Murray, Whitfield, and Gordon counties. Operating at night, they "knock down the doors of the houses of the people, shoot into their homes, and take them out and beat them, and at times it is weeks before they can scarcely walk." According to the district attorney, the whitecappers killed at least fifteen to twenty people in such attacks. In one case they seem to have been able to command loyalty that broke normal kinship solidarity. In 1894, a Georgia informer, "Henry X.," was hanged and, when he escaped, was later shot by local whitecap vigilantes. These gentlemen told both his wife and mother what they were going to do and allegedly received the blessing of both. The wife even berated them for bungling the hanging, and when Henry did die, the mother responded to condolences by saying, "We've never had such peace and comfort in the world as we've had since Henry was killed." "Henry X." is undoubtedly Henry Worley, who was indeed hanged and later shot. His offense was particularly serious: himself a whitecap under indictment, he turned "states evidence" against his fellow vigilantes. His family was more loyal to principle than to kinship.[25]

Despite terror and intimidation, the informer continued to be essential to revenue enforcement. He or she broke the wall of solidarity at great personal risk to bring the forces of the law upon the heads of neighbors. Occasionally informers were enforcing a "moral economy" shared by their community. When corn crops were poor and people were having trouble feeding their families, highlanders did not look upon moonshining with their usual tolerance. When the crop was poor, local sentiment demanded that corn first be made into meal for bread and fodder for animals. In North Carolina, a poor crop in 1881 "will render illicit distillation unpopular" and "induce many. . . who otherwise would be indifferent" to report moonshiners to the revenuers. In Cades Cove, Tennessee, churchgoing farmers generally opposed excessive drinking and moonshining. They tolerated a little stillin' if it were not a person's principal source of income, but "condemnation was instant" if excessive drinking led to abuse of wife and children and neglect of farm work, and "men who made moonshine in large quantities were always in danger of becoming outcasts." Even there, though, moonshining had to become quite extensive before a leading citizen would turn informer.[26]

Revenuers and mountaineers agreed that informers most often were motivated by the five- or ten-dollar reward for locating stills or by personal animosity to the moonshiner they betrayed. "Persons giving information . . . are generally governed by one of two motives—hatred or expected reward," reported one revenuer; a colleague agreed that "no one will give information except for pay or unless some one has a slight or imaginary wrong to avenge." A moonshiner who "should happen to gain the displeasure or excite the malice of a meddlesome neighbor" was in serious trouble, as many people would walk twenty-five miles to swear out a warrant. An old mountaineer catalogued the types of informers: "Sometimes hit's some pizen old bum who's been refused credit. Sometimes hit's the wife or mother of some feller who's drinkin' too much. Then, agin, hit may be some rival blockader who aims to cut off the other feller's trade, and, same time, divert suspicion from his own self. But ginerally hit's jest somebody who has a gredge agin the blockader for family reasons, or business reasons, and turns informer to git even." These personal motives could be calculated, or they could be flashes of anger the informer may have regretted later.[27]

Although many women supported their blockader husbands or sons, and a few stilled themselves, women made up a large proportion of the informers. After a major raid and arrest of Bill Berong and his sons, notorious blockaders of Towns County, Georgia, the wife of one of the arrested men resented that the net did not snare all the local moonshiners. She informed on twenty neighbors, saying, "My husband has gone, and twenty men *must go with him*." Ordinary jealousy was also a motive. In East Tennessee, Sallie P.'s conflict with Bessie B. over the affections of Si W. led to Sallie's reporting the B. family's still to the revenuers. The raid was successful; whether Sallie was able to continue living in the neighborhood is not known. Sometimes wives and mothers opposed moonshining because they were angry at the drunkenness and violence fostered by brush whiskey. One woman "with an edge to her tone" said, "Them men that makes whiskey, and sells it to our boys—I wish I was on the jury, I'd penetentiar' 'em every time." An Arkansas woman fed a posse a substantial meal of hogs' heads and feet with home-baked bread, telling the leader that she had "been praying for years" that neighborhood moonshiners would be arrested. In the early twenties Cades Cove women "begged" leading citizen and mailman John Oliver to report moonshiners; disturbed by the consequences of heavy drinking, he became an active informer, and his house became a base for raiders. He paid the informer's price, losing two barns and their animals and machinery to arsonists. Revenuers "oftentimes" received anonymous letters in women's handwriting, and an assistant district attorney considered women more reliable than men as guides to hidden stills.[28]

Most historians agree that family loyalty was the cohesive element in mountain communities, and it was a powerful force in protecting moonshiners. Nevertheless, it was not absolute, as the extreme case of the Worley incident and the examples of women exasperated by their menfolks' drinking suggest. There are other instances of informers betraying kinspeople. In North Carolina an 1894 raid on the Smith Settlement was guided by Jim Smith, a former blockader. The Lunsford family of Union County, Georgia, seems to have been divided. Thomas Lunsford received a three-month jail sentence because of testimony from Mary J., Tabitha C., and W. J. Lunsford. Thomas in his turn testified against W. J. Lunsford. In 1907 William Foster sought to reform his oldest brother by reporting him. He had threatened family members with death if they gave away the location of his still. Foster wanted the still destroyed but a light sentence for his brother "to convince him that it is impossible to escape punishment." The revenuers destroyed the still, and the judge obliged with a short sentence.[29] Foster was able to use the power of outsiders to teach a lesson to his brother.

Moonshiners were not necessarily firmly loyal to their own communities, certainly not the group of South Carolina blockaders who placed their stills on unsuspecting neighbors' land so the wrong person would be arrested. Nor was there strict loyalty to blockaders as a group. Competitiveness among wildcatters sometimes led to betrayal. Dave Payne from southeastern Tennessee had tried to join moonshiners Silas and Milos Wood, who told him they did not need another man. Payne then became a deputy marshal and arrested Silas and Milos. Silas went to prison, but Milos received only a fine. He told Dave to stay on the other side of the road when he walked by Milos's house and "not to come breshin' up agin his palin's [fence]." Angered, Dave later returned in a drunken rage and shot Milos and his father. Local people, "despising one of their fellows who 'turns revenue'" made up a posse that captured Payne. However, the Judas and murderer escaped from jail, and all the possemen "got out their rifles and still carry them," anticipating Payne's revenge. Most of Dave's kin stood by him, and the mountaineers expected a full-scale feud to develop between the Paynes and the other men "who watch each other like opposing armies." Jim Ashford, killed by revenuers in Kentucky in 1879, seems to have informed on his neighbors to monopolize distilling for himself. He proclaimed his own intention of "never being taken by the officers." Payne and Ashford were looking out for themselves.[30]

Some people were one thing in their own settlements and another thing outside. A group of North Carolina blockaders and outlaws were rumored to be working as revenuers in adjoining South Carolina; one member of the band apparently served as a deputy marshal. Riley Pyle, a notorious Tennessee blockader, was brother of a deputy marshal serving in another district. Campbell Morgan, "the head-centre of moonshiners" in mid-Tennessee and southern Kentucky, became a deputy marshal after he was arrested in 1878 and served his prison term. He worked with revenuer Captain James Davis, earlier his bitter enemy, "arresting his former associates, in which business he has been remarkably successful." Morgan joined Smith in arresting Bill Berong, head of a Georgia moonshiner clan. Berong in his turn promised to help them break up illicit distilling in his neighborhood. Whether the motives of such men were greed or genuine desire for reformation, they helped weaken moonshiner solidarity.[31]

Informing against blockaders could also be part of internal community struggles over other issues. The Hatfield-McCoy feud included some incidents of this type. Both the Hatfields and the McCoys were blockaders, but once members of the McCoy faction informed on Devil Anse Hatfield, an industrious moonshiner, as part of a plan to capture him and claim a reward offered by Kentucky officials. The federal judge presiding over his trial on a charge of illegal liquor selling heard of the conspiracy and told the jurors, who promptly acquitted Hatfield. The judge frustrated the plot by providing a guard of deputy marshals until Anse reached his family's realm. He told the angry McCoys, "When Hatfield gets to his home, I certainly have no objection to any of you arresting him that may want to try it." In another episode of the feud, Roseanna McCoy, lover of Jonse Hatfield, warned him that three of her brothers were plotting to capture him by arresting him for moonshining. In a less prolonged conflict in Neshoba County, Mississippi, not a prominent moonshine area, a minister angered local young men by insulting the reputation of their women friends. The youths tossed a rock

through his window during services, injuring him. The minister's supporters retaliated by reporting that the young men were running wildcat stills,
hoping to avenge the injury by their arrest. The revenue laws could be a
useful weapon in such quarrels.[32]

Highlanders sometimes fought to the death to protect members of their
family or personal friends, but their solidarity rarely went beyond the local
community or kin network and sometimes was broken even within those
boundaries. Mountaineers were divided by individual motives and increasingly during the nineteenth century by conflicting attitudes toward liquor
consumption and manufacture. Such divisions left openings for the informer and prevented the kind of political solidarity and power found
among the white supremacists who overthrew Reconstruction. Mountain
people resisted the revenuer as an outsider disrupting their economy and
culture, but their defenses weakened when people with family or personal
grudges could wreak vengeance by calling in the might of the law against
their enemies. Even the heavy sanctions against betrayal do not seem to
have deterred some people. Punishing a rival with arrest and a possible
prison term upped the ante in what had been locally confined disputes.

Politicians sought moonshiners' votes, but they never organized the total
warfare that white supremacists mounted against Reconstruction. White
supremacy carried a profound psychological and emotional weight that
moonshining never acquired. White supremacists throughout the South
were political brothers, and their leaders were talented politicians who kept
sight of their goals. Mountain people sought to protect themselves and their
kinsmen but were also capable of enlisting the aid of normally despised
outsiders to get back at rivals. Although they could sometimes mount
formidable vigilante organizations, neither traditionalist moonshiners who
simply wanted to be left alone nor modernizers who sought to exploit
expanding markets were able to form lasting political movements. Their
own lack of group solidarity and their minority status within the politics of
their home states prevented effective political organization. They deeply
resented violation of their "right to make a little licker," but that right did
not rise to the level of a sacred unifying principle as did white supremacy.

William F. Holmes has described moonshiners' resistance as a form of
"reactionary" violence.[33] Both entrepreneurial and traditional moonshiners
reacted against extension of federal power that meant either loss of rights

they once enjoyed in peace or the cutting off of new opportunities. In both cases their response was defensive, and they hindered revenue collection with their wits and Winchesters for many years. However, they never drove the revenuer out of the mountains and never silenced all the informers. They fought a continuing battle but could never win. Outwitting and out-fighting the revenuer became part of mountain folk culture and song, one of the highlanders' many confrontations with the changing world.

4 Revenue Enforcement

A Losing Battle,

1865–1877

. . . .

Moonshiners began to evade the liquor tax as soon as revenuers tried to collect it. The earliest reported southern confrontation was in 1865, and evasion soon became extensive in northern cities as well as the mountains of the South.[1] The architects of the revenue system had not anticipated widespread resistance, and revenue collection was inefficient and often corrupt in the early years. Congressmen debating the original revenue bill of 1862 believed they had found a "painless" means of raising revenue in the liquor excise. They used the debates as an opportunity to put their views of liquor and temperance on the record, many arguing that a high tax would promote sobriety. The legislators gave virtually no attention to problems of enforcement.[2]

The original wartime measure set the tax rate and established the enforcement bureaucracy, which did not take its permanent form until after the whiskey ring scandals of the early 1870s. The first measure of 1862 created the office of commissioner of internal revenue and divided the nation into collection districts administered by assessors and their assistants and collectors with their deputies. The assessors had the job of levying taxes by inspecting distilleries and other industries liable to the excise. Their work on the local level was handled by assistant assessors who had the difficult duty of inspection, calculation, and reporting of the taxes due as well as enforcement of the law. Collectors received the tax payments levied by the assessors. They had the power to punish, by seizure of property, tax evaders or delinquents. The collectors could appoint inspectors, paid by fees from the manufacturers, who checked on compliance with the law. In 1863 revenue agents were created to assist enforcement and to supervise local officials. At first there were only three agents, but as the need for supervision and detection of fraud became more obvious, their numbers steadily increased to thirty-five in 1879.

In 1865, Congress appointed a special revenue commission, headed by the economist David Wells, to study ways of improving the efficiency and honesty of the bureaucracy. The commission reported that the Bureau of Internal Revenue was receiving more money every quarter than the entire government took in annually before 1860, but that partisanship in appointments, fraud and collusion with tax evaders, and excessively high taxes were encouraging illicit distilling and costing the government thousands in potential revenue. The commissioners recommended adoption of a civil service system, modeled on the British revenue service, with strict examination of applicants for the various jobs and constant supervision of their activity. The civil service concept was ahead of its time, and Congress responded slowly and incompletely to these recommendations.

The first change occurred in 1866, when the Bureau of Internal Revenue received its own clerical staff, having relied previously on Treasury Department clerks. More importantly, following one of the commission's British-inspired recommendations, the office of solicitor of internal revenue was created. This attorney conducted the revenue bureau's growing number of legal cases. No major changes in the system occurred until 1868, when Congress created the supervisors. These officials monitored the work of several collection districts, to prevent fraud and weed out incompetence. The supervisors could appoint "detectives" to work in special investigations of fraud or evasion. In 1872, their name was changed to "agents," merging them with the previously appointed agents. Calling them detectives had suggested spies and informers. The measure of 1868 also systematized the inspection of distilleries by creating gaugers, who tested and recorded the amount and proof of each barrel of liquor distilled to make sure every gallon was taxed. Storekeepers, who measured and recorded other phases of the distillery's production, were also appointed. They were paid a flat fee per day, but the gaugers were paid according to the amount of liquor they measured. These changes did increase the centralization and efficiency of the system but did not prevent collusion between revenue officials and distillers to evade the tax.[3]

President Andrew Johnson, seeking to build a power base among the federal officeholders, was more concerned with placing his friends in the revenue service than with suppressing illicit distilling. He sought to drive one disloyal revenuer from office by charges of corruption, but Johnson did not bother to check the activities of his own supporters. A Republican congressional investigation in 1866–67 subjected revenue enforcement in New York, Brooklyn, and Philadelphia to close scrutiny and found that "the frauds in those cities are so universal and gigantic; the morals of manufacturers have become so tainted; confidence in the local officers of internal revenue has become so shaken [that] it is manifest that frauds cannot be practiced so generally and so openly without either connivance or gross inefficiency on the part of a large number of revenue officers." Tax evaders, even when caught, could easily pay back taxes, penalties, and legal fees from the profits of years of undisturbed fraud. They never feared imprisonment. One of the worst features of the revenue bureaucracy was payment of distillery inspectors by fees from the distillers themselves, "simply the institution of a farce." In 1869 the *New York Times* reported "wholesale and shameless evasion of the law" under Johnson, and the Democratic *Atlanta Constitution* several years later agreed that immediately after the Civil War there had been "a demoralization in the administration of the law." David A. Wells looked back on this period with amazement: "Under the strong temptation of large and almost certain gains, men rushed into schemes for defrauding the revenue with the zeal of enthusiasts for new gold fields." An extremely high tax rate complicated the picture. The tax rose from 60 cents per gallon when the original revenue act was passed in 1862 to $2 at the end of 1864, and revenues actually fell steadily until 1868. High taxes encouraged evasion, and moonshining took root in the back alleys of cities like Brooklyn as well as in the hollows of the southern Appalachians.[4]

Aided by a drastic cut in the tax rate to 50 cents a gallon, as requested by the commissioner of internal revenue in 1868, the Grant administration began to crack down on small illicit distillers, and revenues rose again. Civilian revenuers and soldiers pursued southern moonshiners, but the prime target was Brooklyn's Democratic Irish of the waterfront district, whose operations were broken up in massive raids aided by literally hundreds of soldiers during the early 1870s.[5]

The Grant administration ignored the main source of low tax revenues in the early seventies until Treasury Secretary Benjamin Bristow exposed it. This was not resistance in the mountains or alleys, but organized evasion by large distillers in the Midwest, the notorious whiskey ring. The ring included high regional revenue officials and reached up to the chief clerk in the Bureau of Internal Revenue and the president's secretary, Orville Babcock. The officials allowed distillers to produce untaxed liquor in exchange for bribes that they at first contributed to President Grant's reelection campaign in 1872 but soon began to pocket themselves. Investigators estimated that between 12 and 15 million gallons of whiskey evaded the tax each year after 1870, costing the government millions in uncollected revenues.[6]

Whiskey ring corruption thrived on defects in the complex system of collecting the liquor tax. The routine business of revenue collection involved monitoring and recording the output of licensed distilleries to make certain that every gallon of liquor was taxed. This regulatory work made distillation the only industry under direct federal regulation of its daily operations. The original revenue measure of 1862 essentially allowed distillers to monitor their own output, but after 1868 two officials were stationed at each distillery. The storekeeper recorded the times of emptying and filling the mash tubs, to meet the requirement that fermentation take place for a maximum of forty-eight hours, with twenty-four-hour empty intervals after each fermentation period. He weighed the grain used in preparing the mash to make sure that the distiller's output matched what was recorded in the official survey of the distillery. This survey described the location of all the distilling equipment and the distillery's capacity. The other official, the gauger, was in charge of the cistern room, to which the spirits were piped after fermentation. He recorded the exact quantity produced and tested the proof of the contents of each barrel. He stamped each barrel with a serial and barrel number, the proof and gallon content, and his name and date. The barrels were then placed in a warehouse—if for longer than a month, the distiller had to obtain a warehouse bond valid for up to a year.

When the liquor was ready for sale, the distiller paid the per-gallon tax to the collector of internal revenue, who supplied the tax-paid stamp with all the information recorded on the warehouse stamp and its own serial number. The distiller kept a record specifying each barrel's various numbers and dates and to whom it was sold. The purchaser, a wholesaler, kept a similar record showing from whom he bought each barrel and to whom he sold it. Many of the purchasers were rectifiers, who produced blended whiskey. A gauger in a rectifying establishment regauged the spirits and provided a rectifier's stamp after seeing that all the original barrels of unblended liquor were emptied and their original stamps destroyed.

This process, involving two officials for each distillery and one for each rectifying establishment, closely monitored the production of whiskey to ensure payment of the tax. However, it was not difficult to subvert the system by bribery. One method of tax evasion required payoffs to the distillery's storekeeper and gauger. Distillers bribed the storekeeper to allow the use of more grain than the law allowed and employment of "quick yeast" to speed fermentation to twenty-four hours instead of forty-eight. This doubled the output of whiskey although the storekeeper's records would show only the legal amount of grain and the usual fermentation period. The gauger was then paid to allow removal of unstamped barrels from the distillery or reuse of old stamps. Using old stamps was safer and was the most common method of cheating the government, although it necessarily involved collusion with a rectifier and payment of his gauger not to destroy the original distillers' stamps received by the rectifier. Another method required the rectifier's gauger to record only half the amount of unblended whiskey received on the stamp stubs, while each barrel of blended whiskey went to market with a legitimate record of its actual contents. If these schemes of tax evasion were widely practiced in his district, the collector had to know about them and share in the profits of illicit distillation.[7]

Seeking to recoup revenues lost during the depression of the 1870s, Secretary of the Treasury Benjamin Bristow searched for the sources of the losses.[8] Acting on tips from informers, he sent investigators to St. Louis to check into reported evasions. Detectives were able to compare distillers' reports of whiskey shipped from the city with the returns of gaugers, storekeepers, and the collector of taxes paid. They found that the excise was paid on only one-third of the whiskey produced in St. Louis. They hired watchmen who reported that distilleries were illegally running at night and that 150-proof whiskey was being certified as 135 proof. They found that stamps were reused over and over and that whiskey was shipped as vinegar.

In May 1875 a carefully planned raid seized St. Louis distilleries and receivers of illicit whiskey from Massachusetts to Texas. The ring, because of Babcock's knowledge of the government's plans, almost escaped the raid because of a telegram sent from Washington warning that "lightning will strike on Monday." It was intercepted before reaching the leader in St. Louis, Supervisor John McDonald. Although Babcock escaped prosecution because he was protected by Grant himself, McDonald and other officials in Chicago and Pittsburgh, the chief clerk in the revenue bureau, and scores of gaugers and storekeepers were punished. Likewise the distillers involved were prosecuted for evasion of the tax. Bristow demanded and received the resignation of Commissioner of Internal Revenue J. W. Douglass, whom he regarded as honest but lazy and cowardly. He recommended and obtained the appointment of Daniel D. Pratt in Douglass's place. The new commissioner predicted in 1876 that frauds on the scale of the whiskey ring operation would not occur in the future because exposure had "been so fruitful of misfortune and pecuniary disaster" for the participants.[9]

Congress responded to the scandal by reforming the revenue system. In 1872 the office of assessor was abolished, and its duties were transferred to the collectors. In the same year, a law provided that gaugers would be paid by the government instead of by distillers' fees. In 1876, the supervisors were abolished, with most of their duties going to the collectors and the agents. The agents were made directly responsible to the commissioner and soon became the backbone of the system, checking up on local officials and often organizing large-scale raids on illicit distillers. As an indication of their importance, Congress raised their number to thirty-five in 1879. The same measure virtually completed the structure of the revenue system by providing that the salaries of deputy revenue collectors, increasingly important in local enforcement since abolition of the deputy assessors, be paid directly by the government instead of from the collector's income. Although the revenue service remained a prime source of political patronage for many years, only slowly coming under civil service rules, these reforms eliminated the worst abuses.[10]

Corruption of individual storekeepers and gaugers and "irregularities" in distilleries continued, but they were isolated rather than systematic. In

1877, honest distillers reported illicit operations that threatened to drive them out of business in Cincinnati. Secretary of the Treasury John Sherman, "profiting by Mr. Bristow's experience and the discoveries he made as to the methods of fraud," quickly moved against the tax evaders. Further south, a group of North Carolina legal distillers produced untaxed corn liquor that they sold in South Carolina, driving legitimate distillers out of business. The operation required collusion of several storekeepers, but the collector and revenue agents discovered it and broke the ring up in 1879.[11]

About the same time the commissioner of internal revenue reduced the minimum legal capacity of distilleries in North Carolina from six to three and a half bushels of corn, a move to encourage moonshiners to become legitimate and to reduce charges that the revenue system discriminated against poor men who could operate only small distilleries. These goals were achieved, but in 1882 a Senate committee headed by North Carolina's Zebulon Vance investigated charges that the policy encouraged collusion between distillers and storekeepers. Small stills were only marginally profitable, and their operators developed a scheme of taking a portion of the storekeeper's pay, often in the form of very high rates for room and board with the distiller in isolated areas. This collusion guaranteed that the small distillery would continue to operate and assured that the storekeeper would retain his job, although at the price of part of his $5 daily pay. The distillers were extracting a subsidy from money intended for government officials. Although the commissioner warned collectors that it "is not to be supposed" that ex-moonshiners' "sentiments were revolutionized in a minute, and you must watch and see that they do not defraud the government through the means of a legal distillery," it was hard to detect collusion because of the isolation of the small stills. He did reduce the storekeepers' pay to $3 a day to make them less willing to share with the distillers.[12]

Several years later, North Carolina and Kentucky distillers cheated the government by producing more whiskey than their official capacity, undercutting their colleagues who obeyed the law as well as depriving the government of revenue. Commissioner John M. Mason dealt with the problem by having the distilleries' capacity tested and recording the actual figures on the survey. Some gaugers tried to protect the distillers by cheating on the testing, and Mason was criticized by people who charged him with favoring prohibition or discrimination against small distillers. He fired the gaugers and answered the complaints by saying, "It may be just possible that I am trying to enforce the law without making trouble for anybody but law-breakers. It sometimes happens, you know, that an office holder has a conscience of his own."[13] Despite persisting episodes of small-scale corruption, generally after 1875 the commissioner enjoyed a cooperative relationship with the industry his office so closely regulated, and which contributed three-fourths of the cost of every gallon it produced to the Treasury. He could now turn his attention to small-scale tax evaders, southern moonshiners whose operations were entirely outside the elaborate regulatory structure.

During the early 1870s, obscured by the issues of Reconstruction and the government's crackdown on the Ku Klux Klan, revenue enforcement in the South was mainly up to the initiative of local officials. They met mountaineers' fierce resistance and developed tactics to cope with it. In northern Georgia, defiance of the revenue laws in 1871 was so intense that "no officer dare undertake to enforce the law, without running the risk of being bushwacked or 'Ku-Kluxed'." The people boasted that "they will let no revenue officer come in there," which encouraged resistance across the line in North Carolina. In some parts of that state, local people believed that "the Government is opposed to the rigid execution" of revenue laws and would not provide men for raiding posses.[14]

In many counties moonshiners were organized to warn each other when deputy marshals were approaching, giving time to move stills to new hiding places. Several times bands of armed men drove the deputies away. In the border counties men from Georgia or South Carolina knew when the deputy marshal was away and entered North Carolina to "run the blockade." These men could never be caught by a law officer known to them. In western Virginia a posse member asked a local man for the whereabouts of a moonshiner he was seeking. The mountaineer replied that the blockader was well armed and was determined not to be captured, adding his opinions: "The revenue laws was oppressive and unjust, and the citizens of Scott [County] had been imposed upon by the Government officers as long as they would stand it, and he expected to hear of Mr. Wilcox [deputy marshal] being killed, every day."[15]

Deputies did indeed die. Some fell in the blaze of fire that sometimes greeted raiding parties; others were ambushed or assassinated in cold blood. In March 1875 Deputy Collector of Internal Revenue Holman Leatherwood of Alabama survived an ambush, but his companion, Deputy

Collector Perry, was seriously wounded. The next month, on another raid, Leatherwood left the party to destroy Marion Newgent's still. He was murdered somewhere in the laurel thickets. Although his killers were indicted, as of 1878 the government had a poor case against them because Leatherwood's body still could not be found.[16] The contest for dominance in the mountains was bitter.

Many revenue men were intimidated by this resistance, or at least reluctant to risk death without extra pay. John McDonald, supervisor of internal revenue for Missouri, Arkansas, and Tennessee in 1870, argued that the government could stop moonshining if it paid collectors for detectives, guides, and possemen. A collector could not be expected to "run the risk of assassination without recompense." McDonald, a principal in the whiskey ring, found other forms of recompense. Some raids were successful, though. In 1869 H. C. Whitley, who later became chief of the Secret Service, participated in a lightning raid against Virginia blockaders: "We dodged from point to point with such rapidity, that the moonshiners had hardly time to catch their breath before we were on to them. We would ride up to a distillery, jump off our horses, pick up an axe, dislocate and thoroughly destroy the copper boilers and worm-pipes, making a clean knockout as fast as we came to them." This success sounds too easy to be true, but it is possible the moonshiners were taken by surprise because raids were relatively rare that early.[17]

Abolition of the office of supervisor in 1876 greatly facilitated operations against blockaders. The agents were now centralized in Washington, directly responsible to the commissioner. This reorganization would prove useful in mounting concerted warfare on moonshiners. Although some officials had organized coordinated raids in border areas earlier, the agents pioneered tactics that would be perfected by Commissioner Raum in his campaign of the late seventies. The most active agent in the South was Jacob Wagner, sent from Washington in the fall of 1875. Wagner developed an "experiment," a twelve-man civilian posse, well supplied with rifles, tents, and camp equipment, that moved "over the country in regular military order." In late 1875 these men seized about twenty-five stills per month. This was a force carefully designed for effective raiding, not a group of local men hastily assembled for a single seizure. Stepped-up enforcement brought revenuers and moonshiners to national attention.[18]

Wagner's posse was an experiment because revenue men during the seventies relied heavily on the army for aid in making arrests and seizing stills. Marshals had long had the power to summon all citizens, including soldiers, as a posse to aid them in making arrests. William M. Evarts, last attorney general under Johnson, acknowledged this power in reply to a confused marshal but cautioned that "nothing can be less in accordance with the nature of our government, or the disposition of our people, than a frequent and ready resort to military aid in execution of the duties confided to civil officers." This aid should be sought only in "extraordinary emergencies."[19]

The Force Act of 1871, aimed at the Ku Klux Klan, spelled out the explicit power of federal officials to summon troops as a posse to aid them in making arrests. The act provided a sort of blanket endorsement of a power that earlier had been exercised only cautiously. Marshals and deputies needing a force to help them serve warrants quickly took advantage of this power. So did revenue collectors, who had the same authority to summon a posse. Neither military officers nor enlisted men had powers of arrest or seizure of stills; they provided a guard for the civil officials to discourage or repel resistance.

As the seventies opened, military commanders were not eager to supply men for revenue enforcement. By 1870 troops were already being used in raids, and General of the Army William T. Sherman sought opinions on the legality of this action. Judge Advocate General Holt replied that the secretary of war based his approval of military posses on a verbal opinion of the attorney general that such employment is legal and proper "whenever it is actually indispensable." Sherman was concerned that if soldiers returned the fire of moonshiners and killed some of them they would be arrested and tried for murder in state courts before juries "composed of the very men against whom they are called upon to act." He felt very strongly against ordering soldiers not in battle against an enemy "to do what may imperil their lives." Holt argued that this danger "cannot . . . be allowed to outweigh the inexorable necessity" for enforcing the laws against all resistance. The commissioner of internal revenue told him that Captain Summerhayes, whose report of a raid aroused Sherman's concerns, was often called upon to aid revenuers. He was "so prudent and judicious that though one of his men has been wounded, he has always avoided firing upon citizens," successfully aiding arrests and seizures "through a firm attitude and fearless display of force, but without proceeding to extremities." If other commanders were as discreet and supplied with enough men, there should be few deaths of moonshiners.[20]

General orders governing soldiers detailed to aid civilian officials incorporated Sherman's concerns about violence. Troops were expected to "use force when specially directed by the civil authority within the limits of their lawful authority to do so, and where, in the last extremity it is necessary for self-protection. . . . They are not, whilst enforcing one law, to be allowed to violate others." Commanders of individual detachments impressed these cautions upon their men.[21]

General Henry W. Halleck, commanding the Division of the South in 1869, objected that revenuers too readily turned to the military for support. "Old Brains" argued that they naturally relied on troops to "avoid danger and trouble, and increase their own emoluments at the expense of military appropriations." Soldiers were a powerful and, from the point of view of revenue officers, free posse. Halleck also had a more important concern, that civil officials came to depend on troops, which increased the anger of moonshiners "at being coerced by a force which they think has been unconstitutionally employed against them." Law-abiding people no longer felt obliged to serve in posses, as they assumed that was the duty of the soldiers. Halleck complained that revenuers could requisition troops at their own discretion, urging that soldiers not be called out as a posse without a federal court order specifying that a proper civilian force could not be obtained. This restriction would compel revenuers to "exert a little more energy in the ordinary civil means for the enforcement of their authority" and relieve military officers from much of the responsibility for "disagreeable duties, which can hardly be said to legitimately belong to the military service."[22]

General John Pope in Missouri similarly opposed revenuers' demands for troops. Supervisor John D. McDonald requested a hundred-man company of cavalry to be stationed at Jefferson Barracks, to be deployed as he desired. Pope would willingly supply small detachments for individual raids, but he stood firm against placing soldiers "under the command of Internal Revenue Officers to be used when, where and how they pleased." He believed that such duty would "permanently convert the soldiers into detectives and policemen, wholly subject to non-military control." Pope's requirement of revenue officers' formal request before releasing troops for raids became the standard procedure. Soldiers' dislike of revenue enforcement even found its way into fiction. A young lieutenant in the story "Moonshiners" expresses his disgust: "It's a cursed business I am sent on, . . . and none of my seeking. Here I am, Lieutenant Harry Norcross, very much at your service, turned all at once into a revenue officer, and ordered to hunt down whiskey distillers in Virginia instead of Indians in Idaho. . . . What the devil do I care whether they make whiskey or not? If it's good, the more the better."[23] Soldiers and their officers did not relish acting as policemen.

Despite fears and doubts, in many parts of the South, especially the Carolinas, northern Georgia, and northern Alabama, revenue enforcement remained the "principal occupation" of troops stationed in local posts. By 1876 aiding revenue officials was a requirement of military duty: a commander told his subordinate that he must comply with civil officials' request for troops, even though a deputy marshal had been drunk on a previous raid.[24]

Squads of the Seventh Cavalry rode out of Opelika, Alabama, and through the Carolinas before transfer west in 1875 to meet their rendezvous with destiny in Montana Territory. The Fifth Cavalry also was active in the Carolinas during the early seventies. Companies of the Second and Eighteenth infantries operated out of Atlanta for raids in northern Georgia. The Eighteenth posted other companies in Spartanburg and Greenville, South Carolina, for work along the Carolina border. The Second Artillery established a new post at Morganton, North Carolina, in 1875 for revenue raids. Other military units, including the Sixteenth Infantry, were active in the Kentucky-Tennessee region.

The infantrymen did not usually tramp through the woods; the artillerists did not fire cannons against moonshiners. Both were mounted on horses or mules that the quartermaster either rented locally or later received from the Bureau of Internal Revenue. Cavalry was clearly best for the rapid movements necessary in raiding. Mounted infantry and artillerymen were a less efficient substitute, but there was really no choice after withdrawal of the cavalry for western service. The typical detachment was small, ten or fewer men led by a lieutenant or sometimes a sergeant. They accompanied deputy marshals or revenuers, dividing into units of two or three men to protect the civil officers in raiding the stills they were seeking. Sometimes the detachments were larger, up to about twenty-five soldiers, and sometimes they went out on "scouts" seeking as many blockaders as possible instead of looking for individuals named in warrants. In 1875, thirty-seven detachments aided marshals and revenue officers in the Department of the South. Between 1870 and 1877, 142 reports of troops supporting revenue enforcement reached the adjutant general's office; there were probably even more operations that were not reported except to the local commander. In parts of the South, chasing moonshiners was as much part of military duty as pursuit of Klansmen.[25]

These military operations were usually routine, with a few stills destroyed or a few blockaders arrested. Most revenuers agreed that the soldiers were not only necessary for protection, but that the officers and men were efficient and cooperative. Many claimed they could not do their job without troops. "I am fully persuaded that unaided by the military I shall find it almost impossible to suppress illicit distilling," a North Carolina collector wrote in 1869; "A few soldiers could in a short time root out the whole matter." Several years later another North Carolina official asserted that "one soldier is worth half a dozen armed men in citizens clothes." A colleague in Kentucky was "satisfied that twenty-five regular soldiers would be of more service than fifty citizen soldiers." Tennessee moonshiners feared only soldiers and "are afraid to murder them," unlike revenue officers whom "some would be glad to kill for pure gratification and others to get what money he might have." Collector Carpenter of South Carolina declared that his success in destroying seventy stills in 1875–76 was due to the "cordial and earnest support of the military" who had accompanied revenuers on "nearly every excursion." In northern Georgia Captain Falck and Lieutenants Miller and Webster of the Second Infantry were "as desirous of suppressing the frauds upon the revenue as any of the civil authorities and are always ready to render any assistance and protection at their command." Gen. Alfred Terry echoed civilian sentiments when he reported that the small detachments were "productive of good results in preserving the public peace and enabling the civil authorities to enforce the law."[26]

Military posses usually provided enough force to protect the civil officers without inspiring violent resistance. Revenuers believed that the mere presence of soldiers on a raid discouraged moonshiner attacks. Large detachments that moved quickly, catching the blockaders off guard, were most effective. Equally valuable was a series of raids in rapid succession, even with small detachments. In Georgia this tactic "demoralized" moonshiners, who came in and surrendered. In Kentucky an officer argued that even unsuccessful raids were valuable because the mountaineers would see that they were "liable any day to be visited by the U.S. authorities and will abstain more or less in consequence from their unlawful proceedings." The commander of the post of Morganton, North Carolina, developed an effective combination of strength and restraint. His men were experienced and effective raiders who knew the countryside and always supported the civil officials. Behind this strength was a policy of "kindness to the people of the mountains, together with severe punishment of any improper act on the part of his men." His conciliation did "very much to allay the hostile feelings so common in this section." Georgians also appreciated the kindness of military officers while respecting the power of the uniform. A report commissioned by the state legislature in 1877 was harshly critical of the actions of deputy marshals but praised the officers and men whose "conduct has been always kind."[27]

Violent confrontations between soldiers and moonshiners were rare, but they did occur. When blockaders died, troopers had to face the prosecution in state courts that General Sherman worried about. A prisoner captured by men of the Second Artillery in North Carolina tried to escape, and they pursued him into a bog. The soldiers ordered him to halt and shot and wounded him after he kept running. State officials indicted the lieutenant in command of the detachment and the deputy marshal for assault with intent to kill, but the case was transferred to the federal court and the men were acquitted. Later the same detachment and marshal went into the South Mountain section of Burke County, where moonshiners fired on the troops and local people again swore out warrants, but again the men were acquitted. The collector of internal revenue emphasized the violence of this area when he said, "Even U.S. soldiers have more than once been fired upon."[28]

In Gilmer County, Georgia, Deputy Marshal Charles Blacker and a four-man military detachment captured a still-house and four local men they found inside. Private O'Grady was stationed outside to halt anyone approaching. According to the army's report of the incident, two men did approach, whom O'Grady challenged three times. The trooper said that one, later identified as John Emory, an old man who owned the still, drew a pistol and fired. O'Grady said that Emory shouted, "Take that you Yankee son of a bitch." Fortunately for the soldier, only the percussion cap exploded. O'Grady shot back, wounding Emory, who was later found dead. Emory's friends had a quite different version of the episode. They said that

Emory was merely trying to find out why the four men were arrested when O'Grady shot him without warning. O'Grady and two other soldiers, they said, then hid the body in a nearby creek bed, covering it partially with brush. Emory's wife found it the next morning. The county coroner testified that Emory's wound was fatal and that he must have fallen immediately. Bloodstains and beaten-down grass indicated that the troopers had dragged the body to conceal it. The men may have hidden the body because they were afraid of military discipline, since their commander had cautioned them against shooting except in self-defense. All the soldiers were indicted for murder by the state, but they were released after transfer of the case to the federal court, where a largely black jury declared them not guilty.[29]

In Kentucky, Corporal Lemuel Davis accidentally killed a moonshiner who ran out the back door of a house during a raid. The trooper's horse bolted, causing his carbine to go off, killing Brandy Hall, the blockader. Davis was indicted for murder, and after a series of legal maneuvers arising from fear that local people would lynch him, he was released by the federal court.[30]

In an 1872 South Carolina civilian death, widely trumpeted by southern papers as an outrage, the army court-martialed the lieutenant in charge for negligence and irresponsibility. He had ordered his men to fire at any of their prisoners who tried to escape, and then he went to sleep in a nearby house. One of the guards shot and killed a young man under arrest as a Klansman; it was not clear whether he was indeed attempting to escape or whether the soldier had ordered him to halt. This is the only episode in which the army punished an officer for a civilian death. This and the cases of Davis and O'Grady are the only instances of soldiers killing civilians that have turned up in the records. Sherman's concern for restraint seems to have prevailed.[31]

Mountaineers firing at soldiers wounded a few troopers, but only two died.[32] In February 1877, a party of revenuers, accompanied by Deputy Marshal Charles Blacker and Lieutenant Augustine McIntyre with four soldiers, rode into the Frog Mountain country along the border of Gilmer and Fannin counties, Georgia. On their way they stopped at the log house of Ayers Jones, whom Blacker hoped to arrest under a warrant for moonshining. Jones was away, but the party remained at the house for rest and food. Blacker was apparently quite abusive to Mrs. Jones, who pleaded with them to leave the cabin. According to the army's account, at about two o'clock in the morning twenty-five or thirty men attacked the house, firing shotguns and pistols, yelling, "God damn your souls, we have got you now!" The raiders returned the fire; during the "brisk skirmish" Lieutenant McIntyre was shot in the heart. Staggering through the back door, he fell dead. Colonel Samuel Williams, sent into the Frog Mountain district by Georgia governor Colquitt to investigate the circumstances of McIntyre's death, argued that the moonshiners had hoped to avoid arrest and had not intended to attack the soldiers, possibly mistaking McIntyre for a revenuer because his uniform was hidden by a raincoat. The army, on the other hand, contended that the raiders were victims of a plot to attack them in the Jones cabin. One of the local people had heard of the army's preparations while in the camp at Ellijay and had raced ahead of the posse to warn his neighbors.

After McIntyre's death the moonshiners forced the revenuers and soldiers out of the house and surrounded them. Reinforcements arrived the next day, who drove off the assailants and rescued McIntyre's body. According to the army reports, the rescuers were fired on amid shouts of "Here is the damned son of a bitch—take him away from here—he is dead where you all ought to be, you dam [sic] sons of bitches you." When they recovered McIntyre's body, the soldiers discovered that his gold watch, other jewelry, and $20 had fallen "into the hands of the enemy."

The next month the army got some revenge, sweeping through the Frog Mountain district and netting fifty prisoners, including a woman, although the actual murderers had all fled. This sweep angered local people and resulted in a state investigation that sharply criticized the deputy marshals involved, but not the soldiers. The governor of Georgia offered rewards for McIntyre's killers, and the federal marshals arrested several men, but the evidence against them was too weak to bring the cases to trial. Ayers Jones and his brother Tom were not captured until 1879. The Joneses were not charged with murder—not a federal crime—but under the provisions of the Ku Klux Acts of 1870–71 as conspirators to prevent Deputy Marshal Blacker from serving his revenue violation warrants against them. They were indicted and tried in federal court, but the jury declared them not guilty. A newspaper reporter described Ayers as "a large, well-formed man of forty, whose face shows the Indian blood that flows . . . in his veins. His long straight hair is parted in the middle, and his face covered with bristling reddish beard." Dressed in "true backwoods style," he wore jeans, a dark green wool shirt, and sturdy brogans. "A pure a specimen of a child of nature as can be imagined," Ayers was illiterate and had never seen a railroad in his life. Nevertheless, he spoke articulately, and he was a substantial local citizen who owned 700 acres of land. Several years later, in 1893, Jones was murdered by his own son.[33]

The other reported death, of Private Crusoe in Kentucky, was a tragedy for all involved. In 1871 a four-man detachment under Sergeant Schrader accompanied a deputy marshal to the house of Cassius Coffey. The marshal demanded to see Coffey to serve a warrant against him. The people inside fired, wounding the sergeant and killing Private Crusoe. Under continuing fire, the detachment retreated. Coffey and his family said that they thought the troops were Klansmen. When he discovered he had killed a soldier, Coffey cried, "I feel as if I had killed a brother." He had apparently been threatened by the Klan and was edgy. The detachment's tactics may have contributed to the tragedy: Private Wilson thought that "what led to the firing was the charging up to the house and getting the people in a fright before they knew what was coming."[34] Though bullets did fly in the mountains, the only two very different soldier deaths suggest that moonshiners greatly preferred to run than to fight the army.

Even when not culminating in a gunfight, raiding was not easy service for the soldiers. Because moonshining was carried on after harvest and before spring planting, raiders frequently traveled by night in cold and rainy weather. Soldiers often had to cover several hundred miles on raiding expeditions, riding over steep, rough trails barely discernible through the underbrush. Mounted infantrymen were inexperienced riders; they often did not know how to saddle or guide horses and became stiff and sore after riding long distances. Usually they carried the regular-infantry long Springfield rifle strapped on their backs. They had to use one hand to guide the horse, the other to brush aside branches. The long rifle constantly caught in overhanging boughs, slowing down the troops when rapid movement was essential, or sometimes was knocked to the ground. Added to these difficulties, parties returning from raids or moving from one place to another had prisoners mounted behind the soldiers. The horses themselves were rented from citizens or livery stables. They were often in poor condition and worn out when returned. Local people constantly demanded exorbitant sums for damage to their animals. Livery stable keepers warned moonshiners when the army rented horses, or they refused to provide mounts because blockaders threatened them. These problems were relieved somewhat in 1877 when the revenue bureau provided short carbines and supplied horses. One officer reported that distillers of Hogback Mountain, North Carolina, gave up moonshining because they could no longer rely on livery stable keepers for warning of impending raids.[35] Even with better weapons and mounts, squads of tired and sore soldiers crashing through the underbrush hardly made an imposing martial image.

Although the record of military success against moonshiners was good despite difficulties, many raids were failures. Sometimes moonshiners received warning of the soldiers' approach, or the guide failed to meet the party or led it astray. A Rabun County, Georgia, resident remembered an unsuccessful attempt to arrest his father, "who of course was not home." The soldiers sat on their horses in the rain by the front gate, cursing "the country for having such muddy roads."[36]

Some expeditions failed because of civil officials' incompetence. The worst fiasco occurred in Tennessee in 1875. When the military detachment arrived near Cookeville, the deputy marshal and deputy collector said they could not stay because they had to appear as witnesses in the federal court at Nashville. The detachment camped in the area for nearly two weeks awaiting their return, during which time the moonshiners hid all their stills and somebody found a list of the men with warrants against them in the town's main street. When the civil officers returned, Lieutenant J. K. Waring suggested that "the proper and usual time" for raids, moonlit nights, would give the men the advantage of a cool march to the blockader strongholds. The deputy collector replied, "The Government does not pay me enough to justify me in losing my sleep and rest by working in the night." When the raid was finally made, Waring's commander fumed that it netted only "*one small still and eight gallons of common whiskey*," observing that the marshal and revenue officers were "*certainly not very efficient*." Added to all this, the train transporting the soldiers back to Atlanta derailed, causing a five-hour delay.[37]

Another detachment commander complained that deputy marshals asked for more troops than necessary and that "as a class they are fond of drink & on this trip gave his men whiskey." A North Carolina deputy marshal always pleaded sickness or other excuses to avoid going out on raids. When he finally went with the soldiers, he got drunk to avoid confronting the blockaders and sent the squad a long distance away so he could stay behind with "fair but frail" Rachel, whom he had met on the way. A Georgia deputy spoke of the troopers in "scurillous, ungentlemanly and insulting language," such as "the soldiers might kiss my arse." Deputy Collector Leatherwood (later killed by moonshiners) accidentally alerted moonshiners by announcing that, after a raid in which he and a deputy collector were fired on, he would return with troops to make the arrests. Of course, nobody could be found to arrest. Finally Deputy Marshal Hodges allowed some prisoners to escape the military guard; another deputy thought "it looked very much as though he wanted the prisoners to escape or get off."[38] Such complaints were directed against individual civil officials; military men usually worked in harmony with both marshals and revenue collectors.

For their part, despite most of their colleagues' reliance on and praise for troops, some revenuers and deputy marshals criticized the soldiers. A few argued that civilian posses were more effective as well as cheaper. Deputy Marshal John Wyatt of Kentucky was unimpressed by military cautiousness in a confrontation between fifty soldiers and thirteen moonshiners in 1865. When Major Long faced the blockaders, he demanded their surrender: "A laugh was all the answer he got." Wyatt said to him, "Major, . . . you don't know the men you are dealing with; it must be either catch or kill." He urged him either to place his men so the moonshiners would be caught in a cross fire or to provide ten men for a surprise attack from the rear. He refused both Wyatt's requests, and the deputy, "disgusted with his cowardice, gave up the fight. . . . Like the King of France, we marched up a hill, and then marched down again."[39]

A revenue collector in Tennessee found that Lieutenant McIntyre could not eat mountain people's food for health reasons and would not allow his men to ride faster than a walk or move by night. The revenue man preferred to raid with his own deputies, who could "do without trunks, cooking stoves or utensils, can ride faster than a walk and . . . work at night . . . and can live 30 days or more on food furnished by the mountain people." Another collector rejected mounted infantry as "of little avail" and assembled a raiding party of his own deputies and deputy marshals. A military officer seemed to be convinced by a deputy marshal's argument that a civil posse would be "more effectual & economical" than even cavalry. The marshal said that with twenty-five "such men as he can pick out, and authority to cross the Georgia line he can do more than could be done by double the force of cavalry." Revenue Agent Wagner's civilian posse of 1875 was effective because the men operated "without uniforms to embarrass their work."

There were other objections to troops as well: Virginia revenuers refused to accompany a military raid because they were "afraid" and "ashamed to ride with Yankee cavalry"; a North Carolina federal judge believed that use of soldiers "produces public excitement and indignation." Commissioner of Internal Revenue Raum came to believe that, despite their contributions to revenue enforcement, "the presence of the troops was a constant irritation to the people, that the use of companies was expensive, and that they moved heavily and clumsily from the very nature of things."[40] Troops reminded some people of Reconstruction-era "bayonet rule," but some revenuers and deputy marshals thought they were more inefficient than tyrannical. At any rate, they never occupied the mountains in large numbers, and as Reconstruction wound down, they were increasingly withdrawn from the South.

After the official collapse of Reconstruction in 1877, the number of troops rapidly diminished, and even during the Reconstruction era, they were diverted from revenue duty to more pressing service. Revenuers had increasing difficulty securing their aid during the 1870s. South Carolina collector Carpenter's district became "overrun with distilleries" while Companies K and D of the Eighteenth Infantry were posted at Columbia and Laurens to guard the polls during an election. In Missouri a detachment aiding revenue officers was suddenly ordered back to St. Louis for transfer west to fight the Indians. Troops remaining in the South in the summer of 1877 were withdrawn to deal with the great railroad strikes.[41]

Although slow, conspicuous, and politically sensitive, military operations against moonshiners did lead to less violence than civilian raids. Most of the federal civil officials appreciated the protection that soldiers provided and praised their cooperation and efficiency. Despite his doubts about the political impact and efficiency of soldiers, Commissioner Raum was glad of their assistance and sought their aid in his battle. Even though Revenue Agent Wagner's civil posse chopped up 133 stills and arrested 131 men, "nearly all" of whom were convicted and serving prison terms, Raum believed that resistance in the Carolinas and Georgia required troops. In January 1877 he wanted the men retained at Morganton, North Carolina, Greenville, South Carolina, and Atlanta and twenty-man detachments at Athens, Georgia, Huntsville, Alabama, and Knoxville, Tennessee. The army complied with his request. Although Raum believed soldiers were a valuable aid, he also thought soldiers were "not desirable where it can be avoided, and should not be long continued." Soon after his request to the army, he notified all the southern revenue collectors that his policy would be "to so strengthen the hands of the Collectors with a large force of Deputy Collectors . . . so that at an early day the military force may be withdrawn."[42]

That day came soon. In 1878 a Democratic Congress attached a rider to the military appropriation bill that prohibited the use of troops as a posse under civil officers. In 1879 the Posse Comitatus Act made the prohibition permanent. Significantly, one of the original sponsors of the act was Representative J. Proctor Knott, a Democrat from the moonshiner stronghold of Kentucky. According to the *New York Tribune*, "it was well understood in debate that one chief object" of the 1878 rider was denial of military support for revenue officials. Senator James G. Blaine and two Republican representatives from Illinois argued that the rider would undermine revenue enforcement. After passage of the bill, Attorney General Charles Devens protested that it "seriously cripples the execution of the laws of the United States when the process of its courts is violently resisted."[43]

The future of revenue enforcement looked grim. Moonshiners were fighting fiercely to protect their economy. Military raids seemed to be effective individually with a minimum of violence, but these small victories did not seem to turn the tide of the larger war. Wagner's civilian posse was proving efficient, but most revenuers agreed that moonshiners were much more violent against deputy marshals or deputy collectors than against soldiers. Nevertheless, the Bureau of Internal Revenue would have to depend on the civil officers to carry on its campaign during and after 1878. Two former military men seemed to hold the key to eventual success. Revenue Agent Jacob Wagner, a major in the Civil War, pioneered the well-armed, rapidly moving civilian posse that became the most important striking force in the mountains. Former general Green B. Raum, appointed commissioner in 1876, developed Wagner's methods into a campaign against illicit distillers on all fronts.

Typical nineteenth-century images of moonshiners. From Donald A. Baine, "Among the Moonshiners," *Dixie* 1 (Aug. 1885): 9–14.

Working a still. The copper still itself, shown in the right center, is enclosed in a stone furnace to hold the heat. A wooden trough, on the left, conveys water from a nearby creek into the barrel enclosing the spiral copper worm, where the vapor rising from the heated mash in the still precipitates as mountain dew. Ca. 1900. From Margaret W. Morley, *The Carolina Mountains* (Boston: Houghton, Mifflin, 1913).

Still in full blast and moonshiners prepared for any emergency. Ca. 1900. From John C. and Olive D. Campbell Papers, Southern Historical Collection, University of North Carolina at Chapel Hill, Album 8, p. 27.

Caves, such as this one in Kentucky, were a favorite place for hiding stills. Ca. 1900. From John C. and Olive D. Campbell Papers, Southern Historical Collection, University of North Carolina at Chapel Hill, Album 8, p. 22.

Moonshining was often a family business. The distilling apparatus includes a "doubler" or "thump keg," the small barrel on a stump next to the still. The vapor from the still passed through the doubler with great heat buildup, removing many oils and impurities before final distillation by passage through the worm, enclosed in the larger barrel to the left of the doubler. The doubler, which appeared around the turn of the century, saved the step of having to pour the "singlings" or first distillation into the still for a second distillation. Fermenting mash is visible in the large barrels in the foreground. The man with a white shirt and tie in the right background is very likely a revenuer or deputy marshal; certainly the other people in the photograph do not look particularly cheerful. Ca. 1900. From John C. and Olive D. Campbell Papers, Southern Historical Collection, University of North Carolina at Chapel Hill, Album 8, p. 4.

Moonshiners sold liquor to miners, loggers, and millhands, adapting well to the arrival of industry in the mountains. Courtesy Professor Lou Athey, Franklin and Marshall College, from collection of Mrs. Frank Brown, Ansted, West Virginia. Post card, ca. 1900.

Revenuer assembling a posse for a raid. From Samuel G. Blythe,
"Raiding Moonshiners," *Munsey's Magazine* 25 (June 1901): 418–24.

Mountain dew that did not reach the customers. Hiding liquor in innocent-looking wagonloads was a common trick to avoid detection. Somebody probably reported this man to the revenuers. From Samuel G. Blythe, "Raiding Moonshiners," *Munsey's Magazine* 25 (June 1901): 418–24.

Fighting for "the right to make a little licker." From Samuel G. Blythe,
"Raiding Moonshiners," *Munsey's Magazine* 25 (June 1901): 418–24.

End of the battle. The still is a large, complicated apparatus, more common around the turn of the century than in the 1870s. With the spread of local prohibition laws, some moonshiners became large-scale operators. From Samuel G. Blythe, "Raiding Moonshiners," *Munsey's Magazine* 25 (June 1901): 418–24.

—OFFICE OF—

United States Marshal,

EASTERN DISTRICT OF TENNESSEE,

KNOXVILLE, TENN., Dec. 31st, 1888.

Five Hundred Dollars
REWARD.

The Attorney General of the United States authorizes me to offer and pay a reward of

FIVE HUNDRED DOLLARS EACH

For the arrest and conviction of the murderers of

Deputy U. S. Marshal THOMAS GOODSON,

Who was murdered near Roan Mountain, Carter county, Tenn., on the night of December lst, 1888. This reward will be paid for the arrest and conviction of either of the parties concerned who were not in arrest before December 27th, 1888.

W. M. NIXON,

S. B. NEWMAN & CO. PRINT, KNOXVILLE.

U. S. Marshal.

Federal officers as well as moonshiners died in gunfights, as evidenced by this handbill. From W. M. Nixon, U.S. Marshal, Tennessee, to Attorney General, Dec. 17, 1888, DJ 9960 '88, box 385, National Archives (thanks to Cynthia Fox of the National Archives for bringing this document to the author's attention). See chapter 7 for a description of Goodson's death.

The spoils of war. Two of the men in shirtsleeves in the upper photograph (not specifically identified) are captured blockaders. The third is probably a guide. Ca. 1900. From John C. and Olive D. Campbell Papers, Southern Historical Collection, University of North Carolina at Chapel Hill, Album 8, pp. 2, 13.

Trials of moonshiners in federal courts were big events in the county seats where the courts were located. People came in from the surrounding countryside to attend as spectators or witnesses and to buy and sell goods at the markets that were often part of court week. From "Law and Moonshine in Western North Carolina," *Harper's Weekly* 23 (Aug. 23, 1879): 665. Engravings from sketches by Frank H. Taylor, courtesy of Nancy L. Gustke.

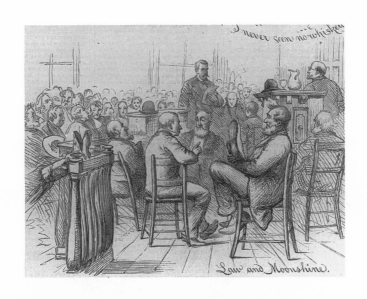

"The Cantrells in Gainesville Jail." Convicted moonshiners who were tried at the federal district court in Atlanta could serve their sentence closer to home in the Hall County jail at Gainesville, Georgia. In the mid-1890s the sheriff allowed prisoners in this jail to wander about the town during the day, and even to drink in local saloons and visit relatives, until the federal judge ordered him to keep them locked up (see chapter 7). Ca. 1900. From John C. and Olive D. Campbell Papers, Southern Historical Collection, University of North Carolina at Chapel Hill, Album 8, p. 19.

5 General Raum
to the Rescue

· ·

Green B. Raum took office as commissioner of internal revenue in
1876, determined to suppress illicit distilling and restore respect for federal
law. Born in Illinois in 1829, Raum was a lawyer who went to Kansas in
1856 as an active opponent of slavery. He soon returned to Illinois and
served as clerk of the state House of Representatives. He was a Douglas
Democrat in 1860 and attended the national convention that nominated the
little giant for president. Like Douglas, Raum was a "war Democrat"; he
made the first speech in southern Illinois supporting the war. He entered
military service as a major of Illinois volunteers, rising to brigadier general
in 1865. He saw active service, leading a successful bayonet charge at the
battle of Corinth in 1862. He participated in the Vicksburg and Chattanooga campaigns and was severely wounded at Missionary Ridge in 1863.
He played an important role in the capture of Atlanta and joined Sherman's
march to the sea. After resigning his commission, Raum served as president
of a railroad company in Illinois. He became a dedicated Republican and
was elected to the national House of Representatives in the 40th Congress,
1867–69. He voted for all the articles of impeachment against President
Andrew Johnson. Defeated in 1868, he remained active in state politics and
was a delegate to the national Republican convention in 1876.

President Grant appointed Raum as revenue commissioner in 1876, and
he served through the Hayes and part of the Garfield-Arthur administrations, leaving office in 1883. Raum surprised even close friends by his
resignation, anticipating the careers of modern bureaucrats, "to join the
large group of lawyers in Washington who have gained, while holding office,
an intimate acquaintance with certain branches of the Government service,
which is very useful to them in the practice of their profession." Liquor

distillers in fact retained him as a lobbyist to work for a bill extending the period whiskey could be stored under bond. Although Raum was "a vigorous politician . . . and his political labors in behalf of himself and others . . . invited criticism from time to time," he was defeated twice for U.S. senator and failed to obtain the Republican nomination for governor of Illinois. These disappointments aroused "a feeling of disgust for politics," which seems to have influenced his decision to leave public life. He was also clashing with Secretary of the Treasury Folger, who apparently did not treat Raum with the respect he thought he deserved. After several years of practicing law and carrying on business operations in Washington, Raum became commissioner of pensions under President Harrison in 1889. Although praised by his superior, the secretary of the interior, Raum was suspected of using his office to further his business interests. One congressional committee cleared him by a three to two vote, but a second upheld the charges by the same margin. Raum's friends accused the Democrats on the committee of trying to create scandal for the 1892 presidential campaign. Raum remained in office until replaced by Cleveland in 1893. He then returned to Illinois to practice law in Chicago.[1]

His photograph shows a large, balding man with a neatly trimmed full beard. His face suggests a combination of mild manners and shrewd intelligence. He looked like one of the "bullet-headed generals" who entered politics under Grant and was apparently so loyal he sent a telegram to Orville Babcock, the president's secretary, congratulating him for escaping prosecution for his role in the whiskey ring frauds. Raum also worked diligently for a third term for Grant in 1880, serving, according to Senator John Sherman, as "the most active and efficient agent of Gen. Grant in the national convention."[2]

As might be expected of such a loyalist, Raum was not a champion of civil service reform; he favored the leading alternative—fixed, four-year terms for federal officeholders. He objected to good-behavior tenure in terms dear to Andrew Jackson and later generations of politicians: "Such a system would create a privileged class removed from the influences of popular sentiment, which in this country is a constantly operating force favorable to honest, efficient administration." He considered himself to be "the most practical civil-service reformer," believing that if officials were paid reasonable salaries and required to carry out their duties faithfully and honestly, they should be allowed "to go forward and to exercise their right as citizens and do whatever political work they can conveniently for their party."[3]

Raum declared that he would "not appoint a Democrat if I knew it; for I think the true policy of party administration is to appoint its friends so as to uphold its principles." He was a strict party man, demanding partisan loyalty from all his subordinates. He tried to remove Revenue Agent W. H. Chapman, who had refused to work for a Virginia congressional candidate the agent considered corrupt. Chapman appealed to President Hayes, and he proved a political survivor who was still on duty in the nineties. Raum was more successful in his campaign against O. P. Fitzsimmons, a Democrat whom Hayes had appointed U.S. marshal in Georgia as a conciliatory gesture. Henry Farrow, the district attorney, charged that Raum and Collector Andrew Clark of Georgia plotted to refuse cooperation with Fitzsimmons and then blame the marshal for the ensuing enforcement problems. Fitzsimmons did not in fact last long, and Farrow had made himself a powerful enemy.[4]

Despite his partisanship, Raum was not a hack. He was among the small group of Grant appointees who were devoted to their duty. He was a dedicated bureaucrat who served his party while maintaining high standards of honesty and efficiency in an era notorious for low standards. The *New York Tribune*, no friend of corrupt and partisan politicians, praised the revenue bureau. Raum used the success of his own agency in defense of partisan activity by federal officeholders. Although Raum had his critics, it was "generally admitted" that his tenure in the revenue bureau was "marked not only by honesty but also by rare executive ability." Apparently "not one cent" of the revenues collected was lost through subordinates' defalcations. He served as commissioner of internal revenue nearly seven years, while the longest term of any other commissioner was four consecutive years (Joseph Miller served eight total years in the two separate Cleveland administrations). Raum's military, legal, and political experience was a good combination for his job and undoubtedly shaped the style of his campaign against moonshiners.[5]

Raum was the first commissioner to call attention to how much money illicit distilling cost the government. He told Secretary of the Treasury Morrill in 1877, in a letter discussed and endorsed in a Cabinet meeting, that 2,000 moonshine stills were operating in the Carolinas, Georgia, Virginia, and Tennessee. They ran at least 20 days per month, 4 months during the year, with an average daily output of 15 gallons. Consequently, blockaders cost the Treasury $2,500,000 annually. In his first official report, Raum lowered his estimate somewhat, saying that the combined losses from both illicit liquor and tobacco were "not less than $2,000,000." Whatever the actual figure, the commissioner was "satisfied" that the annual loss from moonshining almost equalled the cost of collecting the internal revenue tax throughout the entire country.[6]

Raum emphasized the powerful resistance to the whiskey tax, describing organized and armed bands determined to keep revenuers out of the mountains. Resistance was so fierce and casualties among revenuers so high that "many experienced and intelligent officers had come to the conclusion that the fraud of illicit distilling was an evil too firmly established to be uprooted, and that it must be endured." Raum disagreed, and despite the perennial problem of insufficient funds and congressional denial of military support in 1878, he launched a campaign against moonshiners to break their organized resistance. At first the tide of battle went against Raum's men because increased enforcement inspired more resentment and violence. By 1882, though, Raum announced like a victorious general that "the supremacy of the laws of the United States for the collection of its internal revenues has been established in all parts of the country." He owed his success to the "policy adopted to execute the laws firmly and vigorously, but impartially, and in as conciliatory a manner as possible." Although he recognized that illicit distilling could never be entirely eliminated, he thought it could be reduced to insignificant proportions. To record the progress of his campaign, Raum published statistics showing the number of stills seized, blockaders arrested, and casualties among revenue officers. In periods of intensive crackdown, he required monthly reports from the officers in the field. The development of Raum's policy combining strength and restraint, despite many obstacles, represents a unique assertion of federal authority in a period when the government was abandoning its Reconstruction-era attempts to enforce civil rights and fair elections in the South.[7]

Department of Justice officials had hoped to enforce Reconstruction "firmly and vigorously, but in as conciliatory a manner as possible," but they had failed to demonstrate enough vigor or win respect for their efforts at conciliation. Why did Raum usually succeed where they had failed? His first

task was to demonstrate and sustain enough strength to convince blockaders that resistance was dangerous. In his first year of office, he could rely
on troops to protect revenuers on their raids, and the soldiers were active
during 1876 and 1877. However, after Congress prohibited military forces
as posses to aid civil officers in 1878, Raum had to rely on civilian raiding
parties strong enough to protect themselves and defeat moonshiner resistance.

Raum believed that effective enforcement required "such a force of
deputies, armed when necessary, as will demonstrate the ability and determination of the government to collect its revenues and enforce its laws." As
a military officer, he recognized that this strength was insufficient without
careful strategy and effective tactics. Raum inaugurated his campaign in
January 1878 with a general sweep through every county that harbored
moonshiners. The blockaders had imagined themselves secure from harassment in the dead of winter and could not hide out in the mountains for
very long in the cold weather. The "simultaneous appearance of the deputies" throughout the mountains confused and demoralized them: according
to Raum, "It was new and aggressive tactics that they did not understand."[8]

A year later the first coordinated sweep occurred, in which deputies from
different counties moved according to prearranged plans. Raum took personal interest in the campaign's progress in each district, often directing
movements himself by telegraph from Washington. He does not seem to
have imposed unrealistic obligations on his subordinates, because he usually had good information about conditions in the collectors' districts. He
gladly praised raiders' "activity, zeal and courage" but also sent information
about stills to collectors and urged them to take immediate action. He also
criticized poorly organized raids. Observing that "it is somewhat remark-
able that a force should go out searching for illicit stills" in Kentucky with
neither wagons for carrying them off nor axes for destroying them, Raum
suggested to Collector Crumbaugh that he put his force "in charge of some
officer possessing more forethought and better qualifications for that work."
His general policy, communicated in circulars to collectors in the mountain
South, was to try persuading moonshiners to give up their activity and to
warn them that the Bureau of Internal Revenue meant business. When
warnings failed, as they usually did, Raum directed collectors to "thoroughly police" their districts and "take such measures as will convince

offenders that if they continue their former practice they cannot expect to avoid discovery, arrest and punishment; and, after the warning already given they need not indulge the hope of immunity for their offenses."9

The men on the "front lines" of revenue collection were the deputy collectors, appointed by the collector of the district and paid salaries. They were in charge of the routine regulatory activities, far safer and more congenial work, as well as operations against moonshiners. Usually based in the county seat town, they recruited for individual raids special deputies from men who lived in town or nearby. These possemen, paid on a per diem basis, rarely lived near the blockaders, but they usually knew their way around the mountains, and most raids required travel to reach the targeted area. Although anathema to moonshiners, revenue deputies lived in the county in which they operated, like Adolphus and John Wellborn and Jeff Holcomb of Rabun County, Georgia, who raided or reported several local moonshiners in 1881. Revenuers had diverse views of their opponents. Some regarded them as "ignorant, rough, and in many instances, *mean and vicious*"; others thought they were as much "sinned against as sinning." Whatever they thought of blockaders, deputies were willing to risk ostracism and danger to work for the government.10

According to George W. Atkinson, a West Virginia deputy who later became U.S. marshal, governor, and federal district attorney, Captain James M. Davis of Tennessee was the beau ideal raider. Over six feet tall, muscular, and large-boned, he weighed 210 pounds. "He looks like a backwoods man, and he possesses much of the native shrewdness, activity and daring of the Indians." Uneducated, but with "a remarkably retentive memory and keen perceptive faculties," he could patiently track moonshiners into "nearly all the by-paths and deep recesses of the Cumberland mountains." Before his career as a revenuer, Davis had worked for the Tennessee state prison tracking escaped convicts. Physically strong, able to tie up any ordinary man he got his hands on, he could travel for four days without food or sleep. A superb shot, his bullets usually found their mark. So accurate was his shooting, Davis was able to describe the nature of the wound received by a moonshiner who got away, later found dead from the type of wound Davis predicted. Davis was also "a natural born leader and commander of men." Blockaders "quake at the bare mention of his name," but he was "one of the kindest hearted and most gentle natured of men." Once he captured his man, Davis "never fails to win the affection of the prisoner" by kind treatment. He captured over three thousand blockaders and smashed up 618 stills, in all these efforts killing only three men and wounding "about a dozen more."[11]

Davis joined the company of obscure Americans whose names appear as Supreme Court cases. He was fired on during a raid in Tennessee, and when he shot back, he killed a moonshiner, J. B. Haynes. Davis surrendered himself in Tracy City, where, during the state's preliminary hearing, someone tried to assassinate him, killing the deputy who was walking with him instead. State authorities charged him with murder and contested removal of the case to federal courts under statutes providing for the defense of officers acting in the line of duty. The case reached the Supreme Court, which in a divided decision upheld the constitutionality of the removal provisions.[12]

Davis himself died in the saddle in 1882. While on his way to court with other revenuers and a captured moonshiner, he was ambushed in Tennessee near the spot where he had earlier killed Haynes. Davis fell from his horse, only wounded by the first shot. He got up and was walking toward the other possemen when a second shot knocked him down. Several men emerged from the bushes and fired pistols into Davis, leaving his body with twenty bullet holes and a crushed skull. The ambush had apparently been carefully planned in a nearby saloon, and the assailants had constructed a log and brush barricade for the purpose. The murderers do not seem to have ever been captured. Most revenuers hardly matched either Davis's strength or his kindness, but their reports do often indicate bravery and determination. Some deputies, however, were corrupt, cowardly, or brutal and made the work of honest and brave men more difficult.[13]

Revenue posses were led by one or more deputy collectors and deputy marshals. The marshals served warrants on individual moonshiners and could also arrest without a warrant any blockader they caught in the act. The power to arrest without warrant was essential, for as a federal judge said, without it, "No one would be arrested for blockading whiskey or tobacco unless he first sent the Revenue Officers notice of his intention to do so, or carried on his business in front of the Commissioner's office." The revenue officers had the power to seize or destroy illicit stills. Following the precedent of Revenue Agent Wagner's successful raiding parties, Raum made sure that the possemen were well armed and equipped. Sometimes as many as fifty men rode in these posses, but usually they contained about ten to twenty men. An experienced revenuer said that a force of ten men "in a timbered country can cut their way through any opposition which can be set up against them." Raiders often carried both revolvers and Springfield carbines, effective up to 1,000 yards in the hands of a good marksman. Serious revenuers constantly practiced their shooting. On a raid, one man was designated "hatchet bearer," whose job was to smash up a still as quickly as possible, as it was dangerous to stay around a still-house too long. Seizure of stills was preferred to their destruction because they could be sold at public auction. Some raiders did haul off stills, barrels of whiskey, and other material in wagons, but usually transportation was impossible in the mountains. Revenuers routinely destroyed stills, although the practice was not definitely sanctioned by law until 1879. Provided with rubber coats and leggings for bad weather during the usual fall and winter season of their operations, raiders moved by night to escape observation and to surprise the moonshiners at work. During the day, they hid in houses or the woods.[14]

Revenue officers usually relied on informers for the names of illicit distillers, but occasionally they themselves carried out detective work. The easiest method was to follow "smell and smoke," though stills were rarely that obvious. If a revenuer's horse refused to drink from a creek, the rider knew immediately to follow the creek to its source where a still was undoubtedly located. Hogs, on the other hand, loved mash and sometimes betrayed their moonshiner owners. In more elaborate detective work, deputy collectors pretended to be cattle- or fur-buyers traveling through the country, but the strategy eventually "wore threadbare." A stranger asking about cattle or sheep for sale set off a round of horn blowing to warn local moonshiners. A more elaborate, and more successful, technique was to travel through mountain communities selling cheap tinware and looking for stills or asking where a thirsty man could have a drink. Penetrating the most remote areas along mountain streams disguised as hunters or fishermen seems to have fooled the wary mountaineers most often as well as providing a pleasant combination of business and pleasure for the revenuers.[15]

Raids in search of individuals listed on warrants were the most common type of revenue enforcement, but Raum developed two innovations: seasonal sweeps through moonshine country and coordinated raids along state borders. As the distilling season approached, Raum directed the collectors to organize their deputies for annual raids to remind moonshiners of the government's determination. Raiding would be preemptive instead of reactive: "Let that class who have heretofore defrauded the revenue understand that the laws are to be rigidly enforced, and that they cannot expect to escape detection and punishment." Prompt action early in the season would "deter many old offenders and thus save the government much trouble and expense." General Raum believed that it was essential for his forces to *"permanently reoccupy all the ground you have gained,* [sic] and then to push forward with as much vigor as possible." He thought that "active work for ... two or three months" would "produce the desired result." Raiders should reconnoiter the territory to locate all the illegal stills in a county and, led by reliable guides, move into the area with a force "strong enough to seize and destroy every still without fear of being overcome by the illicit distillers."[16]

Counties bordering on state lines were notorious moonshine centers because the blockaders could escape even federal warrants by fleeing to the next state. Local officials had earlier organized coordinated raids along the Carolinas border and the Kentucky and Tennessee line, but Raum developed this tactic into a regular feature of revenue enforcement. Raiders working together on each side of the border would drive fleeing moonshiners into each others' hands. The commissioner personally directed many of these operations from Washington, informing the cooperating collectors of each others' plans and movements himself instead of relying on them to tell each other. "Use the telegraph," Raum admonished the South Carolina collector in one of these operations; "Do not let this movement fail," he warned the officer in North Carolina. In a typical operation along the Kentucky-Tennessee line, Raum directed Collectors Cooper and Woodcock of Tennessee and Collector Landrum of Kentucky to assemble forces of "from ten to twelve sober, reliable, discreet brave men" in Scott and Fentress counties, Tennessee, and Wayne County, Kentucky, on December 18, 1878. The two Tennessee forces worked together and then cooperated with the Kentucky force for a sweep through several border counties. Later in December, Collector Landrum joined Collectors Duval of West Virginia and Rives of Virginia for coordinated operations along those borders. Despite occasional delays, miscalculations, or leaks to moonshiners, the coordinated raids were usually effective. A deputy collector boasted in 1880 that his posse could "penetrate the remotest corners" of moonshiners' territory and "travel over the roughest mountains" to "find out their distilleries no matter how well hidden." Raum regarded these raids as reducing revenuers' reliance on informers; he withdrew offers of reward money for locating stills, because "other and more effective methods for the suppression of illicit distilling . . . are now being put into operation."[17]

Increased government activity at first aroused "a very bitter feeling" among blockaders. West Virginia distillers were surprised by a large-scale raid, but the collector expected them to be "more on the alert, in better organized combinations, and more exasperated than before." Instead of being demoralized, "their aim will doubtless be hereafter to outnumber and outfight any such force as that which recently greeted them."[18]

Gunfights, infrequent when soldiers accompanied revenuers, became common during the first years of Raum's crackdown. Moonshiners died or were wounded in these encounters with often better-armed posses, but their friends usually carried off bodies or helped the injured escape. Consequently, their casualty rates are unknown. In South Carolina, shooting at deputy collectors and marshals became "so common as to excite but little comment, and the officers begin to regard that as an unpleasant performance incidental to the discharge of their duties and are usually prepared to return it." They did not take this lightly, for the stakes were high. In Greenville County "so many officers have been threatened, injured and killed" that able men refused to serve as deputy marshals. One who did serve was Rufus Springs, "an exceptionally good officer," who was shot from behind and killed while accompanying revenuers on a raid. In North Carolina during 1876–77, more officers were shot than moonshiners. Confrontations with blockaders led to the most casualties before 1880. Twelve revenuers were killed and eight were wounded during 1876–77; ten killed and seventeen wounded during 1877–78; and four killed and twenty-two wounded during 1878–79. The casualties declined afterward, with a maximum of four killed (1881–82) and nine wounded (1880–81). In 1879, Georgia was the most dangerous state, with one man killed and six wounded; in South Carolina and Tennessee no officers died, but five were wounded in each state. North Carolina saw one death and three woundings. Most blockaders preferred to hide themselves and their stills, but some moonshiners shot possemen in carefully planned ambushes; others fired when they were cornered and faced arrest and imprisonment.[19]

George W. Atkinson considered the casualty rates low. Moonshiners usually fired at posses from hillsides, and they seem to have been ignorant of the need to aim low, below the knees, to hit their target. Consequently they usually missed, though it seems odd that experienced hunters would not know a simple rule of marksmanship. However, other officers confirmed that moonshiner ambushes sometimes failed because they fired too high from the hillsides. Even when armed with an old Civil War cannon, the mountaineers fired over the heads of a marshal's posse charging up the hill: the load of "pot-metal and nails went crashing through the leafless trees." Whatever the reasons, casualties in the mountains were low compared with the Wild West: in 1890 the attorney general reported that the number of deputy marshals killed in Indian Territory averaged twenty per year.[20]

Whether on duty in the South or the West, federal officers were not protected until 1934 by any statute punishing people who resisted or even killed them. State authorities, rarely friendly in the mountains, were responsible for prosecuting moonshiners who killed deputies. Indictments were rare, successful prosecutions even rarer. During the first two years of Raum's term, about twenty-five or thirty revenuers were killed or wounded; only one of their assailants was prosecuted by local officials, in a Republican district of East Tennessee. Murderers of officers or informers were triable in federal courts only for the lesser offenses of conspiracy or resisting arrest. An assistant district attorney warned that until adequate punishments were prescribed, "the administration of the United States laws and the laws themselves will have little respect." Members of revenue posses were not even compensated for their own horses killed or wagons damaged by moonshiners in retaliation. In 1890 an agent complained that it was hard to recruit good possemen, not because they were afraid, but because they believed the government unjustly refused to compensate them for killed or injured horses or their own injury or death. The best that Commissioner John M. Mason could do for two of his injured men during the early nineties was to have Congress place one on the Union pension rolls and provide the other with compensation for medical expenses. Widows of soldiers killed on duty received a pension; widows of revenuers or deputy marshals did not. All that Commissioner Mason could do for two of them was to urge the collectors to appoint them to clerkships in their office.[21]

Armed resistance was not the only method moonshiners used to frustrate revenue enforcement. County sheriffs, justices of the peace, and state prosecuting attorneys were often their allies, arresting and prosecuting revenuers for murder, carrying concealed weapons, trespassing, and other offenses. Occasionally, as in the case of North Carolina deputy collector W. M. Walker, the charges were meant to harass and embarrass revenuers more than to get them into serious trouble. Walker was indicted in state court for disturbing a religious camp meeting because he allegedly produced "one of those things . . . called a 'cundum' . . . and . . . blowed it up, so as to resemble a man's penis, and showed it to the ladies." This charge was never tried.[22]

The experience of Deputy Collectors Shepard and Lane in Georgia was uglier and revealed the thin line between violence and legal harassment. The two men were arrested for carrying concealed weapons and were confined in a filthy, "loathsome" county jail. They had raided a previously untouched moonshine district, arousing local anger even though "they all admit that his [Shepard's] course has been characterized by fairness and moderation, as well as firmness and discretion." Previously, three civil warrants had been served on Shepard, but he was quickly bailed out, and the cases were transferred to federal courts. Lane was a local man who became "an object of intense dislike to the lawless inhabitants who have pursued him with great malignity, and have several times attempted his assassination." When Lane was arrested, blockaders threatened his friends so no one was willing to put up bail for him. Shepard tried to bail him out, but the sheriff refused to accept his money, and later a crowd stoned him. He was saved from serious injury by his own arrest. Finally both men were released on bail put up by Collector Clark and District Attorney Farrow. Clark complained, "as though it were not enough that government officials in the honest discharge of their . . . duties . . . should be hounded, stoned, bushwacked, and treated with indignities of the most aggravated type, they are thus to be outraged in the *name of law*, which we have been taught to regard as a protection instead of an unrighteous oppression."[23]

Raum reported that 165 revenuers were prosecuted for various offenses in state courts between 1876 and 1879. Georgia was far in the lead with 48, Tennessee and North Carolina following with 36 each. The old troublemaker South Carolina was a somewhat distant third with 18 prosecutions. Nevertheless, Marshal Wallace of that state spoke for his colleagues when he said that "one of the most serious difficulties with which we have to contend is the universal hostility of the democratic State officials" whose obstruction of federal law enforcement inspired moonshiners to resist. One state judge in the piedmont town of Greenville charged the grand jury to indict every federal officer who "had infringed the rights of a citizen and he would see that they were tried and punished." He may have been legitimately concerned about civil liberties, but revenuers, like policemen in general, saw his views as harassment.[24]

Federal officials did have some protection against state harassment: the district attorney could remove their cases to federal court by a writ of habeas corpus. This was a common feature in both Reconstruction and revenue legislation, but the process was slow and frequently obstructed by state officials who challenged its constitutionality. Even under South Carolina's Republican Reconstruction government there was confusion about the removal power. The state prosecutor, Samuel Melton (who later became U.S. district attorney), argued that a revenue man charged with murdering a moonshiner should be tried in state court because murder was a state, not federal, crime. Deputy Collector Alex Mattison languished in jail for six months while federal judges waited for Congress to clarify the removal provisions. He wrote to Attorney General Williams, "I would much prefer that someone else be the victim of a test-case." He finally was released a year later by Judge Bond's decision that the killing was in the line of duty. When South Carolina returned to Democratic rule in 1877, state officials actively resisted removal of murder and other cases to federal courts. The Greenville judge who charged jurors to indict federal officers added that they should proceed "without regard to any order of the United States Circuit Court to transfer their cases to that court."[25]

J. J. Mott, revenue collector in North Carolina, had to fight every case in the state courts because the judge had indicated he would not allow removals to federal jurisdiction. Mott employed prominent Democratic lawyers to argue for removal, which "had a very good effect indeed." The cases aroused considerable anger, and the deputy marshal was afraid to deliver the writ of habeas corpus. Mott was able to secure a commission as deputy marshal for himself and personally delivered the papers to the state judge. Eventually the North Carolina Supreme Court upheld the power of federal courts to try cases of officers charged with offenses in the course of their duties. The *Tennessee v. Davis* decision of the United States Supreme Court in 1879 upheld the removal provisions in a ringing affirmation of federal supremacy: "The general government must cease to exist whenever it cannot enforce the exercise of its constitutional powers within the states by . . . its officers and agents." The decision did not forbid state prosecutions, which continued, though less frequently than before the ruling.[26]

Moonshiners and their supporters denounced removal to federal courts as merely guaranteeing revenuers and marshals immunity from punishment. The Department of Justice, responsible for securing removal of cases against federal officials, was careful to make sure it was protecting officers against charges clearly arising in the course of normal duties. Attorney General Devens denied removal when a deputy marshal mistakenly arrested a man not named in an indictment, and he endorsed a district attorney's refusal to defend an ex–deputy marshal charged with grand larceny. The government was unwilling to protect irresponsible or dishonest officers.[27]

A South Carolina case that dragged on from 1878 to 1882 illustrates the difficulties of protecting federal officers. In early June 1878, Special (temporary) Deputy Collectors Kane, Moose, Scruggs, and Durham (who was also a deputy marshal) headed for Rocky Bottom, Pickens County, hoping to arrest the outlaw moonshiner Lewis Redmond who had led a raid on the county jail to release some fellow moonshiners. The posse hid in the woods of a mountainside near a house where Redmond was supposed to live with a woman named Ladd. After several hours, a shrill whistle and a knock heralded a meeting at a fence between a man and "one of the women (known as Redmond's women)." Judging from "his actions toward the woman and her child," the revenuers concluded that he was Redmond. Instead of chasing him immediately, with good chances for escape, they decided to wait for him to return to the house and capture him inside. The next morning two men, including the person they had seen earlier, entered the house. The revenuers charged the cabin, hoping to arrest the two men. At the door Kane encountered Amos Ladd (Redmond's brother-in-law, who had been with him in the jailbreak episode), who "snapped" his gun at him, jumping from the door to flee. Durham then shot him twice and killed him. The other man, thought to be Redmond, also fled. Scruggs captured him, but he broke away and escaped. The deputies, fearing for their lives if they remained in Rocky Bottom, left for Pickens Court House to surrender to the local sheriff. However, they worried about the risk of staying in Pickens jail, and the possemen continued on to Greenville where they surrendered.

State officials moved quickly. The sheriff of Pickens County sent what Revenue Agent Jacob Wagner called a "ruffianly dispatch" to the police chiefs of Greenville and other towns to arrest the revenuers while they were on their way to surrender. The state authorities charged that the possemen mistook Ladd for Redmond, "giving no quarter or time for identity." The deputies claimed that they actually had a warrant for Ladd, though Kane's original report made no mention of it. This would later prove to be a sticky point.[28]

Collector Brayton reported that the defense lawyers "say that the government could not have a more favorable case to carry to the Supreme Court to test the validity and binding effect of the federal law providing for the transfer of cases against revenue officers prosecuted in the state courts." He lamented that "in any other country the people would praise and honor" the officers "instead of hating and persecuting them." William E. Earle, one of the defense attorneys, told Attorney General Devens, "The press of this State is united in the cry for the blood of these men. And its popular effect has been immediate. A trial means conviction," and the grand jury would definitely indict them. The prosecutors, revealing as much about themselves as about the deputies, attacked their character. Moose was supposed to be living "in open adultery or marriage, with a black woman of low degree, has children by her and is not a person of good character." They said that Durham was convicted and sent to the penitentiary in 1872 and since then had been "engaged in selling whiskey to the colored people." Kane was "brought here from the North by ex Gov [sic] Frank Moses, and is of bad character." Although defended by District Attorney Northrop and by Earle, now his special assistant, the men were indicted. Earle succeeded in having the case transferred for state trial outside of Pickens County, to Anderson.[29]

Meanwhile he and Northrop petitioned to have the case removed for trial in the federal court; the circuit court issued a writ of habeas corpus, but the sheriff ignored it, refusing to release Kane and the others from jail. State judge Kershaw did not allow the transfer, holding that the federal court lacked jurisdiction in the case. Despite concern about forcible resistance to getting the deputies out of the county jail, which prompted the attorney general to list all the options for Earle, from a marshal's posse to a presidential proclamation of insurrection, the second attempt to transfer the deputies to federal custody proceeded peacefully in August. Clearly this was a major case, involving the ability of the government to enforce its laws. As Attorney General Devens said, attempts to punish federal officers for "alleged misconduct in the performance" of their duty "have become so numerous that it must be definitely determined whether they are liable elsewhere than in the courts of the United States, when acting under their authority. If they are it must lead to serious embarrassment in all attempts to enforce the revenue laws in parts of six or seven states where such laws are unpopular." The *New York Tribune* argued that "the collection of any tax can easily be prevented, the levying of any tax can be entirely nullified, and it can even be made impossible to find reputable and worthy men who will undertake to act as Federal officials" if the government cannot protect its officers in the performance of their duties.[30]

Although the jurisdictional quarrel was favorably settled, the next step, actual defense of the deputies against state charges in the federal court, almost collapsed because of suspicion that a false warrant had been prepared after Ladd's death. Apparently the possemen carried a general warrant charging Ladd and others with conspiracy, a misdemeanor that did not justify use of force in attempting Ladd's arrest. District Attorney Northrop alleged that, at Earle's request, a U.S. commissioner issued a warrant charging Ladd with illicit distillation in order to strengthen the case for transfer to the federal court. This commissioner supposedly confessed to Northrop, who was embarrassed and feared harm to the government from exposure of the fraud. He warned that a Greenville editor was already suspicious of the warrant. Devens admonished Earle that if the defense rests on "a false, forged and antedated warrant," the government should immediately withdraw from the case. "The United States will not countenance anything but a straight-forward honest defense." If Earle attempted to use a phony warrant, he should resign immediately. Earle emphatically denied that the deputies ever carried any warrant for Ladd and that none was prepared after the moonshiner's death. He charged that the district attorney was frustrating his efforts to defend the men. Since the two officials could not work together, the attorney general accepted Northrop's suggestion that he withdraw from the case and leave its conduct entirely in

Earle's hands, "untrammeled by any association" with the district attorney. Earle assured Devens "in most positive terms that in no way will he countenance any thing which is in highest degree wanting in good faith," and the attorney general was satisfied that the controversy was settled and the defense could go forward.[31]

The case went forward very slowly. The trial was postponed several times because the prosecuting attorneys could not find their witnesses, who had gone "somewhere in the Mountains of North Carolina." Collector Brayton, following Raum's general directive to pay men who had cases pending against them, appointed Kane, Moose, Scruggs, and Durham as deputy revenue collectors while they were out on bail. This aroused a storm of protest, including a letter from U.S. senator Wade Hampton. Finally, in April 1882, William E. Earle was able to report a trial and acquittal of the four men.[32]

Collector Brayton said that Kane and his fellow revenuers "are not saints, for they are not engaged in works of piety," but they would compare favorably with any police officers. He seemed to suggest that one should not demand high standards from police officers. Former attorney general Amos Akerman commented, "It is impossible to get men of sensitive feelings to do the work of deputy-marshals in the mountains of the South. They have to deal with a rough, desperate set of men, and none but rough, desperate men can be induced to undergo the hardships and take the risks." Earle, defender of the deputies in court, denounced the conduct of revenuers in general terms: they were "as a rule" "not only destitute of character and principle, but are harsh and brutal and utterly indifferent to the rights of citizens in the enforcement of the law. Instead of one of these men being killed the wonder to me is that any of them are left alive."[33] Many southerners shared his attitudes toward revenuers, and indeed their conduct sometimes justified such hostility.

Southern newspapers condemned the tyranny of revenue enforcement. Editorializing against Kane and the other deputies, a Charleston paper fulminated: "For several years past these officers, some of whom are known . . . to be men utterly depraved in character and unworthy the high position they now disgrace have claimed for themselves and exercised powers and privileges more in harmony with the blind and despotic governments of the East than with the institutions of a free and enlightened Republic." The officers seemed to take "peculiar delight . . . to oppress the helpless and to torment and bedevil both the innocent and guilty." They scoffed at local laws and "openly boast" that if prosecuted by the state they will be "dismissed unwhipped of justice" by transfer to federal courts.[34]

The Georgia state legislature commissioned an investigation of the conflict in the northern part of the state in 1877 that strongly condemned the arbitrary, harsh, and corrupt conduct of deputy marshals who made revenue raids. They refused to show people their warrants, forced prisoners on long marches to jail, stole or destroyed property, cursed and frightened women and children, and offered to release people who paid them substantial sums of money. A meeting of 100 citizens of Fannin County, where Lieutenant McIntyre was killed, regretted his death but charged that "all the trouble in our midst has been caused, not by the attempt to execute the laws . . . but by those who have been employed to execute them," all but one of the deputy marshals having been moonshiners themselves who tyrannized over their neighbors for "pecuniary benefits or to gratify some personal animosity" against their victims. Charging deputies with being blockaders or in collusion with them was fairly common. Georgians complained that the government's policy seemed to be "to terrify the people into obedience," leading to "gross outrages upon person and property, to a disregard of the authority of the state to protect its citizens, to the frequent employment of desperate and unworthy men as deputies." The *Atlanta Constitution*'s choice epithets were "the bashi-bazooks who train under Andrew Clark and oppress the people of North Georgia by their demoniac yells and worse than Turkish vindictiveness," "Clark's cavaliers," or "Clark's buccaneers." An Alabama paper hinted that citizens should resist revenuers if the government did not check their abuses: "If the United States Government is not willing to protect its citizens, but persists in allowing such drunken vagabonds as some of these men are to be clothed with the authority of the law when they themselves are violators of the law which they pretend to enforce, then such conduct should not be tolerated by the communities through which these armed and lawless rabbles [*sic*] pass; when patience is thus abused and protection is sought in vain from the strong arm of the government, then it becomes time, in accordance with nature's law of self-preservation, to take care of ourselves."[35]

The Alabama state legislature sent a memorial to the United States Congress complaining that revenuers "raided over the country with large bodies of armed men and, regardless of law and decency, have abused and insulted the people without cause," stealing from them, breaking down fences and shooting their farm animals, and firing their guns "into the yards and around the dwellings of defenceless females, for the brutal gratification of terrifying them." Deputies acted "as if they were the ruthless myrmidons of a power at enmity with its people, and whose laws were enacted, not to shelter and protect, as well as punish, but only to harass and destroy." Representative Emory Speer of Georgia joined in with perfervid oratory: "Sir, the people of these United States have never relished an undue exhibition of armed strength on the part of the Government in time of peace, and such visitations are not more palatable to the people of the mountains of Georgia than to any other section of this free country."[36]

In a single, rolling sentence the North Carolina legislature summarized all the criticisms: "The present system of internal revenue laws is oppressive and inquisitorial, centralizing in its tendencies and inconsistent with the genius of a free people, legalizing unequal, expensive, and iniquitous taxation, and, as enforced in this state, is a fraud upon the sacred rights of our people and subversive of honest government, prostituted in many instances to a system of political patronage which is odious and outrageous, corrupting public virtue and jeopardizing public liberty, and sustained by intimidation and bribery on the part of the revenue officials to debauch the elective franchise." Campaigning against the revenue laws in 1876, Zebulon Vance of North Carolina denounced revenuers in more folksy terms as "red-legged grasshoppers." Holding up a specimen of the voracious insect preserved in alcohol, he orated: "This fellow . . . eats up every green thing that God ever gave to man, and he only serves the universal dissolution. The time has come when an honest man can't take an honest drink without having a gang of revenue officers after him."[37]

Much of this denunciation was undoubtedly politically motivated, and Zebulon Vance led a Senate committee probing the revenue system as an instrument for advancing the Republican party. He and other critics charged that revenuers had to contribute a month's salary to the Republican campaign fund and that they spent their time building up the party machine when they were not oppressing local citizens or conniving with distillers to cheat the government. Georgians took a partisan view of a revenuer's killing a moonshiner while fighting an ambush as "the murderous policy of the Republican administration."[38]

Despite the partisanship of many of the charges, revenue officials themselves criticized deputy collectors' and deputy marshals' abuse of power and arbitrary conduct. Revenue Agent Olney described the deputies in Tennessee as "generally the roughest sort of illiterate men, who are unnecessarily severe." Four special deputies were chosen because "they are 'fighting men' and consequently are men of no polish, education or brains. It is not wonderful that they meet resistance." An assistant district attorney agreed about such Tennessee deputies: "Some of them are the most arrant of cowards, and, as might be expected, these are the most energetic of all in efforts to establish reputations for being 'bad men from away back.' " Agent Olney also criticized deputy marshals in Kentucky who "go out to make arrests, with a loud noise—their arms unnecessarily conspicuous—they go with the avowed intention of bringing in their men dead or alive. They love the sport, as a bloodhound loves to track and capture a run-away negro." Naturally they angered local people, "and the least appearance of resistance causes an explosion of oaths, and immediate exhibition of shotguns revolvers &c. In fact the deputies are delighted. It is just what they wanted." Marshal Fitzsimmons of Georgia said, "Permit me to suggest that one cause of the trouble in Rabun county is the employment of persons who have made themselves obnoxious to the people." A federal grand jury in Georgia called for suspension of two deputy marshals and "an extensive examination into the official conduct" of all the deputies. South Carolina district attorney Northrop listed mountaineers' complaints of brutality, illegal searches, and possemen forcing farmers' wives and daughters to cook meals for them. He urged official investigation to show the people that the government cared about abuses. He wanted to sift truth from rumor because "a crisis has come, in which, unless we prove these charges false or remedy them if not false, the Government will be put to constant and extraordinary difficulty and *expense*."[39]

Revenue records do not reveal such investigations or their results. However, Raum responded to criticisms in Tennessee newspapers by reminding the collector, "The important thing in enforcing any law where seizures and arrests are made is to perform the duty in such a manner as not to offend well-meaning citizens. The offense usually is not in the doing of the act itself, but in the manner in which it is done, for a lawful act may be done in so brutal and offensive a manner as to render the officer unpopular." He expected the collector "will observe the law yourself in seeking to make others observe it, and I trust you will impress the importance of this upon your subordinates." Telling Collector Brayton of South Carolina that his "earnest desire is that collectors of internal revenue shall appoint to office as their subordinates men of intelligence, honesty, fidelity, experience, and sobriety, so that the laws can be enforced not only with vigor, but with moderation and discretion," he requested removal of men against whom there was "any just ground of complaint." He affirmed the principle that "it is the experience of mankind the world over that laws are properly enforced in proportion to the moral support given the officers of the law in the community where they are called upon to perform their duties, and that is of the first importance to enlist the sympathy and support of well-meaning citizens in the enforcement of the laws." He strove to implement this precept in all the southern states and expected collectors to follow it also.[40]

Even more serious than abuses committed by individual officials, because it was built into the law enforcement system, was arbitrary arrest for the sake of making fees. Revenue collectors and their regular deputies were paid salaries, and men appointed special deputies for raids received a per diem payment. However, United States commissioners (equivalent to justices of the peace) and deputy marshals received their income from fees for issuing and serving warrants. Commissioners received $5 for each case they heard, and dimes and nickels for providing the paperwork. The routine case of William Green brought in $7.40 to a Georgia commissioner. In 1877 one commissioner heard about seventy-one cases, committing twenty-one people for trial; he received his fees in all of these. The deputy marshal in the Green case collected $4.70 for serving the commissioner's warrant, guarding the prisoner, and attending the hearing. These amounts do not seem large, but they were substantial then, especially in the mountains. Fee payment encouraged deputies to swear out warrants on doubtful testimony, leading to the arrest of innocent men. Sometimes deputies arranged with a commissioner for prisoners to be brought exclusively to him for a hearing. This often meant that arrested moonshiners had to travel long distances from home for a preliminary examination, and it gave deputies an opportunity to bill the government for unnecessary travel expenses. A mountain Republican newspaper charged that "the long trains of poorly-clad, half starved men . . . under the conduct of guards and deputy marshals" did "more to bring the government into odium . . . than any other agency."[41]

Some deputies not only took advantage of their legal powers but participated in more complex forms of corruption. In Virginia, deputies suspected to be in league with moonshiners swore out large numbers of warrants against innocent people. They made their fees and never attempted to "penetrate the remote localities of illicit distillers." Raum told the attorney general about this scam, and the offenders were sacked after an investigation.[42]

A ring of Georgia deputy marshals in 1873 supposedly arrested illicit distillers under dubious warrants and then extracted payment from them to settle the cases out of court, which they had no legal power to do. The marshal denied Revenue Agent Norris's charges, and they were investigated by a federal grand jury, which did not find any indictments. Nevertheless, the evidence seems strong that the deputies were engaged in dubious practices. In 1879 another revenue agent charged Georgia deputies with encouraging "illiterate colored, and white men" to "scour the country to obtain warrants for some mere technical violation of law." These men received fees as witnesses, and the deputies and commissioners received their fees. Often these "strikers" encouraged a mountaineer to sell them a glass of whiskey or a few chews of tobacco. If the person refused to accept payment, the visitor gave some coins to the children. The unsuspecting mountaineer was soon under a warrant for retailing without a license. Usually discharged upon preliminary examination, he returned home "only to nurse his wrath against the laws and the officers, if not before he now becomes a law breaker in fact." Even federal juries were refusing to convict moonshiners in Georgia, saying that the prosecutions were "simply a scramble among the officers for costs." Collector Wade ruefully "admitted that the expression does not appear to be wholly devoid of truth."[43]

Deputy marshals were the usual culprits, but revenuers were often charged with abuses they opposed or tried to prevent. A revenue agent in Georgia urged a commissioner to refuse to issue warrants based on the testimony of a notoriously unreliable informer. The commissioner refused to do so, probably to make the fees, and the revenuers took the blame from local people. Because deputy marshals were often appointed special deputy revenue collectors, mountaineers considered arrests for the sake of fees part of the tyranny of revenue enforcement. Also, until reform of the system in the 1870s, revenue officials had received part of the proceeds from the sale of any property they confiscated. This "moiety system" was abused by revenuers and became a bad memory among local people, who continued to charge them with raiding stills for the sake of money they could earn.[44]

Under Commissioner Daniel Pratt, Raum's predecessor, the revenue bureau had prohibited its salaried officers from receiving witness fees for testifying in federal courts. Commissioner Raum opposed fee payment of commissioners and deputy marshals as a "vicious" system "tending to demoralize the service." Attorney General Williams had recommended salaries for both district attorneys and marshals in 1874, inaugurating an almost unbroken stream of pleas to do away with fees stretching into the nineties, when the problem was partially remedied. In 1878, a congressman from Texas proposed a bill to abolish fee payment.[45]

Some people, though, argued in favor of fees. Attorney General Benjamin Brewster asserted in 1882 that fees provided encouragement for enforcing unpopular laws in a hostile community. Federal judge Robert P. Dick in North Carolina, even though he had dismissed several commissioners who participated in a fee ring, shared this view. He claimed that salaried deputy revenue collectors had little incentive for dangerous duty. "If all officers were paid by salary, we would soon live in good quiet times, and Redmond and his gang would soon . . . own the mountains, and whiskey would soon be as plenteous as in olden times, and the Government would not collect tax enough to pay the local officers of the revenue." By 1884, though, Attorney General Brewster changed his mind, recognizing that fee payment invited fraud and arbitrary arrest, making the government "odious" and the people "hostile to the courts of the United States." Presidents Arthur and Cleveland urged salary payment in annual messages, but Congress did not act.[46]

Though the fee problem persisted, both revenue commissioners and attorneys general worked to keep it under control. Raum's predecessor, Daniel D. Pratt, wrote to the attorney general in June 1876 to suggest that federal judges require approval of the collector or district attorney before commissioners could issue warrants in revenue cases. Raum directed all collectors to examine revenue charges carefully before reporting them to the district attorney for prosecution, and Attorney General Charles Devens called marshals' "attention to the fact that there is much reason to believe that many causeless and idle prosecutions have been brought in some districts, apparently only for the purpose of making fees. Great injustice is thus done to individuals and the Government." Raum believed that such instructions and cautions "greatly diminished" the number of prosecutions "instituted apparently for the creation of costs only."[47]

Federal judges issued court orders limiting commissioners' warrants; collectors and district attorneys sought to improve their quality or demanded to see them before they could be served. For example, District Attorney George Andrews in East Tennessee warned commissioners in 1875 not to make their courts into "engines of oppression and malice" filled with "trashy and insignificant cases" of merely technical violations of the law.[48] However, such efforts to control fee abuse stirred up a hornet's nest of jurisdictional disputes in some states. Commissioners were angry over lost power and income; sometimes the collector and district attorney quarreled over who had ultimate judgment of a warrant's validity, and both objected to some aspects of judges' orders.

Perhaps the earliest of these fights occurred in eastern Tennessee in 1871. District Attorney Camp objected to Judge Trigg's highly restrictive rulings that a person could not be charged with illegal retailing of liquor unless it were his "means of livelihood" and that only owners of stills, not paid employees, could be charged with illicit distilling. Camp appealed to Circuit Judge Emmons, who overruled most of Trigg's decisions but insisted that employees of moonshiners had to have known the operation was illegal before they could be prosecuted. Blockaders took advantage of the ruling to declare that they were mere hirelings, ignorant of the illegal nature of their work. Camp's successor, George Andrews, objected to a routine effort to curtail deputy marshals' and commissioners' abuses. This was Attorney General Williams's 1875 directive that all revenue violators be taken to the nearest commissioner for preliminary hearing. The requirement sought to prevent deputies from colluding with individual commissioners to secure all the cases and fees, including mileage for travel, for themselves. District Attorney Andrews, however, directed deputy marshals to ignore the order when they thought that taking prisoners to a neighboring commissioner would encourage rescue attempts. After an investigation of fee abuses, the Justice Department in 1880 again ordered that prisoners be taken to the nearest commissioner. This time the circuit judge, John Baxter, who had made the original charges prompting the investigation, objected to this solution. He warned that it would encourage rescues and "breaches of the peace" because arrested people would remain among sympathetic neighbors.[49]

The controversy over revenue warrants in North Carolina reflected a different configuration of disputes among federal officials. Part of the battle there was between District Judge Robert P. Dick, a curmudgeon who fought against corruption, and the U.S. commissioners. The judge also ran up against the Department of Justice's efforts to save money. In 1873 Dick issued instructions for the commissioners, who "should be impressed with the dignity and honor of their position, and should not regard their offices as mere means of making money." He required marshals to take arrested people to the commissioner nearest to where they were apprehended, not necessarily the commissioner originally issuing the warrant. Later he limited warrants to those based on the testimony of federal officers who verified informers' statements. He discovered rings of commissioners and dishonest witnesses who swore out warrants for the sake of fees. He sacked some of the commissioners implicated and published a list of disreputable witnesses. In 1875 he added further restrictions. At the preliminary examination, commissioners had to inform defendants of the charges and their right to counsel and refusal to testify. He put deputy marshals on notice that they would be dismissed for excessive rudeness, force, or obtaining confessions by promise or threat. Warrants should not be issued for petty sellers of liquor or tobacco without an affidavit that they were frequent violators. Affidavits supported by revenue officers now had to be first sent to the collector and then to the district attorney for approval. The judge was working to minimize a problem that frequently came up in his jurisdiction.[50]

Despite such restrictions, Dick by no means opposed revenue enforcement. At one point he allowed commissioners to appoint special deputy marshals to pursue moonshiners fleeing while the regular deputy marshal was absent. He hoped to defeat their strategy of leaving the state to escape prosecution, but the Department of Justice overruled him because it had no money for the special deputies. Consequently he had to order nonprosecution of about fifty revenue cases. "Your Department insists on a reduction of expenses," he complained to Attorney General Williams; "the Commissr of Int Rev [sic] insists on an energetic enforcement of the Revenue laws. I cannot satisfy both requirements and I determined . . . to save expenses and let many offenders against the law go unprosecuted. The Commissr [sic] must look to your Department for explanations."[51]

Although Judge Dick's rulings must have curtailed some of the worst abuses, Attorney General Devens nevertheless had to call the district attorney's attention to Raum's complaint about commissioners' practice of issuing warrants for the sake of fees. Soon afterward another North Carolina district attorney complained that a court ruling requiring approval of revenue warrants by the collector placed "the whole subject within the power of the Collector of Int. Rev. [*sic*], gives them the fullest opportunity to protect offenders, to persecute enemies, to take black mail and to freeze out objectionable District Attorneys." This complaint only got him into trouble with Attorney General MacVeagh, who told him that he himself had drafted the ruling. There was still a problem with warrants, because deputy revenue collectors obliged deputy marshals by signing as witnesses in warrants actually based on false charges. Collector Cooper cautioned deputies that they were personally responsible for all warrants under their name and they must be satisfied that all the facts were correct. It seemed they needed frequent reminders.[52]

In neighboring South Carolina, deputy marshals evaded restrictions in a different way. There they got themselves appointed deputy revenue collectors so they could verify their own warrants. Raum cautioned Collector Brayton that "such appointments are inconsistent with the Order of Court, which should be in good faith respected, and which was intended to correct an abuse." Since the deputy marshals' income depended on their fees, they were quite resourceful in collecting them.[53]

In Georgia the controversy over warrants for the sake of fees dragged on for years and was part of a political and personal feud between District Attorney Henry P. Farrow and Collector Andrew Clark. Problems with the number and quality of warrants first appeared during the Reconstruction years. Georgia blacks, unprotected by the courts of a state "redeemed" by white-supremacist Democrats in 1870–71, turned to the federal commissioners for protection of their rights. The commissioners, some of whom were also black, signed "hundreds upon hundreds" of warrants with little understanding of the limits of federal civil rights jurisdiction. In 1875, District Attorney Farrow advised against issuing warrants in most of these cases. Three years later, after complaints from a Democratic congressman and upon the attorney general's advice, Farrow required that all charges involving conflict between blacks and whites be sent to him for approval before issue of a warrant. Previously, Farrow had requested commissioners to clearly establish the facts from witnesses before signing a warrant. Now he followed the 1877 court order of Justice Bradley requiring all warrants to have the district attorney's consent. By this time the question was shifting from civil rights to revenue enforcement. Justice Bradley ordered that warrants had to be based on evidence provided by the actual accuser, either by affidavit or by examination under oath. This policy sought to eliminate warrants based only on what an officer had heard from an anonymous informer, which clearly opened the way for abuse and charges for the sake of collecting fees. The *Atlanta Constitution* endorsed Bradley's order: "It is possible that by exercising this degree of caution" some guilty people would escape, but it was preferable to the former oppression of innocent people.[54]

This attempt at reform only drew the battle lines. Collector Andrew Clark objected because requiring the testimony of the actual accuser of moonshiners forced informers to reveal their names. The whole enforcement system would be disrupted because informers would obviously be afraid to come forward. Clark hoped the ruling would be modified.[55]

Warrants based on direct testimony of revenuers and deputy marshals did not require the district attorney's approval. Farrow tried to persuade the district court to require his endorsement of these warrants as well, but the court refused to go that far. Later the commissioners revolted against control of their work and convinced the federal court to weaken its original order, narrowly interpreting the district attorney's consent to mean examination for correct legal form but not for evaluation of the evidence. Revenue Agent Somerville blamed Farrow himself for the large number of dubious warrants, charging that "sixty percent" of them "should not and would not be issued if the Dist. Atty. [*sic*] was as careful of the public interest as he assumes to be." The charge seems to have been unfair, for Farrow escalated his crusade against excessive warrants by asking Marshal Fitzsimmons, a Democrat who agreed, not to *serve* warrants without his consent. This policy got Farrow into a running feud with Collector Clark and ex-marshal Smyth who had become a U.S. commissioner. Clark and Smyth were leaders of the radical Republican faction, and the warrants fight was part of a larger power struggle with Farrow, a former Confederate and a moderate Republican. The radicals had tried to remove Farrow several times.[56]

Each side enlisted different federal courts in its cause. Farrow relied on the circuit court, staffed by Supreme Court Justice Joseph Bradley; Clark counted on the district court and Judge Woods. In 1879 Woods ruled in favor of Clark and Smyth, requiring the marshal to serve all warrants given to him. The *Constitution* backed Farrow, commenting on the decision, "Uncle Sam is rich . . . and now for wholesale arrests for the fees!" Farrow bounced back, obtaining two restrictions from the circuit court. One prohibited arrests of petty sellers of liquor for a single violation; arrests were allowed only if they "frequently" sold liquor illegally. This was clearly aimed at the entrapment scheme described earlier. The other order required commissioners to give to the circuit court full reports of all warrants they issued. Presumably the extra paperwork would inhibit signing of dubious warrants. However, the first order brought Commissioner Raum himself into the fray. He said that no such order existed in any other revenue district, and "it is only by punishing offenses as they occur that the Government can hope to secure observance of the law." Attorney General Devens did not like the restriction either, arguing that it prevented action against first offenders that would deter them in the future, or against repeat offenders for whom only one sale could be proven. He urged Farrow to "assent to the reversal of the order." The scrappy district attorney did not, and the order stood. Federal judges in other states later followed its precedent.[57]

Farrow, protesting all the way and accusing Raum and Clark of helping to cover frauds by ex-marshal Smyth, finally lost his job in 1880, partly due to Raum, who told the secretary of the Treasury that "it is impossible to enforce the laws with this man in office." The warrants problem did not disappear with him, however. In 1881 Marshal Longstreet, an ex-Confederate Democrat, and U.S. commissioner Mollin protested a court order forbidding warrants unless supported by an affidavit of revenue collectors or the district attorney. Longstreet complained that the order "would seriously cripple the operations of this department, and extend aid and comfort" to illicit distillers. In 1883 revenuers were directed to prosecute by filing informations (charges and testimony by officials) instead of obtaining a grand jury indictment of moonshiners. District Attorney Emory Speer, who as a Democratic congressman had led the attack on revenue enforcement, argued that bypassing the usual process of warrant followed by indictment undermined the primary motive for prosecuting revenue offenders. That was none other than the fees that deputy marshals and commissioners no longer collected under the new procedure. These officials lost "all of that inducement to active prosecution." He took a sanguine view of motivations for prosecuting moonshiners: "The general sense of patriotism which every citizen is presumed to have . . . has not been an apparent element in those Internal Revenue prosecutions which I have observed." Speer also complained that informations could not be filed until the session of the district court met, giving offenders time to escape. Service of a warrant meant that the arrested person was bound over for trial and witnesses were secured. He persuaded the attorney general to approve returning to warrants.[58]

By 1886 the circuit court ruled that warrants could be issued in revenue cases only if revenue officers or the district attorney swore that they had carefully investigated complaints of private citizens or deputy marshals. During the 1890s the process acquired more safeguards. Returning to a modified version of the 1877 order requiring testimony of the actual accuser for revenue warrants, the informer had to submit an affidavit that he personally knew of the violation. The requirement was "strictly enforced," and the commissioner was responsible for investigating the character of the accuser. The informer received some protection because his name did not appear on the actual warrant. The commissioner then sent the affidavit to the district attorney for his approval. After approval, the statement was submitted to a deputy revenue collector, who made a formal complaint based "upon information and belief." Only then did the commissioner issue the actual warrant. This warrant itself then had to be sent to the district attorney for approval before it was given to the marshal for execution. This strict, time-consuming policy reflected the guidelines set by the Democratic attorney general in 1896. Though this was the last word in Georgia, the warrants and fee problem cropped up in various places in later years.[59]

Judges, district attorneys, and revenue officials sought to check abuses of the fee system, but they sometimes conflicted. Each group sought to maintain control of what was happening in their jurisdictions; each thought that their methods of eliminating fee abuse were the best. Despite conflicts, collectively they seem to have reduced corruption of the fee system over the years. The problem, though, would not finally be solved until deputy marshals and commissioners were no longer paid by fees. As long as they depended on fees, they still could find ways around restrictions of their power.

General Raum faced formidable obstacles to his program for containment of moonshining: violent resistance, intimidation or sympathy of block-aders' neighbors, prosecution of his subordinates by state officials, some-times arbitrary or unreliable subordinates, the fee system for commissioners and its inducement for abuse, and jurisdictional disputes among federal officials. His strategies would be tested in mountain hollows and court-rooms throughout Appalachia.

6   Moonshiners
in Retreat

. . . .

Despite casualties, inadequate legal protection, state harassment, and public anger over arbitrary conduct, the revenue posses rode into the mountains. General Raum's campaign, like General Grant's during the Civil War, moved forward all along the line. The triumphs and setbacks of revenuers' efforts in northeastern Georgia were typical. The Georgia confrontation prompted a resolution from the House of Representatives requesting the secretary of the Treasury to explain "the necessity for the employment of armed men at the instance of the Internal Revenue Bureau." Raum swamped the legislators with over 200 pages of printed letters and reports on Georgia that also covered all the other districts where illicit distillers resisted revenue collection.[1]

Raum took office in August 1876, and the problems in Georgia became acute during his first distilling season, the fall and winter of 1876–77. Collector Andrew Clark reported that the "immense corn crop," the largest in fifteen years, contributed to making northeastern Georgia perhaps the worst moonshine district in the United States: "more illicit distilleries, and in the hands of the most desperate men; besides, the whole white population, with a few exceptions, can never be relied upon to aid a revenue officer in discharge of his official duties, and the colored people dare not give any assistance." Clark did not have enough deputies to carry on the normal business of monitoring the legal distilleries as well as to pursue blockaders.[2]

Raum organized a revenue force under Agents Chamberlin and Grimeson to assist Clark and his men, and the detachment of soldiers at Atlanta was detailed to accompany the revenuers on their raids. This campaign netted eighty-four moonshiners and thirty-three stills during the first part of February, but it was during these operations that Lieutenant McIntyre was killed in the Frog Mountain district. The revenuers and soldiers persisted, continuing to scour northeastern Georgia for moonshiners and their distilleries. This sweep prompted charges of oppression and corruption that were investigated by the Georgia legislature. Its report was sharply critical of the deputy marshals involved.[3]

Agent Chamberlin and his men rode through Murray, Cherokee, Gilmer, and Fannin counties, and "after I clean out the distillers and murderers in that section," he proposed to operate in the counties bordering North Carolina. During early March these raids captured sixty-five moonshiners and destroyed twenty-one stills. A sign of their effect was the surrender to the deputy marshals of twenty-three blockaders, "tired of being hunted down, and fearing arrest and punishment," who came in from distant strongholds. Chamberlin believed, "The opinion is spreading that it is useless to longer resist the enforcement of the United States Laws; the vigorous operations now being prosecuted are having a wonderfully good effect. . . . A few more telling blows, such as have already been struck, are all that is necessary to produce the desired result and add immensely to the revenue."[4]

The blows, however, were suspended. Leading Georgia politicians and other citizens petitioned President Grant for amnesty to illicit distillers if they promised to obey the laws in the future. The president offered clemency to all moonshiners who appeared in court and pleaded guilty, leading to dismissal of 792 people. Their guilty pleas probably accounted for an apparently impressive surge of revenue convictions, rising from 42 percent of cases in 1875 to 68 percent in 1876 and 84 percent in 1877, the highest ever reached in northern Georgia. Nevertheless, moonshiners kept at their business and resistance continued. During the early summer of 1877 President Hayes replaced the Republican marshal with a Democrat in hopes that mountaineers would be more inclined to obey a Democratic officer. However, Raum reported that "illicit distillers . . . , when put to the test, resisted, bushwacked, and shot Democratic and Republican officers with rigid impartiality."[5]

By December Collector Clark's special deputies were traveling through their districts as a patrol looking for illicit distilleries. Since extension of the amnesty in April, revenuers had captured forty-two moonshiners and thirty-five stills. Clark believed that things had improved compared with a year earlier, since five times as many illegal distilleries had been operating then. Some of the improvement he credited to the increasing willingness of local people (including leaders of temperance societies) to support revenue enforcement, but he disagreed with District Attorney Farrow, who called the amnesty Grant's "last kindness to Georgians" and claimed that it had been successful in encouraging obedience to the law. Clark argued instead that the winter offensive and his deputies' continuing patrols had convinced moonshiners that making wildcat whiskey "was not a safe business." In addition, fruit brandy was so abundant and cheap that there was little demand for whiskey from Georgia tipplers. However, Clark noticed that the supply of brandy was running out in some areas and moonshiners were returning to making whiskey. He expected to be busy by the end of January.[6]

Indeed, his deputies had already seized forty-one stills in December 1877, "unprecedented in any one month in this district since the enactment of the revenue laws." Federal law did not yet give explicit sanction to the destruction of stills, so Clark's men made every effort to carry them off instead of breaking them up. Often the distilleries were so far from roads that deputies had to carry them on their shoulders for up to three miles, frequently through rain, snow, or sleet. They still encountered armed resistance and ambushes, and Clark exclaimed that he had not met "such bitter hostility to the laws as now exists in the section traversed in making these seizures" since he entered the revenue service in 1869. He had hoped during the 1877 winter offensive that "we had reached the beginning of the end of our troubles with illicit distillers," but the experience of the 1878 season frustrated his expectations.[7]

Throughout the winter and spring of 1878 and 1879 the familiar pattern of ambushes, rescues of seized stills, state prosecution of revenuers, and harassment and murder of guides and informers continued. In March 1879, Congress finally made life somewhat easier for revenuers by authorizing the destruction of stills they were unable to carry away and by clarifying deputy marshals' power to arrest without a warrant distillers caught in the act. More importantly it provided an appropriation large enough for Raum to organize a full-scale offensive during the 1879–80 distilling season.[8]

Georgia mountaineers defended themselves bitterly. In mid-November 1879 Deputy Collector John C. Hendrix rode out of Dahlonega with a posse of twelve men. After traveling all day and into the early morning of the next day, they reached the Hightower River, Towns County, bordering on

North Carolina. The revenuers dismounted and walked five miles to the house of Bill Berong, "the notorious Hightower distiller," for whom Deputy Marshal Robinson had a warrant. At dawn the posse surrounded the cabin, but Berong heard them and ran out, dressed only in a shirt. They collared him, but immediately "the family (and a very numerous one) began to scream from every door, and would not stop halloing either from orders or threats." Neighbors answered from all directions, blowing horns and gathering in large numbers. The revenuers decided to retreat with their prisoner to where they had left the horses. After walking for two miles followed by a growing crowd of mountaineers, the posse found itself in a narrow pass surrounded by thirty or more armed men. After trying to find a way to escape a pitched battle against ever stronger enemies, the deputy marshal agreed to turn Berong loose. The posse was able to return to camp, cook breakfast, and start out for Union County, twenty-five miles distant, for operations against distillers there.

In Union the marshal arrested two men, the posse seized two stills, but most of the moonshiners were able to flee and pull out their stills. The next day the posse again ran into trouble. The revenuers divided into two groups of six to raid different distilleries during the night. Hendrix's squad heard someone shouting ahead of them, "Come on, boys." Thinking the caller was their own guide, Deputy Collector Pool rode ahead, and other posse-men soon followed him. They met a large group of armed men and ran back to warn the officers who had stayed behind with the wagon used to transport their prisoners. They heard sounds of a man being pulled and pushed, with shouts of "Bash him up, damn him," which made the posse think that Pool had fallen into the mountaineers' hands. They called to Pool and held their fire, fearing they might kill him. Just before reaching the wagon, which the revenuers had made their fort, the moonshiners "dodged out into the bushes and disappeared from sight." Soon the other half of the posse returned, and the larger force began to search for Pool. About daybreak they found a man staggering in the road, who looked so black that Hendrix thought he was "a colored man." He soon turned out to be a severely bruised Pool, whom the mountaineers had beaten unconscious and thrown over a fence, thinking he was dead. They had robbed him of pistol, cartridges, and money. The posse learned that the moonshiners had posted themselves in a narrow pass a mile ahead to ambush the revenuers. Hendrix and his men changed direction and returned to Blairsville, where Pool received treatment for his wounds. Hendrix assessed the results of his "trip" as "a comparative failure, so far as results are concerned, but has given us information of the status of things in the mountain counties, which is, in the opinion of our party, that *these counties over the Blue Ridge are in armed rebellion against the government in the enforcement of the revenue laws.*"[9]

Hendrix's colleague W. O. H. Shepard met even stiffer resistance in Rabun County. After seizing two distilleries, the posse was worn out from long hikes on foot and decided to rest until daybreak. As soon as they lit their fire, someone fired a shot at them. They doused the fire and waited for dawn without the warmth they had anticipated. The next day, bushwhackers hidden in a swamp fired into the posse, severely wounding two men and slightly wounding a third. The revenuers returned the fire until the mountaineers were driven off. Shepard later received warning that "*if he ever crosses the mountains again he is a dead man.*"[10]

Raum responded immediately to this resistance, authorizing Collector Andrew Clark to recruit 150 men if necessary "to assert and maintain the supremacy of the law." Clark replied that fifty men armed with breech-loading rifles would do a better job than a hundred armed with less efficient weapons, requested that the guns be sent by express, and began to organize his force in cooperation with Revenue Agent Wagner. He hesitated to send too many men into the mountains because the moonshiners had hidden their stills and sent "spies out in every direction watching for the 'big raid.'" Guides or detectives Clark had sent into the area around Dahlonega had not returned when expected, probably because of the "vigilance of the law-breakers." The collector decided to attack the region from the north-west, remaining long enough to "either arrest or drive out of the country" every illicit distiller. After "giving the section a thorough purging," Clark would station a permanent deputy north of the Blue Ridge with sufficient men for any emergency. Traveling over the mountains exhausted both men and horses and took deputies from their own districts where they were needed.[11]

When moonshiners could not drive out the revenuers, they turned their attention to guides and informers. Cherokee County mountaineers failed to rescue prisoners from a posse because the deputies "loaded their carbines and made preparations to fight, if necessary, and as they approached the mobbers, drove quietly along." The would-be rescuers, "perceiving the determination of the officers," let them pass through, saying, "Give our respects to the parties who led you in here, and tell them never to be seen in this country again." The moonshiners then rode to Marietta and threatened the livery stable keeper who had rented horses to the posse, vowing that if he did so again he would "suffer for it." They next ransacked the homes of informers. Pointing cocked pistols at men and women they met along the way, the vigilantes demanded "production of the witnesses, whom they swore 'should never reach Atlanta alive to testify for the G–d d–n revenue department.'" The witnesses had escaped to a neighboring swamp, where they had to hide for several days while the vigilantes picketed the roads and ferries to prevent them from reaching the federal court. They also, for good measure, swore out civil warrants against the informers "to improve their chances for obtaining possession of them before they reach Atlanta." Collector Clark was able to have four ringleaders arrested, and sent his deputies to rescue the men hiding in the swamp.[12]

After Collector Clark reported that moonshiners were organizing to resist, consolidating their distilleries, picketing the roads, and sometimes adopting passwords, Raum decided in January 1880 that it was time for a coordinated sweep along the Georgia-Carolinas border. He left the local details to Clark, who arranged meeting points and movements with Collectors Brayton and Mott. After some initial confusion and failures to meet at appointed places, the coordinated posses began seizing stills and making arrests. Deputy W. O. H. Shepard's force moving through Rabun County went without sleep for eighty-five hours and ran into firing from hillsides on January 16. The revenuers' long-range carbines kept the moonshiners far enough away so no possemen were shot. However, they were forced to halt for the night because the mountaineers could have sneaked through the brush close enough to make their weapons effectual. Shepard and his men decided to camp in an abandoned farm building and soon found themselves under fire from all sides. The battle continued all night, with the revenuers firing when they saw the flashes of moonshiners' guns, then changing position to deceive them as to how many were in the building. The blockaders approached within close range to shoot at where they thought possemen were positioned. The next morning, the posse was able to leave without opposition and joined forces with a deputy marshal's force and a revenue posse from South Carolina. The combined posse then went out in search of people for whom the marshal had warrants. Clark believed that "the presence of so large and respectable a force of revenue officers . . . will serve to impress the people with the power of the government to protect its officers and enforce the law at any hazard."[13]

Bill Berong was not particularly impressed. When the posse under Deputy Collector Hendrix approached his neighborhood in January 1880, he assembled a force of seventy-five of his friends to drive them off. A revenuer described the road to Berong's house as "hemmned in for the greatest part of the way by mountain slopes and laurel thickets, running through narrow defiles, and as crooked as the Ganges." As the posse approached a church, "a yell ascended from a knoll on our right, taken up from one on the left, and thence was echoed along the defiles of this road." They realized that a man waited in ambush at every bend of the road. The revenuers decided, although they had "a squad of good men, as good as had ever been in that country," to avoid a fight under such circumstances. They believed that "while we might whip in the fight, and a fight was inevitable, still it would be attended by the loss of several of our best men, and probably the greatest part, for we saw... that we would be bushwacked at every turn, with no chance to turn upon the enemy."[14]

Berong had won the day, but Deputy Hendrix proposed to return with a larger force, and other revenuers eventually arrested Berong. In May 1880 Captain James Davis of Tennessee and the reformed moonshiner Campbell Morgan led a squad of ten men into Towns County. The raiders hid overnight, planning to capture Bill Berong and his two sons when they came to their house for breakfast. At dawn they spotted two men coming across the fields and moved in to capture the two sons. Berong's daughter tried to "stampede" the revenuers by asking, "Is that some of the reserve force upon the hill?" Surprised, the possemen replied, "Why no." She added, "Well, I didn't know, I saw a big crowd of men coming this way with guns in their hands, and thought it must be some of you-uns." Davis just laughed at her deception. He treated the two sons so "kind and good humored" that they showed him the still they had buried. Less than two days later Bill Berong himself surrendered to Davis, who was surprised to meet "a diminutive, dried up old man." He said, "Arms to arrest this man! Why, I could pick him up, and carry him out of the mountains on my shoulders." At his examination, the U.S. commissioner asked Berong how he pleaded to the charges. His reply was also a surprise: " 'Guilty, if I am hung for it,' said Berong without a quiver of his voice. 'I am through with this blockading business. It has given me a fame that I don't deserve. They talk about my resistance, but

I'll take my oath that twenty men have turned me loose, when only my three sons cried from the bushes, "release him or we'll shoot." I threw forward my hands, and said to them, "off with these hand cuffs, or every man of you dies." They took them off, and that is the way I resisted the United States Government.'" One wonders whether the old blockader read dime novels, and it was obviously in his own interest not to mention the crowds of armed men and threatened ambush described in the revenuers' account of the incident. On the other hand, the possemen could have exaggerated their opponents' strength to cover their embarrassment. Whoever was right about Berong's escape, the old man was released on bail and invited Davis and Morgan to spend a week at his house, promising to help break up illicit distilling in Towns County.[15]

Neither Raum nor his subordinates could proclaim a resounding victory, but they kept up the fight. By the spring of 1880 Deputy Hendrix noticed much more cooperation from local citizens in his work and in June pronounced that "the trouble is now over, and . . . no further resistance will be offered to our policing the country." In Rabun County, "You can hardly realize what a change has been produced here in the last month." Collector Clark believed that enforcement reduced moonshining by 80 percent during the past two years. Conviction rates, after plummeting from 84 percent of cases after the 1876 amnesty to only 34 percent, after 1880 remained above 60 percent for six years. Though a large proportion, if not most, of these were guilty pleas, the government was clearly in a stronger position than in 1878, when the district attorney actually discontinued more cases than he secured convictions. Many blockaders gave up, turning to operating legal distilleries because illicit distilling was too risky and costly. Even newspapers that had denounced revenue enforcement had fallen silent.[16]

Democrats, though, preferred not to credit Republican Clark and his men. They believed that the conciliatory policy of District Attorney Farrow and Democratic Marshal Fitzsimmons persuaded moonshiners of the futility of resistance and was more effective than armed posses. Farrow appointed a new U.S. commissioner in Fayette County, which relieved moonshiners from traveling to Atlanta for hearings. Fitzsimmons rejected revenuers' offers of armed posses. He appealed to law-abiding citizens to use their personal influence to convince moonshiners to give up, so "that it may not become necessary to use harsh and severe measures in inforcing [sic] the law." He preferred to send only one or two deputies, who persuaded blockaders to surrender, into allegedly dangerous areas. However, Raum said that Fitzsimmons's deputies were shot at as much as those of Smyth, his Republican predecessor. He also believed that "we would have had peace in Georgia at least twelve months ago" but for what he considered the marshal's and the district attorney's obstruction of Clark's efforts. Confrontations with moonshiners and political conflicts would continue, with the Georgia state legislature entering the fray by urging repeal of the revenue laws in 1882 and 1885. Nevertheless, the days of organized bands were over until the outbreak of whitecapping in the late 1880s.[17]

Containment of blockading in Georgia, despite setbacks, depended on strength, organization, and persistence. Raum demanded these qualities from his subordinates and deemed them essential to enforcing the law. However, he also sought to balance the strength with leniency. He admitted that President Grant's executive clemency was a failure in Georgia, but Raum developed his own methods of mitigating the law's rigor. The usual moonshiner's sentence of two months in prison and a fine of $100 that could be "worked off" in jail at 75 cents per day was a genuine hardship for poor mountaineers. Since they rarely had cash for the fine, moonshiners could remain imprisoned for over four months away from their families. Cooperating with the attorney general, Raum developed a policy of suspending the sentence of minor offenders if they paid court costs and promised to obey the law. He was determined that this not become permanent, which would lead moonshiners to take official leniency for granted, but a concession that he could implement or withhold according to the level of illicit distilling and resistance to federal officers.[18]

Many of the men in the field objected to any leniency for moonshiners. Marshal Wallace of South Carolina drew upon his "more than ten years experience in dealing with them" to argue against the district attorney's belief in the benefits of clemency. His "firm conviction" was that "nothing but the strong arm of the law will ever effect a change. Sufficient force must be employed to overcome their resistance and bring them before the courts, where the heaviest penalties must be enforced." Well-intentioned amnesty "would encourage men to repeat their offenses and others to join them, hoping for another amnesty to release them from responsibility." He added that "nothing but the fear of punishment will work upon the feelings of many of the ignorant and vicious people engaged in distilling in the mountain regions." A few years later, District Attorney Northrop agreed with the marshal: "After trying for a long time the policy of kindness . . . it became apparent that defendants cared very little for the consequences of a law, which could be avoided so cheaply." Collector Fannin in Georgia believed that most released moonshiners "returned to their homes to brag of their easy escape and resume their illicit work." His colleague Clark believed leniency was "detrimental to the public interest" because it "emboldened violators of the law and made them more defiant." Federal judge Rives in Virginia had long given light sentences to moonshiners, but he realized that they returned to their stilling as quickly as possible. He became more strict, sentencing them to penitentiary terms in hopes that they would realize the government meant business.[19] These men were acutely sensitive to the danger of kindness being interpreted as weakness, but typical of policemen everywhere, they were suspicious of leniency toward men they had taken so much trouble to arrest and prosecute.

Commissioner Raum, having learned from the failure of presidential clemency in Georgia, was also aware of the dangers of weakness. Both he and the attorney general applied leniency carefully and selectively. Ideally, as a district attorney put it, "The sentence suspended over [moonshiners'] heads like the sword of Damocles will keep them in order and cause them to use their influence with others." Raum believed that leniency should be exercised only after raids had demonstrated the government's power and determination. The first element of the strategy was "vigorous measures, to force violators of the law to the wall." After moonshiners "were overborne by the efforts of our officers, and found that further resistance was in vain, and manifested a determination to observe the laws in future," Raum "never hesitated to favor the most lenient proceedings" if "satisfied that their professions were sincere, and that a lenient course would result in encouraging a public sentiment favorable to the observance and enforcement of the laws." Between 1877 and 1880 2,506 sentences for revenue violations, mostly illicit distilling, were suspended in Georgia, western North Carolina, Tennessee, South Carolina, and Alabama. Raum emphasized, "Such wholesale jail deliveries cannot, of course, be continued from year to year. No system of statutes with heavy penal provision can long be maintained where all offenders are turned loose without punishment." To convince moonshiners that they had to keep their promises, repeat offenders were sent to federal prison on a bench warrant without a new trial.

Generally the number of suspended sentences in all the states declined after 1879 and 1880.[20]

Raum was willing to suspend sentences for moonshiners too poor to pay court costs, but he made clear that anyone who resisted federal officers would not receive clemency. Both he and the attorney general were determined to avoid anything like a blanket amnesty. Attorney General Devens read in the newspapers that "a general amnesty" was to be given North Carolina moonshiners. He dashed off a letter to the assistant district attorney telling him that "this is entirely unauthorized, and that you will be expected to prosecute the offenders vigorously." The attorney general informed Representative John D. White of Kentucky that an investigation by the internal revenue office and the district attorney concluded that "it would be improper and inexpedient to grant the general amnesty you asked for." Raum had "serious doubt whether any permanent good will result" from suspending the sentences of men recommended by Tennessee's senators. He feared that they would "regard it as an exhibition of weakness on the part of the government, and go forward in violations of the law as heretofore."[21]

As much as possible, the commissioner sought to control suspensions himself. Federal district attorneys and judges, overburdened with cases and perennially short of funds, or in some cases not fully committed to revenue enforcement, sometimes too eagerly recommended or handed down suspended sentences without consulting Commissioner Raum or the attorney general. To adopt a period metaphor, they took the bit into their mouths and ran away. During his ongoing feud with Georgia's federal district attorney Henry Farrow, Raum sharply condemned suspension of sentences on the district attorney's own initiative. He charged that the release of 134 revenue violators in 1879 "was such an exhibition of weakness on the part of the government that, I have no doubt, the spirit of lawlessness and resistance to authority recently exhibited . . . have been encouraged thereby." In South Carolina District Attorney Northrop mistakenly announced that sentences would be suspended for moonshiners, implying pardon for illicit distillers who had not yet been indicted. Local commissioners encouraged moonshiners with warrants against them to come in and surrender. Northrop's announcement was "hailed with joy," and scores of mountaineers camped outside the court at Statesville in expectation of "amnesty." The attorney general had directed suspension of sentences and payment of costs only for people under indictment, but it was too late to change the policy. In the next term of the federal court, the correct policy would be followed. However, moonshiners themselves ended leniency. After armed men forced a revenue posse out of Abbeville, Raum directed that no more suspensions would be allowed in South Carolina. Raum listened to the complaints of men on the scene, and in 1880 approved District Attorney Northrop's decision to recommend suspension only in very minor revenue violations. He was later able to use the promise of suspension to persuade state officials to drop prosecutions of revenuers. Similarly, the North Carolina state district attorney abandoned his prosecutions of revenuers in response to suspension of sentences.[22]

During the Reconstruction period, a similar policy of clemency had signaled official weakness, which white supremacists exploited. Moonshiners also sometimes took advantage of leniency, repeating their offense several times even after prison terms. One such repeater was astounded when the judge asked him how long he was going to keep "coming" to court. The blockader exclaimed that he never "came" on his own; "They fotched me!" and he might be fetched again but did not intend to come if he could help it. Mountaineers had a reputation for keeping promises once made, but sometimes they interpreted their promises very narrowly. One moonshiner promised the judge that he would "neither make nor meddle with illicit whiskey" while the judge remained on the bench. He kept his promise, but as soon as the judge retired, he went back to business and was killed during a raid. Though some individuals refused to reform, leniency did not signal the collapse of enforcement efforts as it had during Reconstruction.[23]

Some moonshiners continued to resist and took advantage of leniency, but there is evidence that restraint won support from law-abiding citizens who had previously sympathized with moonshiners as victims of oppression. Even Marshal Wallace of South Carolina, who advocated toughness, observed that clemency would encourage support of the government. The South Carolina district attorney credited the policy with dampening public anger against Kane, Moose, Scruggs, and Durham, the revenuers charged with murdering Amos Ladd. A newspaper from upcountry South Carolina praised the "magnanimity and clemency of the government," urging distillers to obey the law. Similarly the North Carolina district attorney reported hearing "frequent expressions extolling the Government for its liberality and contemning the violation it's [*sic*] laws, coming from sources, a month since in sympathy with the violators of the law and contemning the Government for enforcing it." A federal judge agreed that leniency had made revenue collection less of a political issue in North Carolina. A revenuer reported some very practical benefits of clemency: raiders could not obtain lodging or food at any price, but by 1882 they were "countenanced by the better part of the people" who now accepted their money for room and board.[24]

Raum supplemented selective leniency in prosecution of moonshiners with efforts to encourage legal distillation, a policy that some local collectors had pursued earlier. Tough enforcement compelled some moonshiners to open legal distilleries, but Raum also hoped to persuade them of the advantages of complying with the law. The negative and positive incentives could operate simultaneously, as when Revenue Agent Tracie sought to strengthen enforcement in one Kentucky district and encourage legal distillation in another. Raum directed the collectors to "call attention to this matter in the public press" and have their deputies "talk the subject up while they are policing their divisions," making sure that the requirements of the law were clear to the new distillers. Raum believed that "it is far better in respect to public morals that spirits should be made openly and in accordance with law and taxes paid thereon than that they should be made illicitly, in defiance or evasion of law, and to the great injury of the government in respect to its revenues." In western North Carolina, Collector J. J. Mott suggested that reducing the legal minimum capacity of distilleries from six to three and a half bushels of corn would end an old complaint that poor men were barred from distilling because they could not afford to set up large stills. Many blockaders, some of whom had been offered suspended sentences if they established legal stills, took advantage of the new policy. A revenuer reported that in the South Mountains of Burke County there had been no legal stills at all, only moonshine operations, but between 1878 and 1880 several were established. Another officer argued that legalizing small stills contributed to improved public order. Local people clustered around moonshine stills drinking, and the distiller could not drive them away because they could take their revenge by informing against him. However, legal distillers could refuse to serve them and not fear being reported. Since small distillers were undercut and sometimes driven out altogether from areas where blockaders were active, Collector E. M. Brayton of South Carolina observed that they, "in self-interest, become the friends of the Government." Several Georgia legal distillers wrote to Raum expressing their appreciation: "The active pursuit by the revenue officers of illicit distillers and dealers during the last year, although it has not stopped all, has prevented so much that our trade has been vastly benefited." The number of registered distilleries rose significantly in the moonshine districts, from 158 in 1878 to 430 in early 1880. By 1879 revenues from these areas exceeded 1877 tax collections by 99 percent. Although the increase of small, in some cases marginal, distilleries introduced new problems and new complaints, in general, Raum achieved his goal of more legitimate distillers and more tax money.[25]

Evidence of increasing support for the government came slowly and unevenly. As early as 1877 Raum congratulated Collector Rives in Virginia because in areas "formerly infested by illicit distillers, the actions of the state officers encouraged by a healthy public sentiment" contributed to reducing moonshining. In Lee County, "substantial citizens" petitioned Raum for money to suppress blockaders and urged that "steps be immediately taken to break up these illicit distilleries, and to bring these pests of society to justice." Collector Rives reported that the help of these citizens made his raids successful. In Arkansas local citizens formed "clubs" to aid revenue officers. These people warned moonshiners to stop their activity before the area was raided, responding to a deputy collector's warning that they would have no peace until illicit distilling stopped. In Alabama, Collector Booth reported that "many good citizens" aided his raiding party and "the local civil officers . . . gave us much information." Similarly, six months later the "county officers are in full sympathy with the revenue officers, and are giving them aid and encouragement in their labors." Such assistance would have been impossible a year or two earlier.[26]

A Dahlonega, Georgia, newspaper urged citizens to obey the revenue laws despite their unpopularity: "While our sympathies are with that class of men who suffer most from this iniquitous law, we would impress upon their minds the importance and wisdom of submitting to the same until it is repealed or modified." Later the editor commented on the ambush of a revenue posse: "While it is true that the revenue laws is [sic] obnoxious to certain classes of our people, yet the good people everywhere frown upon its violation, especially upon such underhanded revenge" as the blockaders sought. Another Georgia paper declared, "Public opinion in the mountains is setting more firmly than ever against all forms of lawlessness. The people are condemning illicit distilling." Leading newspapers of Walker and neighboring counties in Alabama published articles "condemnatory of illicit distilling." Collector Booth reported that "the illicit distillers are no longer regarded as a 'persecuted class' " and the "best citizens are in sympathy with the Government."[27]

The "better portion of the citizens" of Henry County, Tennessee, invited moonshiners to a "grand barbeque." Senator Isham Harris and Representative J. D. C. Atkins addressed the crowd of about a thousand people and "impressed upon them the disgrace being brought upon their country [state], and warned them that a stop would be put to such illicit business by the most vigorous means." The result was voluntary surrender of many blockaders in exchange for suspended sentences. Fortunately the attorney general advised Marshal Waldron, a guest along with Collector Patterson, not to serve warrants against some of the distillers at the meeting! At the end of 1878 in Fentress County, a blockader stronghold, it became easier to discover hidden stills and make arrests because there were "always informers to be obtained." People apparently were less frightened by the threat of moonshiner retaliation.[28]

Even South Carolina could produce a federal grand jury "composed of white men, of the most pronounced democratic type," willing to indict Lewis Redmond, the famous blockader leader, and a leading accomplice. Apparently the outlaw himself, still at large, was "advising the people to quit distilling and to obey the laws." During the winter "most of the better class of citizens" regretted a raiding party's departure because they were impressed by its "discoveries, the determination to discharge [its] duties, and the character and good conduct of the men employed." At first the posse had been "looked upon with distrust and dislike." If South Carolinians could change their attitude toward federal officials, there certainly was hope for the other states.[29]

However encouraging these early reports were, they may have been overoptimistic. Some followed successful raids and reflected only their immediate impact rather than long-term changes of sentiment. Others may have reflected the hopes of local people opposed to moonshining, or officials' efforts to prove they were on the job. Enclaves of organized resistance remained.

After 1880 an increasing number of accounts of improved public sentiment suggests more lasting results. Even northern Georgia was beginning
to yield. Revenue Agent Chapman reported that the longer the revenuers
operated in Rabun County, Georgia's moonshiner stronghold, the more
friendly "the best people" became. They were worried that the posse would
leave soon, placing them under outlaws' power again. He believed that
moonshiners who resisted federal officers could be tried and convicted in
state courts; "you can hardly realize what a change has been produced here
in the last month." Even the county sheriff helped the revenuers. In nearby
Union County citizens and local officers asked to be deputized to arrest
Newton West, an outlaw who had assaulted and robbed Deputy Collector
Pool. The *Atlanta Constitution*, usually sympathetic to moonshiners, encouraged respectable citizens to suppress illicit distilling.[30]

A paper in Charleston, South Carolina, supported revenue enforcement
in language very unusual for that locality. Although moonshiners were "very
hardly dealt with in many instances, and the character of the revenue force
has brought the Government into contempt," until the whiskey tax is repealed, "it is due to the dignity and authority of the Government that it
should be impartially and firmly enforced. . . . The Government owes it to
itself to stop the infamous traffic in illicit whisky, whatever the cost may be."
A Greenville paper, reporting the killing of Deputy Collector T. L. Brayton
(brother of the collector), was sympathetic to him, praising him as an
"efficient and popular officer and citizen," victim of "a deliberate and
desperate murder." In 1882 Collector Brayton still contrasted South Carolinians' "deep seated prejudice" against revenue officers with the "moral
support which the government may rely upon at the North." Nevertheless, it
was "safe to say . . . that these relations are improving, while a friendlier
sentiment prevails with the people."[31]

Outside of the old rebel state respectable citizens were also beginning to
support the revenuers. Collector Woodcock of Tennessee reported in 1880
that armed resistance "ceased over a year ago" and "public opinion has
undergone an entire revolution, and is now in our favor. The newspaper
press, with a few unimportant exceptions, and the leading men of all shades
of politics and religion, insist publicly that the law must be obeyed." In one
district of North Carolina the collector could declare in 1881 that the "very
best citizens" will support his work and that his deputies indicated that
there were "no efforts made now to oppose the enforcement of law any-

where in this district." Effective raids in Kentucky "greatly diminished" moonshining, and there was now "a disposition on the part of the better class of people to inform on the violators of the revenue laws." Even in the mountains there was "at this time, but little resistance to the enforcement of the laws, and a feeling, constantly growing stronger, in favor of law and order." In Arkansas there was in 1882 "a general disposition among the people of this district to comply with the internal revenue laws, and willful violations of the laws are very rare," limited to individuals "without organization or combination." Finally, an Alabama federal grand jury was able to report in 1883 that "the illicit distillation of fruit and grain has almost entirely ceased. Public sentiment has greatly aided federal authority in the suppression of this class of offenses." Any public sentiment aiding federal authority in the South, which had recently overthrown Reconstruction, was impressive.[32]

Impressionistic reports and editorials seemed to be confirmed by a high rate of convictions in moonshine cases. According to Department of Justice statistics, federal prosecutors won more convictions during Raum's term than earlier.[33] Conviction rates in the moonshine districts rose above 50 percent for the first time in 1876, just before Raum took office. After he began his crackdown, they remained above 55 percent throughout his term, reaching 74 percent during the great campaign of 1878–79. In 1877–78, the moonshiner judicial districts accounted for 48 percent of the nation's revenue cases. Their average proportion of convictions was 57 percent, better than the 42 percent conviction rate in the remainder of the nation. The mountain districts' average from 1877 through 1883 was about 60 percent, considerably better than the average for Ku Klux Klan prosecutions between 1870 and 1877, which was 34 percent.[34]

Conviction rates reflected many factors, most of which Raum and his men could not control. The averages concealed considerable variation among the states. The toughest spot for moonshiners, in terms of chances of conviction, was the eastern judicial district of Tennessee, where convictions made up over 55 percent of revenue cases during all seven years of Raum's term. The blockader's paradise was undoubtedly West Virginia, where convictions reached 50 percent of cases in only two of the seven years. This state would remain a haven for illegal makers or sellers of liquor, convictions exceeding 50 percent only three times in the eighteen years to 1900.[35] Once cases reached the federal courts, they were in the hands of district attorneys and federal judges, who varied in their ability and attitudes toward revenue enforcement. Raum could influence such matters as whether to extend clemency, and the attorney general usually listened to him. Though he criticized district attorneys he thought insufficiently zealous, they were not responsible to him. He usually could not influence the attitudes of federal judges and sometimes tangled with them over their procedures or decisions. In the case of Judge Robert Dick of North Carolina, who allowed defense attorneys to attack the personal character of revenuers, Raum threatened to remove all moonshining cases to the circuit court, which would deprive all Dick's court officers of the fees they earned from each trial. This move caused revenuers to "be treated with a great deal more respect."[36] Raum's leniency policy had some influence on the readiness of moonshiners to plead guilty, but he had little control over the willingness of local juries to convict or the ability of blockaders and their friends to prevent witnesses from providing evidence in court.[37] All of these factors influenced the prosecutor's ability to obtain revenue convictions.[38]

Whether his success is measured by changing public sentiment or by conviction rates, Commissioner Raum accomplished something the Department of Justice was unable to do during Reconstruction: secure support from the "better citizens" who disliked illicit distilling or believed in law and order for its own sake. Civil rights enforcement had never won such support: respectable southerners may have disliked racial violence, but they accepted its goal of white supremacy. Unlike white supremacy, moonshining itself was becoming increasingly disreputable, and many people did not accept the violence employed to defend it.

There were important long-term or underlying factors in this attitude. The national economic depression ended in 1879, and it is possible that many people who sympathized with moonshiners as poor farmers in the grip of the depression became less sympathetic as the economy picked up again. An Alabama newspaper made an explicit appeal to wealthier citizens: "It might be well to remember that the Government cannot be without a revenue, and if that revenue cannot be collected from whiskey and tobacco, it will have to be collected from assessments on lands, incomes and other property, of which fact all property holders who sympathize with the 'persecuted' class may as well take notice." During the early 1880s, industrial development of the mountains quickened, and the new professional and managerial elite looked down upon mountaineers and sought to maintain law and order to encourage business investment. Members of the town elite, and the smaller shopkeepers and artisans who served them, increasingly supported local-option prohibition to make the towns less rowdy and the mill or mine workers more reliable. Suppression of moonshining was an important part of that goal.[39]

Democrats, who had taken the lead in denouncing the revenue laws as federal tyranny, gained control of both houses of Congress in the 1878 elections. They had their chance to lower or repeal the obnoxious taxes, but despite continuing rhetorical barrages, they left the system intact. Democratic stump speakers had encouraged local resistance, but the national party's failure to support mountaineers' demands forced many people to become reconciled to the revenue system. A Chattanooga paper, calling moonshiners "simply gangs of lazy, bad men, who from a state of general worthlessness and a temper of pure cussedness, have degenerated into desperate cut-throats, and hill-top brigands," warned Democrats that the government under a Democratic administration would still need its revenue from the whiskey tax and still need "to keep in order and to punish" violators. Politicians who courted the moonshiner vote were "pestilent demagogues who use the press and the hustings to obtain the votes of the criminal classes. Democrats who resort to such methods need not hope long to keep themselves in power." A Knoxville paper similarly reminded its readers that revenue collection had become a bipartisan concern: "Does any political party desire to come into possession of a Government whose revenue laws are set at defiance in a whole section of the Union? Is any man fool enough to believe that whatever party comes into power, it will not be compelled to pursue substantially the system of revenue now in vogue?" Collector J. J. Mott in North Carolina reduced Democratic opposition by letting Democrats have some responsibility for revenue collection. He appointed Democratic officers and discovered that many people sought the positions and that both complaints of partisanship and blockading itself decreased.[40]

Newspaper editorials, optimistic reports, and high conviction rates do not prove that the tide had permanently turned in the mountains. They do suggest, though, that the mountain people's solidarity in defense of moonshining was dissolving. Raum's campaign against moonshiners seems to have convinced many southerners that the government was determined to collect its taxes. Some responded to raiders' power and persistence, realizing that resistance was useless. Others objected to blockading and came to believe that it was safe to do so with decreasing risk of retaliation. General Raum was able to report in 1882 that illicit distillation and sale of tobacco "in the districts where they have hitherto most prevailed have become the exception rather than the rule. There is no longer organized resistance to the authority of the government, the people render obedience to the laws, and the taxes are collected without unnecessary friction." He was fully aware, and repeated in his last official report, that success depended on "continuing the firm, energetic, and impartial enforcement of the laws which now prevails, with such leniency to offenders as circumstances may seem to justify." He had defeated widespread, organized resistance but knew that "it is too much to expect" that illicit distilling could ever be "wholly eradicated." To control moonshining, "it will be necessary to continue the system of careful policing."[41] His men had won the major campaigns and penetrated the mountaineers' strongholds in the Georgia-Carolinas border and along the Kentucky-Tennessee line as well as all other moonshine districts.

Raum's drive intimidated and isolated many blockaders, but some continued to carry out individual guerilla warfare against the revenuers who were in the mountains to stay. For example, Revenue Agent Tracie reported that "nearly all the blockaders" of Harlan County, Kentucky, registered as legal distillers "or signified their wish to do so" in 1883, but in Letcher County four or five blockaders on Carr's and Poor's fork were waiting for the new corn crop to begin again, "sustained by friends, well armed."[42]

After Green B. Raum resigned to lobby for the whiskey trust, would his successors continue the fight to maintain the government's authority? Was the victory of the early 1880s only Raum's personal success or a permanent establishment of governmental power?

7 Holding the Ground,

1883–1893

. . . .

Revenuers held their ground in the mountains, although moonshiners continued to challenge them during the two-year term of Raum's successor, Walter Evans, a Kentuckian who like Raum was a stalwart Republican.[1] Evans's appointment set a precedent of both parties' giving the commissionership to men from the southern mountain states. He had to cope with persistent moonshiners, but his officers were active, making 902 arrests and seizing 377 stills between July 1883 and July 1884. More arrests than seizures suggests that few moonshiners escaped during raids. These arrests were much more easily accomplished than at the height of Raum's battle: during the same period there were no revenuers killed or wounded, the first time since casualties were reported. During the next year one officer was killed and one wounded in West Virginia, but revenuer deaths would never rise above one a year until 1893. During 1884–85 fewer moonshiners were arrested (669) and fewer stills seized (245). The number of moonshiners may in fact have been decreasing, the conclusion revenuers usually drew from such figures.[2]

Prosecutors were busy and did well in the moonshine districts, reporting convictions in 61 and 62 percent of their cases during Evans's two-year term. Exceptions still included West Virginia, where convictions reached 50 percent in only one year. Sentences continued to be suspended in revenue cases, 774 in 1883–84 and 547 in 1884–85, but hardly at the level of the peak year in Raum's term, 1879–80, with 2,974 suspended sentences. The number of revenue cases rose, breaking the pattern of decline since 1879 and inaugurating a general upward trend that would sharply peak in 1896.

Revenue enforcement remained a battle, but it was much less dangerous for deputy revenue collectors and marshals on the front lines.[3]

Collecting the whiskey tax was no longer a pressing concern for the federal government, which found itself rapidly paying back the Civil War debt and accumulating a mounting surplus in the Treasury. Seeking ways to reduce the surplus, President Arthur in 1882 recommended abolition of all internal taxes, including those on tobacco, but urged continuation of the tax on distilled spirits. Ignoring mountain southerners' attitudes, the president described the whiskey excise as "that portion of the system of internal revenue which is least objectionable to the people." He recommended that it be retained to cover the mounting expense of Civil War pensions. The whiskey tax had become the leading source of internal revenue, rising from 30 percent of the collections in 1868 to 63 percent in 1884. The whiskey tax seemed to be a permanent contributor to an expanded government's daily functioning.[4]

By 1888, however, the Republican national platform actually recommended abolition of even the whiskey tax if a surplus remained in the Treasury after removal of the other excises. The Republicans were thoroughly committed to the protective tariff, which they would not touch as a way of reducing revenues. Congress was in a mood to shrink the revenue bureaucracy. Legislation reduced the number of collection districts from 126 to 85, with consequent dismissal of collectors and subordinates, mostly in the North and West; lowered the pay of storekeepers and gaugers in small distilleries; and decreased the number of revenue agents from thirty-five to twenty. Commissioner Evans objected at length to these reductions, charging that they would destroy the revenue service's efficiency. He argued that the agents were "absolutely essential" in moonshine districts "where enforcement of the law is so hazardous that the local officers shrink from it." Congress listened to him enough to drop the original plan to slash the number of agents to only five. If the Republicans were willing to sacrifice revenue enforcement because of political pressure to reduce Treasury surpluses while preserving a high protective tariff, what would the Democrats, who had long opposed the internal revenue system on principle, do when they came into power after Grover Cleveland's election to the presidency in 1884?[5]

Democrats were as committed to reducing the tariff as Republicans to maintaining it. Cleveland's revenue commissioner, Joseph Miller, was "an ardent tariff reformer." Consequently Democrats in power found themselves depending on internal taxes rather than tariffs for government funding. Green B. Raum, writing for a Republican campaign handbook in 1888, chastised the Democrats for blocking excise tax reduction. Moreover, they discovered the patronage value of all those collectorships, deputyships, and storekeeper and gauger jobs scattered throughout the nation. Clerks, storekeepers, and gaugers did not come under civil service rules until 1894, and deputy collectors not until 1896, a move by outgoing president Cleveland probably meant to keep Democrats in office. Collectorships remained major political appointments, and the commissioner had exclusive power to appoint and remove the agents. As Raum put it, after 1885 Democrats no longer held "up to contempt the hated internal-revenue officer. This person is now a Democrat, and of course must be regarded as a gentleman." Democrats in Burke County, North Carolina, did not regard any revenuers as gentlemen but confirmed Raum's observation by fretting that local compatriots were "fishing" for jobs in the revenue service. These were the same people "who swore that a decent man wouldn't hold a revenue office." Patronage seemed to exert a greater pull than campaign promises. Having inherited a system of taxation and the bureaucracy to enforce it, both devised by Republicans, Democrats now needed the money and the men. Revenue enforcement was becoming bipartisan.[6]

The new revenue commissioner, Joseph Miller, was a thirty-seven-year-old West Virginian prominent in state politics and "very popular among those who know him best," including many Republicans. He reported that "it does not appear that the illicit manufacture of either whiskey, tobacco or cigars is carried on in any part of the country to such an extent as to occasion material losses to the Government." However, revenues from the whiskey tax did drop over $9 million between 1884 and 1885 and did not rise to the levels of the last Republican year until the Republicans were back in power in 1890. Numbers of stills seized dropped between July 1884 and July 1885, but most of that period was under the Republicans. Moonshiners and their supporters may have hoped Democrats would harass them less than Republicans: the editor of a mountain paper counseled Democratic revenuers that they were obliged to enforce the laws but there was "no need to do this rigorously." He and other southern Democrats were in for an unpleasant surprise. A few months later another editor declared that "the odium of the internal revenue is now shifted from Republican to Democratic shoulders; and it is indeed an onerous burden, wide-spread and far reaching in its ramifications." Arrests and seizures seemed undiminished, and some Democratic deputy marshals had been indicted for shooting at moonshiners. A joke current during these years depicted Cleveland replying to a delegation of blockaders hoping for easier treatment: "I understand the matter thoroughly, I think, gentlemen, and there is but one of two things for you to do: you must either quit this business entirely, or move your stills farther back from the big road."[7]

Democratic officials indeed carried out this no-nonsense attitude. Seizures more than doubled between 1885 and 1886, the first full year of Democratic rule. They declined by over a hundred during the next year but rose close to 1885–86 levels in the Democrats' last full year, 1888–89. Likewise arrests soared between 1885 and 1886, nearly doubling, but dropped drastically (from 1,214 to 211) during the next year, rising significantly in 1887–88 (from 211 to 812). These figures are difficult to interpret. The initial surge may have reflected new officials' efforts to prove they were doing their job or moonshiners' increased activity under false expectations that Democrats would ignore them. The next fall could register relaxation of enforcement activity or blockaders' realization that they still had to be careful. The subsequent increase of arrests might have meant that having realized the Democrats would do them no favors, moonshiners began to return to normal activity and officials responded in kind. Whatever the explanation, arrests would not reach this level again until another Democratic year, 1895, in the midst of an upsurge in moonshining. Democratic district attorneys handled a larger number of revenue cases than their Republican predecessors and secured a similar proportion of convictions. With variations among the states from over 60 percent to well under half, convictions averaged about 60 percent between 1885–86 and 1888–89. In 1885–86 the conviction rate of 61 percent was much better than outside the moonshine districts, where only 30 percent of revenue cases resulted in convictions. The blockader regions accounted for 83 percent of the nation's revenue cases.[8]

If ex-commissioner Raum had looked at the records of his old bureau under Miller, he would have found Democratic officials doing their duty and facing familiar moonshiner resistance. There were fewer of the massive sweeps of Raum's day, and posses generally were smaller. Most raiding parties seem to have been made up entirely of deputy marshals and revenuers, without recruitment of local people as possemen. The revenue agents organized most of the larger raids as they had under Republican Commissioner Evans. Miller was not a civil-service reformer, but he retained all the agents despite his power to fire them if he wished. He wisely perceived that "the success of his administration depends largely upon the retention of expert subordinates" who could lead the fight against blockaders. The agents were becoming true professionals. Representing the outside central government even if under Democratic control, the agents were not popular among local people who still hoped their own officials would be more lenient toward distillers. "Almost invariably appointed from the North," an editor complained, "they come down South assuming the authority of the President himself." Local revenuers "must bow and tremble in their presence, and their bread and meat is in nosing around and discovering some technical violations, whether there is any intent to defraud or not, and in many instances innocent men suffer from reports made by these heartless dignitaries." Even when Democrats were in charge, Washington's priorities were more important than local sensitivities.[9]

The political change in 1885 swept out an army of experienced deputy revenue collectors and marshals. A revenue agent reported that the new officers in Kentucky were mostly "inexperienced and incapacitated for the hardships attending these raids, while the bulk of them seem to have no appetite for the dangers attending this particular work." Scrutinizing these deputies more closely, the agent found that they varied in zeal and ability. Deputy Hogg of the second division, eighth district of Kentucky, was a "very good" and "very honest man" who "did not seem to know much about his division." Although he "had heard of illicit distilleries, did not know how many[;] if any had been seized and destroyed he had not heard of it." He had not reported any revenue violations since his appointment. Similarly, D. D. Sublett of the sixth division was "not doing much of anything," spending too much time in his office saying the weather was too cold for outdoor work. This division needed "a number one man" because in Letcher and Perry counties it was "dangerous to be a revenue officer." Other deputies, though, were more active and effective. W. E. Farnum, fifth division, was "an active intelligent young man" who destroyed several moonshine stills and "in a short time will have the last one broken up." Henry Magee of the seventh division was "a very steady honest old man, not afraid of outlaws of any kind," who had broken up more stills than any other deputy. The agent spoke to all the deputies, whom he inspired to greater efforts against moonshiners, except Hogg, whom he did not think "will ever do that kind of work. He is a good man but he could not do that kind of work, if he wanted to." For each Hogg or Sublett reluctant to confront moonshiners, there were others like Farnum and Magee who met the challenge.[10]

Most Democratic revenuers seemed to be as ready to do their duty as their Republican predecessors. Despite the problems with some of his deputies, the collector in Kentucky's eighth district was prepared to suppress anticipated moonshining in the fall of 1885. He apparently needed to convince the blockaders that he was in fact determined; if they learned that a Democrat would do his job, they would "to a very great extent refrain" from stilling. In many areas, though, they were still shooting at revenuers. Commissioner Miller organized a special raiding party along the Tennessee-Georgia border to capture moonshiners who fired on possemen in earlier raids. The raiders led by Agent W. H. Chapman seized several stills and captured Riley Pyle, who had killed U.S. commissioner McDonald. Old moonshiner strongholds continued to give trouble: the Dark Corner of the Glassy Mountains in northern Greenville County, South Carolina, was "inhabited by a population more inclined, apparently, to illicit distilling than to any lawful occupation." Local wildcatters resisted raiding parties that frequently invaded their territory. One one occasion in 1888 they wounded a deputy marshal and a guide. They later tried to intimidate the son of a deputy marshal by shooting at his house, and they wounded two other guide-informers. In Tennessee, armed men also confronted the posses; local people refused to provide information because of intimidation by "a crowd of outlaws and desperate characters." Deputy Marshal Thomas Goodson, "an energetic and courageous officer," had been threatened many times but continued to pursue moonshiners. One night in December he traveled to Lost Cove in the mountains of Carter County to summon two witnesses and talk to a mountaineer who promised information about distillers. On his way he was ambushed by men who beat him unconscious with clubs and killed him with two shots from his own pistol. State officials arrested one of the murderers, George Hunnicutt, but several others remained at large despite a $500 reward for their capture. The all-out warfare of the late 1870s seems to have evolved into scattered guerilla actions, which certainly could be deadly.[11]

All these reports would have been familiar to ex-commissioner Raum, but there were some differences from his time. A revenue agent describing conditions in North Carolina emphasized that the blockaders were not well organized for sustained resistance: "The 'moonshiner' invariably runs on the approach of an officer, and they are as utterly without organization, & almost as wild, as the foxes & wolves which roam among the 'crags & crannies' of the Blue Ridge." He argued that only three people were necessary on a typical raid: a guide, a revenue officer to seize the still, and a deputy marshal to make the arrest. Three-man posses, which would not have been considered sufficient in Raum's day, did in fact make successful raids in North Carolina and Georgia. A Georgia deputy collector was actually making seizures alone; Collector Crenshaw thought this dangerous but asked for only one salaried guard to accompany him. Certainly the Georgia revenuers were busy, as indicated by a report of raids during 1886–87. At least five posses went after northern Georgia blockaders during December 1886, six in March and seven in May 1887, and again seven in December 1887. September, October, and November 1887 each witnessed four raids. Other months in 1887 saw from one to four raids each. An important innovation of the Miller years was appointment of special revenue "raiding deputies" who could concentrate on seizing stills. They provided "the continuous presence . . . of a suitable officer, striking promptly whenever and wherever developments may render it necessary." These deputies became a permanent part of the revenue system in the South.[12]

Most federal officials seem to have shared the views of Georgia collector T. C. Crenshaw: "Any laxity . . . will have the tendency to embolden the lawless fellows and make the risk to officers greater." Some, though, advocated lenient treatment of the moonshiners. Emory Speer of Georgia, who as congressman had opposed the revenue system, became a federal judge who routinely handed down mild sentences. Collector Crenshaw told Speer that Commissioner Miller had authorized him to say that the judge was too lenient. Speer thundered from the bench, "This court knows where justice ends and oppression begins. You say to the Commissioner that if he comes down here and says to me what you have said that I will put him in jail for contempt of court. I know what these people are, and I know what is oppression for them." One deputy collector developed an easygoing conception of his duty that reconciled his sense of responsibility with local people's code of morality. "Greatly respected" by his honest farmer neighbors of Georgia's Tallulah district, the deputy "promptly and fairly" investigated all informers' reports of illicit stills but never went out of his way to discover a moonshine operation on his own. As a former blockader himself, he was "zealous in prosecuting an offender against whom a charge has been sustained" but had "all of his old-time contempt for the informer." To his neighbors, this man was clearly the sort of Democratic "gentleman" Raum had spoken of.[13]

In a different form of clemency, an agent proposed that some distillers agreed to be arrested and the case settled by payment of a compromise fine if they were permitted to keep their stills and register them as legitimate operations. He observed, "It is the destruction of their property, not the arrest which provokes them to violence." He proposed to send a deputy collector to one of the blockaders to persuade him to surrender and register before a deputy marshal, "who does not warmly favor my plan" because it would deny him his fee, went after him. The agent made clear that he did not expect moonshiners to be "exempted from the consequences of a violation of the law." Another leniency arrangement had tragic consequences for two men who held up their part of the bargain. Alabama congressmen arranged for suspended sentences for about a hundred moonshiners who promised to cease illegal activities and "give information of all violations that came within their knowledge, and assist the Revenue officers in enforcing the law." Two men, Banister and Terrell, carried out these terms but were killed by moonshiners because of the information they provided. Local citizens and state officials believed that capturing and trying the murderers was up to the federal government, arguing that "the Govt. [*sic*] should protect a citizen as well as an officer, who aids in enforcing the law." Unfortunately, federal officials lacked jurisdiction over such murders.[14]

Revenuers generally worked well with deputy marshals, although the old fee problem caused some difficulties that were not apparent in Raum's day. Deputy marshals accompanying revenue raids received no pay if they seized stills without making arrests. Deputy McDonald was always willing to go on raids in Alabama; during September 1886 he made four "trips" in which several stills were captured but no blockaders arrested. Not only did he not receive his fees, but he was out $28 for traveling expenses. This problem occurred "so frequently" that deputy marshals were reluctant to accompany revenue raids, which needed them to make arrests. Revenuers sought to accommodate them by waiting at the still (not a very safe procedure) until the moonshiner showed up and could be arrested. Agent W. H. Chapman thought that participation in fruitless revenue raids encouraged deputies to make arbitrary arrests for the sake of fees to cover their losses. Mentioning that the revenue agent in North Carolina seemed to have a fund for paying deputies for raids that resulted in no arrests, he wished to pay similarly deputies in Alabama and Georgia. Commissioner Miller and the attorney general, who provided the money, approved this proposal.[15]

Chapman reported in 1887 that payment made deputy marshals "do very excellent service for the Government," and he was "convinced that the work of suppressing illicit distilling has never received so much attention in the Northern Dist. [*sic*] of Alabama as within the past year." The marshal in Georgia concurred, saying that the payments "enabled this Department to do more efficient work than heretofore." The marshals were so pleased with the innovation that they were tempted to appoint more deputies than necessary for revenue raids; Chapman required that all such appointments receive his approval. When the money ran out in December 1887, the Alabama marshal could not persuade his deputies to go out on raids. When it became available again they cheerfully pursued the blockaders. Sometimes deputy marshals arrested the distiller but left the still behind, arousing suspicion that they deliberately allowed it to operate so they could arrest moonshiners over and over again to earn fees. On the other hand, though the law did not authorize them to do so, deputy marshals aided revenuers by seizing stills even when they were acting on their own. Payment of deputies for raids in which they made no arrests was only temporary (although it appeared again in North Carolina in 1891) and only a supplement to the usual payment by fees. It also seems to have been limited to certain areas.[16]

Fee payment continued to invite corruption. Attorney General Garland pointed out that fees received for warrants and other duties of the deputy marshals actually went to the marshal, who paid the deputies only a portion of the fee income received. Many marshals did not provide the deputies with enough money to cover their expenses, encouraging them to multiply warrants to make up for their superior's parsimony. Garland unsuccessfully urged Congress to require that at least half of the marshal's income from each warrant or other activity of the deputies go to the deputies themselves.[17]

Some revenue collectors appointed deputy marshals as "special deputy collectors" who had the power to both arrest moonshiners and seize their stills. These deputies continued to rely on fee payment according to the number of arrests they made. They were on their own, without direction from revenue officials, which an agent regarded as "most unreliable and pernicious." "Thorough work by officers of character, properly compensated, and kept under watchful and efficient supervision," was necessary. Deputy marshals doing double duty as revenuers undoubtedly contributed to people's impression that the revenuers were also paid in fees and participated in arbitrary and corrupt methods of increasing their income. Not until 1896, in his second term, did Commissioner Miller prohibit this double service.[18]

In Alabama and Tennessee mountaineers themselves got into the fee racket. Often a moonshiner brought before a commissioner swore out warrants against "every one he can think of," naming himself as the witness. This of course would usually be a dangerous business, except the wily blockader had an arrangement with his friends to everybody's profit. When the deputy marshal was ready to make his arrests, the "witness" told his friends where to meet the lawman. Members of this ring of mountaineers each acted as a witness against one of their friends, with the result that the government paid all of them witness fees and travel expenses. They all had a "big time" coming to court. They pleaded guilty and were fined $100 but never had to pay because they took the "pauper's oath" that they had no money. This was a clever way for blockaders, who returned to their stills, to make money off the government. The witness fee of $1.50 per day and mileage compensation of 5 cents per mile (when the real cost was only 3 cents) were substantial to people who saw very little cash during the year. One day an Alabama man came to visit Deputy Marshal Eichelberger, asking if there was a warrant against him. When he was told there was none, he replied, "Well *there ought to be*, I have been stilling, if there ain't any, one must be issued, as *I want to go to Montgomery*."[19] Similar rackets occurred in other areas.[20]

In 1888 Congress finally dealt with these problems by imposing some restrictions on the issuing of warrants. Representative Henderson of North Carolina attached a rider to an appropriations bill that forbade payment of fees to commissioners and deputy marshals unless the facts alleged in the complaint were personally known to the complainant. Warrants on information and belief could be sworn only by revenue officers; all warrants had to have the circuit judge's or the district attorney's approval before or after the arrest. These requirements reaffirmed the rules of some states like Georgia or North Carolina. They did not eliminate all the problems, but by 1900 stricter rules and payment of salaries to commissioners had reduced witness-fee rackets as well as arrests and prosecutions for the sake of fees.[21]

Asserting federal authority in the mountains became routine for Democratic officials, a sort of state of alert with forays against the elusive enemy. Though officers had to keep up the fight, Raum's campaign had firmly established the revenuer's position and, despite continued violence, made it possible for three-man posses to seize stills and arrest blockaders. Mountaineers were being forced deeper back into the coves and hollows and became even more secretive and cautious. Occasionally they struck back at deputies and informers, but the days of widespread "Ku-Kluxing" seemed to be over. Though revenuers were still hated by mountaineers, even in South Carolina "the better class of citizens countenance[d] and aid[ed] the revenue forces."[22]

When the Republicans returned to power in 1889 revenue enforcement continued as a dangerous but necessary and inevitable routine for officials in the South. Despite the 1888 platform promise of abolishing the whiskey tax if the Treasury surplus continued to grow, the tax remained, and the moonshiner continued to be harassed. Republicans retained the excise because government expenses were rapidly increasing to support not only the building of a modern navy but especially Civil War pensions, which rose from $54 million in 1880 to $107 million in 1890. The Pension Bureau, appropriately housed in its massive red brick building, had become an immense bureaucracy headed by the quintessential bureaucrat, Green B. Raum. In his first annual message, President Benjamin Harrison recommended abolition of the tobacco tax and the excise on spirits used in manufacture. He did not mention the whiskey tax and proposed no reductions in internal revenue in later messages. Some of the taxes on tobacco manufacturers and dealers were abolished or reduced in 1890. Whiskey tax revenues rose steadily throughout Harrison's administration.[23]

Harrison appointed as revenue commissioner John M. Mason, a West Virginian Union veteran, lawyer, and "aggressive Republican" active in the party's national committee but respected by Democrats. When he took over the office from his fellow West Virginian Miller, the outgoing commissioner presented him with a bung-starter, a long-handled mallet used for pounding the plug into a whiskey barrel. The two men had long been friendly, and the passing on of the bung-starter aptly symbolized the bipartisan nature of revenue enforcement. Mason developed a reputation for systematic business methods and was particularly proud of reducing the costs of collecting the taxes during his term.[24]

Like Miller, Mason valued the services of experienced workers and did not replace revenue agents or general deputies, whom he could appoint personally, because of their politics. Both Mason and Miller were politicians who took their patronage responsibilities seriously, but they also appreciated professionalism. When Mason left office he wrote General Deputy W. W. Colquitt, a Democrat, praising him as entitled to the "commendations and respect of everybody in the service without regard to politics." When vacancies among the twenty revenue agents opened up, Mason sought men who had the "special kind of talent" essential for the work. He found himself "completely overrun" with applications for positions as agents, with about a hundred applications for twelve openings. Some politics entered this process, for the agents were supposed to be distributed as evenly as possible among the states, but Mason allowed himself only one exception to a strictly professional standard. This was his own brother, whom he sent to Agent Thrasher in Chicago for training since he had "no experience whatever in revenue matters." Thrasher's teaching seems to have been successful, for A. B. investigated frauds among licensed distillers and financial irregularities in a collector's office, and he organized raids against West Virginia moonshiners. Despite this nepotism, Mason did not appoint his brother as an agent but as a general deputy collector who worked under various agents. The commissioner received a steady flow of letters from West Virginians and others seeking positions in the revenue service. He had to remind most of them that deputy collectors were appointed by the local collector, and storekeepers and gaugers only on the collector's recommendation.[25]

Mason made a few exceptions to his usual rule of refusing to pressure local officials to appoint subordinates of the commissioner's own choosing. He was determined, for example, to fire the widow of a Democratic lawyer who had defended election rioters in 1882, who was serving as a clerk in the South Carolina collector's office. Mason sought to replace her with the widow of Deputy Collector Brayton who had been killed by moonshiners. In another instance he was more directly partisan: hearing that an Alabama storekeeper was a Democrat, he asked Agent W. H. Chapman to find out if there were any local Republicans to take his place.[26] A partisan activist like his predecessors, Mason managed an intricate patronage network, but he shared their concern for efficiency and competence as well as political loyalty.

The officials Mason and his subordinates appointed were busy, seizing more stills each year—many more in 1891–92 than their Democratic predecessors had ever captured. On the other hand, their arrest totals did not exceed those of their predecessors, except in the case of the Democrats' low year of 1887. Republicans arrested 236 moonshiners in 1889 compared with the Democrats' low of 211. However, their high of 386 in 1890–91 never matched the Democrats' higher arrest levels. Casualty figures remained low, but the total number of revenuers killed (3) and wounded (7) exceeded the totals under the Democrats (2 and 4, respectively). In short, revenue raiders under Commissioner Mason seized many more stills than under his Democratic predecessor but made significantly fewer arrests. Although, after Raum's warfare, it had become "a rare occurrence that the officers are met with pistols and shotguns," they were resisted somewhat more than Miller's revenuers. Conviction rates suggested some trouble for the Republicans as well. They averaged about 54 percent, lower than under the Democrats, and after a rise from 54 percent to 63 percent in the Republicans' first full year (1889–90), declined steadily to 43 percent, their lowest point since 1873. In 1890–91 the moonshine districts' conviction rate of 58 percent was actually less than the rate in the remainder of the nation, 63 percent. Acquittals did not vary significantly; most of the decline was accounted for by a rise in discontinued cases, an indication of the district attorney's inability to secure witnesses or evidence. In 1892–93 discontinued cases rose to the highest point (39 percent) recorded since 1872 (43 percent). In the previous administration, the total number of cases had been trending upward, though the increase was not steady. Now the number rose steadily, sharply increasing in 1892–93 (from 4,667 to 6,117). This increase may reflect the zeal of newly appointed prosecutors, but it was also a sign of trouble—the growth of moonshining and sharper resistance in the early nineties—which the returning Democrats would have to confront.[27]

Commissioner Mason, determined to break up illicit distilling, "cost what it may," warned revenuers that they would "be required to thoroughly canvass their divisions and make the necessary seizures, and if they do not do it they will be removed and their places filled by men who will." Although newly appointed, inexperienced deputies sometimes hampered revenue enforcement, battle-hardened agents like W. H. Chapman continued their work of organizing and directing raids. Chapman, realizing that deputies in Alabama were new to their work, carried out raids with two veteran Georgia revenuers. After the initial period of adjustment, revenue enforcement settled into familiar routine. In Georgia Chapman rode out on raids with one or more deputy collectors and up to three deputy marshals. Blockaders caught in the act usually "expected such a visit all along and made up their minds to surrender quickly." Though they entertained "the bitterest ill will" against the raiders, they went to jail peacefully.[28]

By 1891 Georgia blockaders were aware of the relatively light penalty for minor offenders and usually pleaded guilty. The maximum penalty was three years in the federal penitentiary, but that was reserved for persistent violators. Moonshiners were careful not to be arrested more than twice, because their sentence increased with each offense. The minimum penalty was one month in jail, with sentences less than a year being served in Atlanta's Fulton County jail, or sometimes other county jails if the blockader could pay the transportation costs from Atlanta. Most moonshiners served the briefer sentences, with a $100 fine, which they could escape by the "pauper's oath" that they could not pay. The jail term could be reduced by five days per month for good behavior, and the Fulton County jailer seems to have been generous in his definition of good conduct. He recommended William Bowen of Rabun County for the reduction, adding to the printed phrase that he had "uniformly conducted himself with propriety" the remark "except that he once tried to escape." A reporter for the *Atlanta Constitution*, which in the past had waxed eloquent about revenue tyranny, made the mountaineers' jail experience seem like a social occasion. "See the jovial, romping moonshiners," he wrote, "as they engage in their various sports, playing cards with their greasy packs, skipping about, playing marbles, leap frog, hide-and-seek, catch-as-catch-can, cracking jokes or recalling reminiscences, dancing to the accompaniment of an old-time banjo, in the hands of a darky, and up to any mischievous fun." Moonshiners described a month's jail sentence as "a pleasant recreation." They missed their homes and families but enjoyed a life of "no work, all play, and a good fare."

After this interlude the mountaineer packed up his old valise, shook hands with his friends, and returned home to his family. A few days later he may have been back at his still. Life was even more pleasant in the Hall County jail at Gainesville until the federal district judge heard about it. Prisoners had to be in the jail only to eat their meals and sleep; otherwise they were free to lounge around town drinking the "red eye" sold at local blind tigers or even to visit their nearby homes. The judge "got after Sheriff Munday with a sharp stick" and made him keep the moonshiners locked up.[29]

Lest this image of good times in county jails make moonshining and its suppression seem pleasant for all concerned, there were places where the game was deadly enough. Some moonshiners were so violent that large raiding parties were necessary to break up their operations and overcome resistance. Howard County, Arkansas, was "infested" with blockaders who were ready "to take any risks, or resort to any measures of violence" to stay in business. Cleaning them out required a general sweep of the area by a large posse. Pursuing the Adams-Slone gang, who operated several stills in a closely guarded house, Deputy Marshal Wireman died in an 1889 Kentucky gunfight. The blockaders of Lauderdale County, Alabama, were "desperate men." Deputy Collector W. W. Colquitt, after two Alabama deputies failed to meet him, went ahead on a raid with only two men, one armed with a small pistol and the other with no weapon. They were driven off by the blockaders' fire, and a citizen who had aided them later had his house burned and his life threatened. Returning to the area on a later raid in 1888, Agent W. H. Chapman was wounded while approaching Harvey Reynolds's still. Chapman always suspected Reynolds but could not get him into court until 1891 when a local informer provided enough evidence for an indictment. Some moonshiners were still shooting.[30]

Familiar forms of corruption, both oppressing moonshiners and conniving with them, continued beneath the normal routines of revenue enforcement. The *Internal Revenue Record*, official newspaper of revenue officers, complained that fee rings among commissioners, deputy marshals, and "professional witnesses" caused the service to suffer "deeply in the estimation of the people in some localities." A Kentucky revenue agent believed that "the people of these rough mountain counties uncouth and ignorant as they are have been 'sinned against as well as sinning.'" Deputy marshals received the same fee for arresting a "wanton and foolish boy" for selling whiskey as for arresting "the outlaw who sets on the cliff overlooking his distillery and guards it with his 'Winchester.'" Since the marshal could make the same money with little danger, he was more likely to arrest the boy and leave the desperado alone. The agent argued that the arrest of one innocent person, taken to a commissioner eighty or a hundred miles away only to be discharged, outweighed the value of arresting a dozen guilty blockaders. As for the local deputy revenue collector, he was a candidate for Congress accused of fraternizing with the moonshiners for their votes.[31]

Attorney General W. H. H. Miller charged that East Tennessee commissioners and deputy marshals were part of a fee ring, which included members of local families who alternated roles as witnesses and defendants. The district attorney, resenting Miller's complaint that he had not been zealous enough in controlling such abuses, replied that he had in fact prosecuted and convicted several of the false witnesses for perjury as well as requiring deputies to have a sworn statement from witnesses before summoning them to the hearing. The district attorney had the satisfaction of receiving a commendation from Miller for the prosecutions.[32]

In Alabama, Deputy Collector M. W. Carden and his posse drank the mountain dew seized on raids and, according to a revenue agent, were frequently drunk on their return as local newspapers charged. Carden seems to have been protecting a large illicit operation, taking seized stills to his home without destroying them. Carden sought numerous warrants against moonshiners who were not his friends, and he worked with marshals and commissioners cooperating to make fees in revenue cases. Commissioner Mason had actually met Carden on an official visit to Alabama and had been "well pleased with him" as an "active, intelligent and industrious" man but would not excuse his drunkenness. He demanded that the reluctant collector fire Carden because "the men in this service must make up their minds to quit drinking or quit the service."[33]

A North Carolina citizen wrote to President Harrison charging that revenuers operated stills of their own, raiding those of their rival distillers. Sometimes they arrested their friends and let them off after "sham trials." This letter sounds cranky, but the *New York Times* also criticized North Carolina revenuers, charging that deputy collectors and marshals ignored moonshiners while arresting a few purchasers of their liquor. In two North Carolina districts only "1/9 of a man" was arrested for every still seized, whereas in Georgia "about 4/5 of a moonshiner" was arrested for each seizure. A local Republican congressman openly courted the moonshiner vote. The commissioner did in fact admonish deputy collectors in North Carolina that they should not leave raiding to the agents, and a collector chastised his deputy for "not giving this work the care, vigilance and fidelity to the interests of the Government that you should give it."[34]

Amidst such irregularities, there were officials who did their duty carefully and efficiently. One of these was U.S. commissioner J. L. Thornley, who had been holding hearings at Pickens, South Carolina, since 1874. He took care not to send trivial or dubious cases for grand jury investigation, dismissing 101 of 198 cases between July 1889 and April 1891. Most of the warrants he reviewed were based on deputy revenue collectors' "information and belief" rather than personal knowledge of the facts. On the surface it seemed that Thornley was hearing a large number of cases to make fees (which averaged about $14 for each case), but actually he sought to send up only cases with sufficient evidence to secure a grand jury indictment. About 75 percent of Thornley's cases resulted in an indictment, and about 66 percent of those in conviction. This was a better record than the other commissioners in South Carolina, even though in the February 1890 term of the federal court the grand jury contained many "sympathizers with, and advocates of, the cause of the violators of the Internal Revenue laws." One Department of Justice investigator believed that if there were only fifteen commissioners in the district following Thornley's procedures, instead of the existing thirty-five who were less rigorous, handling of revenue charges "would be more economically and effectively done."[35]

Republicans had one problem that was unique to their administrations. They continued to appoint blacks to patronage positions in the South, including the revenue service. In Raum's time James T. Rapier, a former U.S. congressman, was collector in Alabama from 1878 to 1883; L. M. Pleasant, a prominent leader of Georgia's blacks, served from 1882 to 1883; and "a fair proportion" of Kentucky deputies and three active Republican deputies in Virginia were black in 1881. In Mississippi two of the four regular deputy collectors were black during Commissioner Mason's term. As might be expected, their color added to the normal dangers of their job when pursuing moonshiners. Prejudice in Mississippi was so intense that only the white revenuers could seize stills and return alive. In Georgia, taking a black deputy on a raid would "not only endanger his own life but the lives of all the members of the posse." Local people, willing to feed the white revenuers, would give no food to the black officer. In 1889 white North Carolina deputies refused to work with Henderson, a new black appointee. The man soon lost his job because of "the continuing fight that has been made against him . . . on account of his color." A white supporter, calling him an efficient officer and a valuable worker for the Republican party, urged his reinstatement. Commissioner Mason took a personal interest in the case and worked for Henderson's reappointment, but many months elapsed before the collector found an opening for him, and he still encountered prejudice from fellow revenuers. National patronage managers continued rewarding blacks for party loyalty, but southern white Republicans gained local support only by distancing themselves from the blacks.[36]

At the end of 1892, while Grover Cleveland prepared to reoccupy the White House and Joseph Miller to resume his duties as commissioner of internal revenue, the patterns and problems of revenue enforcement had become familiar. Small posses continued to raid stills throughout the mountain South, sometimes encountering violent resistance but usually making routine seizures and arrests. Moonshiners usually ran rather than shot, but there were pockets of guerilla resistance that seemed impossible to eradicate. Both the moonshiner and the revenuer seemed to be permanent elements of mountain society. Deputy marshals' abuse of fee payment and revenue deputies' varieties of corruption also seemed to be permanent, but the majority of both officials were ready to do their duty and risk their lives if necessary. Whether Republicans or Democrats were in power, revenue enforcement continued. Some people believed, as did North Carolinians, that "Cleveland was rough on the 'blockaders', but Harrison lets us have our own way." In other states, people shared the *Atlanta Constitution*'s conviction that the Democrats were "lily-white" compared with the Republicans, even if under them the law was harsh and some of the officers corrupt. By 1894 both parties had come to accept the revenue system, and many old opponents counseled mountain people to give up their resistance and "bear their part in building up" a new South.[37]

But the mountaineers did not give up their resistance; during the 1890s they escalated their struggle against "the revenue" to crisis proportions. The Democrats inherited the crisis, but they also helped protract it by raising the liquor tax. Republicans also had to cope with it when they returned to power in 1897. The guerilla actions of the 1880s seemed to be expanding again into full-scale battle. Organized movements once again terrorized informers and even revenuers themselves. Not since Raum's day had the government faced such a challenge to its authority. If Raum had to cope with a second whiskey rebellion, this looked like a third.

8   Crisis and a

Continuing Battle,

1893–1900

· ·

Grover Cleveland returned to the presidency in 1893 under gathering clouds. A financial panic had precipitated a nationwide industrial and agricultural depression that dragged on until 1897. The government faced increasing expenses while the surplus in the Treasury drained away and revenues declined because people were buying fewer taxable commodities. Between 1893 and 1894 whiskey revenues dropped over $9 million and the next year declined by nearly 5 million. The Supreme Court ruled the 1894 income tax unconstitutional, leaving the Treasury with $30 million less revenue than anticipated.

Seeking to recover funds without raising the tariff, the Democratic Congress increased the whiskey tax to $1.10 per gallon in 1894. David A. Wells, the economist who developed the original revenue law during the Civil War, warned against setting the tax level too high. Too stiff a levy encouraged evasion because the profits made by not paying the tax could cover the expenses of seizure and arrest. The government, expecting more revenue, actually cheated itself of income it would have made with a lower tax rate. The new tax certainly did not bring in more funds, because licensed distillers who anticipated the increase released huge quantities of liquor that had already been taxed at the old rate and stored in their bonded warehouses. This flooding of the market led to reduced output in the first year of the new rate. Moonshining by both large-scale, sophisticated operators in cities and southern mountaineers increased dramatically. In 1896 the government estimated that between 5 and 10 million gallons of illegal whiskey and other spirits were produced annually, a tremendous loss of potential revenue.

Whiskey revenue recovered only slightly in 1895–96, finally rising in 1897 but not surpassing 1892–93 levels until 1899. According to the *New York Times*, "There is more illicit distilling and trading of 'blockade' whisky in this country than ever before . . . and, consequently, the revenue officers were never more active than at present."[1]

Commissioner Joseph Miller, reappointed from Cleveland's first administration, received the bung-starter from John M. Mason in a friendly, unofficial ceremony. The outgoing commissioner found Miller's appointment "entirely agreeable . . . personally." West Virginia's leading Republican paper thought Miller was "one of the best Commissioners the country has ever had" and called him "a just and honorable officer who, with his added experience, will improve the good reputation he made during his previous term of office. . . . It is a distinctive triumph for the cause of good government." West Virginia Democrats had opposed his appointment because he was insufficiently partisan, but Cleveland had "a warm personal regard" for Miller and made him an exception to his general rule of not reappointing officeholders from his first term. Mason was relieved to leave office but probably would not have wished the difficulties Miller experienced upon his friend.[2]

Miller's appointees were active. Between 1893–94 and 1896–97, seizures of stills increased from 1,016 to 2,273. Arrests, at 487 in 1892–93, reached 871 in 1894–95, the first full year after the tax increase. They dropped to 839 in 1895–96 but remained above predepression levels. Until 1902 there was a greater divergence between seizures and arrests than at any earlier time, suggesting active revenuers but agile moonshiners who made their escape.[3]

Prosecutors were also busy, with the number of revenue cases reaching an all-time high (7,078) in 1895–96. Overall conviction rates in the moonshine districts, according to district attorneys' reports, averaged 60 percent during the Cleveland administration, better than the Harrison administration's 54 percent. The revenue commissioner's figures reveal that the moonshine districts accounted for 56 percent of the nation's liquor cases in 1893–94, the conviction rate of 65 percent being markedly better than the 29 percent rate in the rest of the country. This was a recovery from the Harrison years, when the moonshine districts' convictions were below the outside rate.[4]

Northern Georgia's conviction rate average (59 percent) was close to the moonshine region's overall average, better than the district's less than 50 percent rate in the later 1880s. In northern Georgia there had been 211 moonshining cases in the federal courts in 1892–93, but during the next year, even before the tax increase, there were between 700 and 800. The territory of illicit distilling seemed to be widening, and the old offenders did not appear to have given up their stilling. During the crisis Georgia revenuers were losing strength when they needed it the most. In March of 1894, seventy-five raiders were available but fifteen were let go and another fifteen in July to save money. Georgia federal district attorney J. S. James reported in 1897 that after the tax increase internal revenue violations steadily rose. The general depression certainly contributed its share, as indicated by the increase of moonshining even before the new tax rate. Farmers, unable to sell their products for a decent price, turned to moonshining to make a little money. Georgia moonshiners were "seedy specimens of hard times" who would "scarcely be able to make a living" without income from brush whiskey. The mountaineer was caught between low prices and the high liquor tax. Worthless on the market, his corn repaid his efforts when it was made into mountain dew.[5]

However poor the moonshiners were, collectively they provided stiff competition to small legitimate distillers. In some areas, licensed distillers banded together to prevent tax collection. Distilleries seized for nonpayment could not be sold at auction because local people refused to bid or offered only very low bids. Honest distillers had other problems too, for their industry was increasingly becoming dominated by a few of the largest firms. The "whiskey trust" of the late eighties and early nineties controlled two-thirds of the nation's output of neutral spirits, used in blended whiskies. The depression of the nineties encouraged a new wave of consolidation in many industries, and the small distiller was caught between the giants and the five-gallon-still moonshiners. Many of them may well have given up the legitimate business and taken to the woods, some very likely former moonshiners who had responded to the government's encouragement to go legitimate.[6]

Liquor manufacturers, sellers, and drinkers were also caught in an advancing wave of local prohibition during the 1890s. Prohibition probably encouraged more open opposition to blockading and created a more favorable climate for informers, but it also gave a tremendous boost to moonshining, widening the market even while it encouraged production of a poor-quality product to increase profits.

Statewide prohibition did not reach the South until the early twentieth century, but township and county prohibition had begun its advance in the 1870s, accelerating in the eighties and nineties. Prohibition expanded from special legislative acts outlawing the sale of alcohol within a certain radius of schools or churches, then within townships when local people petitioned for the measures; finally, local-option elections were authorized in counties requesting them. Another measure, adopted first in South Carolina in 1893, established state liquor stores or "dispensaries" to put the saloon out of business. Prohibitionists, though, were not pleased with state sponsorship of vice. The governor of South Carolina, Benjamin F. Tillman, had in fact worked for the dispensary law to head off growing support for absolute prohibition. The prohibition campaign was directed mostly at saloons, but in the early twentieth century it began to focus on manufacturing as well. States, in the years immediately before statewide prohibition, enacted laws against distilleries located outside of towns—"hell-kettles"—a direct attack on licensed small mountain distilleries as well as moonshiners. By the time state prohibition laws were enacted in the early twentieth century, most of the counties in several southern states had been dry for years.[7]

Liquor control became a major state political issue, and the maneuverings of both Republicans and Democrats became incredibly convoluted in their efforts to win the growing dry constituency without alienating the wets too deeply. The federal revenue system, long an issue in the mountain districts, became embroiled in the politics of state liquor legislation. In eastern Tennessee, District Attorney Camp was active in the Knoxville temperance society. One of his assistants, A. H. Pettibone, campaigned for a prohibition amendment to the state constitution and argued from his experience with moonshiners that Republicans should support prohibition. R. B. Glenn, North Carolina's Democratic federal attorney during the 1890s, was an ardent dry and became the state's "prohibition governor" who signed the state law with great ceremony in 1908. The men with whom he was supposed to cooperate, North Carolina federal revenue officials, had joined the liquor dealers in a campaign against statewide prohibition as early as 1881. They hoped to split the Democrats and gain control of the state legislature as well as win back the black vote that the Democrats had come to dominate. Whatever Collector J. J. Mott's political motives, he argued reasonably that prohibition would encourage moonshining and resistance to authority "which happily have almost been eradicated from our state." Democrats argued for prohibition with familiar antirevenue appeals: outlawing manufacture of liquor would rid the state of "the corrupting influence of those internal revenue officers who debauch our young men and use their offices to cloak crime and practice fraud." The wets won the referendum, and statewide prohibition was not enacted until 1908. In Kentucky the political picture was different, for in 1884 the Republican political boss was an ardent prohibitionist who alienated many mountain Republicans who would lose their jobs as employees of the internal revenue service.[8]

Mott and the anonymous Kentucky revenuers confirmed many prohibitionists' objections to the whiskey tax, that it made the government dependent on the liquor interests for revenue. This view gained ground during the eighties as local option accelerated. Earlier, most temperance advocates had favored a high tax to reduce consumption by raising the price of liquor, calling the excise "a tax not merely on a luxury, but upon the most depraving of all luxuries," that would "suppress vices or unnecessary indulgence." Prohibitionists began to argue that it had no effect on consumption and that the organized liquor interests regarded the tax as protecting them against prohibition because the government would go bankrupt without its revenue. The Woman's Christian Temperance Union criticized Commissioner John M. Mason in 1892 for an official tour in which he discussed problems of taxation with leading distillers, with whom he was on friendly terms. The prohibition group disapproved of the "attitude of the Government toward the people engaged in this business" and deeply regretted the commissioner's "personal activity and approving interest in this business." Henry D. Scomp, a leading Georgia prohibitionist, charged that the excise was "the strongest barrier ever erected across the pathway of temperance in the United States," claiming that its abolition would tremendously aid the prohibition cause. Such arguments, though not exclusively southern, of course fit nicely with longstanding southern objections to the revenue system and indicated that prohibitionists were in touch with general popular dislike of the revenuer.[9]

Prohibitionists had more specific reasons for objecting to the revenue system. Local federal officials, backed by both Democratic and Republican revenue commissioners and supported by federal court decisions, actually obstructed enforcement of prohibition laws. State officers regarded a receipt for the federal special tax on retailers as evidence of violation of the prohibition laws. Federal revenue officials, however, obstructed state authorities' examination of their list of taxpayers and refused to produce the records in court as evidence against them. Collector T. C. Crenshaw of Georgia declared he would "use every effort to defeat" use of the records by the state, announcing, "I am a tax collector, not the guardian of the prohibition laws. I am not here to suppress liquor making or liquor selling." In an odd turning of the tables, state authorities were now frustrated by federal refusal to cooperate, and in some states revenue officials found themselves in jail, not for suppressing moonshiners, but for refusing to aid prohibition enforcement.[10]

One would expect the mountain regions of the South, where many revenuers as well as moonshiners lived, to be wet. Their divergent interests would seem to unite against drying up both groups' source of livelihood. From the moonshiners' perspective, state and local prohibition would add another set of officials looking for stills to break up and people to haul into court. Nevertheless, many mountain counties supported prohibition, including areas known for moonshining. Despite the party's opposition to prohibition in North Carolina's referendum of 1881, white Republicans living in the western counties tended to be dry, giving the strongest minority support for prohibition in the state. Maps prepared by Leonard Blakey in 1912 revealed the spread of prohibition between 1877 and 1887. In the first year there were no dry counties in northeastern Georgia and only a few of the circles Blakey used to indicate local no-saloon areas. South Carolina's Oconee and Pickens counties had no dry areas within them in 1877; likewise the entire state of West Virginia. Western North Carolina had the most dry districts. Ten years later the Georgia mountain counties, including blockader Fannin, Habersham, Rabun, Towns, Union, and Whitfield, were dry along with most of the West Virginia counties. Although western North Carolina did not adopt countywide prohibition, the number of local dry districts had greatly increased. Oconee and Pickens in South Carolina had now acquired some dry areas. Eastern Kentucky had also become drier, with several counties outlawing the saloon. In an 1887 statewide referendum in Tennessee, prohibition carried twenty-three of twenty-five of the eastern mountain counties, several of which were moonshiner strongholds.[11]

Moonshiners themselves were not likely to vote for prohibition, unless they cynically calculated how much it would improve their business. Horace Kephart did in fact argue that blockaders liked to see the end of licensed distilleries and saloons because moonshiners then became the sole suppliers. Under prohibition, thirsty drinkers did not set very high standards, and "mean whiskey" was largely a by-product of prohibition. Moonshiners could dilute a gallon of mountain dew with water and fortify it with "cologne spirits or other abominations" and sell it for $1.50 a quart. Kephart said that blockading increased "by leaps and bounds since the mountain region went dry." A *New York Times* reporter described a North Carolina mountain area as " 'dry,' so dry in fact that 100 gallons of blockade whisky serves a small town of 150 inhabitants of all ages and both sexes for a week's consumption, . . . and 50 gallons provide for the festivities of the Fourth of July. The prevailing thirst due to the 'dryness' of the towns is amazing." In dry towns the outvoted wets relied on "the man who comes down from the mountains with his hidden jug." A liquor industry newspaper declared that "such an inviting market has been opened up by Prohibition that the moonshiners are willing to run any risk to reap the benefit thereof." In Georgia there was a "marked renewal of illicit distilling . . . especially in the Prohibition counties."[12]

The towns housed most of the saloons and their patrons but also probably most of the prohibitionists in the mountains. There the influence of the churches, which had early pronounced in favor of prohibition; schools that began providing lessons on the evil effects of alcohol; and groups like the Woman's Christian Temperance Union were most felt. Members of the growing town commercial and managerial middle class regarded the rural folk as desperately needing reform of their manners and mores; prohibition was one means to that goal.

Such reformers joined in denunciation of blockade distilleries as "places of vice and sin . . . , maelstroms of the neighborhoods which they infect, into which nearly all that is good is swallowed up. . . . These places of shame and lawlessness destroy utterly the peace of a home, the plenty of a whole section, the organization of a strong church, and make out of the home a den, out of the section of country a lurking place for law breakers." Several voices in Georgia joined to criticize blockaders. A Populist leader challenged moonshiners' arguments about inalienable rights: "A man has no right to so use his products as to injure all of his neighbors and to the hurt of the entire community in which he lives." A newspaper editorialized, "There is no calculating the amount of trouble which a blockade distillery causes in a neighborhood," later criticizing moonshiners for spending their time in jail instead of "at home working on their farms in place of their wives and little children." A Georgia grand jury charged that the results of blockading were "the youth of the county ruined and murdered, and crime of every kind traceable to these horrible distilleries." South Carolina's Charleston *News and Courier*, never friendly to revenuers, charged that "whisky is a worse foe than Radicalism, and it brings worse ills in its train. To the women of South Carolina . . . we appeal, for the State and the name of the State." A committee of Cherokee County, North Carolina, citizens reversed the usual pattern of local complaints about revenuers. They charged that deputies, who "loved government money more than the morals of our Country," were too lenient toward blockaders. Many people were distressed by the deadly results of confrontations between drunken young men.[13]

Churches tended to reflect the attitudes of local people about drinking and moonshining. Some churchgoers and reformers were able to clean up rowdy communities like the mica-mining district of Mitchell County, North Carolina, or the gold-mining boomtown of Dahlonega, Georgia. Although some ministers were moonshiners themselves, others worked to "put the fear of God" into moonshiners' hearts.[14]

Prohibition increased the pressures on moonshiners. They were now pursued by two sets of officials, federal and county or state. Local officers sometimes even worked with federal revenuers instead of against them. In Arkansas Sheriff Jennings led a large posse that included two deputy marshals. They encountered John Putnam, a moonshiner, and his young nephew, who died in a gunfight at their still. State officers also acted on their own initiative. South Carolina constables surrounded a wagon loaded with blockade whiskey; the moonshiners fired, killing one of the officers. They shot back, killing two of the distillers, who "died on the whiskey barrels." The local coroner's jury supported the constables, who refused to testify, by declaring that the men were killed by "persons unknown." In the Dark Corner district, where "the authority of Sheriff Gilreath is yet recognized because he is personally popular, but B. R. Tillman and Grover Cleveland are out of date," the confrontation was less lethal. The sheriff led a posse against two members of the Howard clan of moonshiners, but they did not show up at their still because the worm had broken and "the two boys had taken a holiday and gone seining." On the second raid the possemen realized they had been carefully tracked by the mountaineers, and when they tried to surprise the Howards in their cabin, a barking dog alerted the moonshiners. Soon the family chickens came upon the sheriff and his men in the brush and joined in, the rooster sounding to a local journalist as if he were crowing, "struck, struck, struck a stranger." The raiders had to retreat to the sound of the blockaders' horns. Other state officials did not get away so easily. A Kentucky sheriff arranged a truce with moonshiners he had been battling after they had wounded both him and his deputy. When he mounted his horse to leave, they shot him in the back.[15]

State measures sometimes led to violent protests from people who believed their basic rights were being violated. Tillman's dispensary system in South Carolina included inspections by special state constables seeking illegal retailers and relied on evidence supplied by paid detectives or informers. In Darlington, a day of searches and growing anger led to a confrontation in which two citizens and two constables were killed; a crowd chased the remaining constables into the woods and surrounded them. Tillman, calling up his supporters in rural state militia units, clamped down in an exercise of authority that angered many firm believers in the Carolina tradition of individual rights and local autonomy. Liquor distillers, licit and illicit, sellers, and drinkers faced an unaccustomed challenge from their own state officials as well as from the more familiar federal interlopers. Many moonshiners feared arrest by state officers more than by revenuers because punishment for violating the prohibition laws was more certain than for federal tax evasion. Sometimes moonshiners who served their time for the federal offense returned home to find a levy against their property to pay a state fine for violating prohibition.[16]

Agricultural depression, a higher liquor tax, and local prohibition made the lives of drinking mountaineers more difficult. The combination of these factors provided a wider market for moonshiners. The stakes were high: some sought survival, others profit, but all were determined to resist destruction of their livelihood. Whether traditionalists who continued to brew a pure mountain dew for their neighbors or profiteers on impure white lightning, many turned once more to organized resistance.

Moonshiner violence and vigilantism were part of a larger intensification of conflict in the late-nineteenth-century South. Ordinary assaults, murders, and robberies began to crowd the dockets of county courts. The nineties witnessed a wave of lynchings of blacks that paralleled the political movement to deprive them of their votes. The rise of Populism among discontented farmers threatened the dominant elites, who sometimes responded with violence and electoral fraud reminiscent of Reconstruction days. In the mountains feuds seemed to be even more vicious than earlier. Logging camps and mining towns witnessed fights among displaced young men and conflicts between the workers and their bosses. Whitecap vigilante groups were organized in the cotton regions of the South as well as in the mountains. Mississippi farmers donned the white mask and rode at night to protest the crop-lien system, driving hired laborers from fields merchants had obtained through mortgage foreclosures. In Georgia cotton areas, whitecaps threatened to destroy the gins of merchants who refused to wait for a price increase before processing farmers' cotton. In some regions they carried on the old Klan function of punishing blacks. Like the Klan, whitecaps served local needs rather than a single, general purpose. Moonshiners had joined the Klan to protect themselves, and they joined the new organization, which southerners commonly referred to as a reincarnation of the Klan, for the same purpose.[17]

Georgia whitecaps were most active in the northwestern counties of Gilmer, Gordon, Murray, Whitfield, and Pickens. Pickens, Murray, and Whitfield were dry in 1887; though Gilmer voters turned down prohibition in 1886, the county had not granted a retail license for ten years. Gordon was wet. Although these counties had long been moonshining areas, they were at the opposite end of the state from some of the old trouble spots of Raum's day, Fannin, Habersham, Union, Towns, and Rabun. Gilmer, though, had been a conspicuous target for earlier revenue raids. As early as 1888–89, Murray County blockaders had formed a secret organization called the Distillers' Union. Gilmer soon had its Working Men's Friend and Protective Organization; Pickens, the Honest Man's Friend and Protector; and Gordon, the Gordon County Grangers. These groups required members to swear that they would help each other by supplying alibis for arrested members and never finding a member guilty if serving on a jury. They promised to force informers to leave the area and to kill those who refused. Members of the Honest Man's Friend and Protector (who, though called whitecaps, wore black disguises) signed the oath with the names of local people they suspected of informing. Each vigilante was responsible for watching his namesake and organizing punishment. Soon the groups broadened their goals to include disciplining people whom they believed violated conventional moral standards. The members were poor mountain and hill people, landless or owning marginal farms. Gordon, Murray, and Whitfield counties had the highest proportion of tenancy (50 percent for Gordon; 43 percent for Murray and Whitfield) in northern Georgia. Gordon and Whitfield had the smallest average farm size (102 and 101 acres, respectively). Some of the whitecap leaders were more substantial landholders, a pattern that had existed in the Klan as well.[18]

Although Georgia whitecaps' war against informers had begun under the Republicans, it intensified when Paul B. Trammel, the new Democratic collector, inaugurated a crackdown on distillers in 1893. Revenuers and deputy marshals "hunted down the moonshiner and dragged him into federal court." Unfortunately, many deputies practiced familiar forms of corruption that only exacerbated mountaineers' anger against them. According to a Justice Department examiner, they "carried on affairs in a high handed manner and falsified their accounts in every possible way." They were also "instrumental in 'trumpeting up' cases against innocent people for no other purpose than making fees." Sometimes the deputies told people that there was no case against them, or defendants cooperated with the deputies by providing their own witnesses, for which the marshal charged the government as if he had subpoenaed them himself. Deputies also paid professional informers to provide evidence against innocent people. Others apparently accepted payoffs to leave stills alone. The investigator asserted that "a large amount of the recent reign of terrorism in this District was due to these unscrupulous officers of the law." Rebecca Felton, politically influential wife of a former congressman and independent Democrat leader, denounced Deputy Tom Wright as "a rapist and a drunken desperado," selected to "maltreat innocent people" and not surprisingly bring "*disrepute upon an already discounted service, by a dishonest enforcement of the laws.*" Such conduct encouraged whitecaps to attack not only informers but deputy marshals themselves.[19]

The Georgia federal district attorney estimated that between 1891 and 1894 over 150 people had been whipped by whitecaps, and at least fifteen to twenty murdered. Thinking this estimate exaggerated, William F. Holmes, the expert on whitecapping, documented sixty-six whitecap attacks between 1889 and 1894. The great majority of these were beating or whipping of informers or destruction of their property, but some were attacks on federal officials. Deputy Marshal J. T. Lewis had spearheaded raids on moonshiners around Fairmount, Gordon County. He had captured the noted outlaw Veal, who had provided information against other blockaders, including Will Morrow, killer of a county sheriff. Veal's betrayal led to the arrest of Morrow and his crowd, which embittered local moonshiners. Receiving news of a planned raid, they plotted to ambush Lewis on the way. However, the posse was delayed in setting out, and their plan was frustrated. Later, a woman warned Lewis that if he did not release an arrested man, Lewis's barn would be burned. Soon after, whitecaps carried out the threat, destroying the barn with its animals and stored crops inside. Another deputy marshal named Goodson was also a target of terrorists. In the fall of 1893, D. J. Atkins, "a red-faced mountaineer of the double-jointed, supple-sinewed type," dynamited the house of Goodson's son-in-law, hoping to murder Deputy Marshal Wright, probably the same man denounced by Mrs. Felton, and his posse as well as Goodson, whom he thought were spending the night at the house. Nobody was injured, but in December nightriders destroyed, again with dynamite, Goodson's own valuable steam engine. Whitecappers were determined to punish their enemies.[20]

Alabama whitecaps were concentrated in piedmont Cherokee and Cleburne counties, the one dry by 1898 and the other containing only state-run dispensaries. More mountainous De Kalb and Jackson and Lauderdale, the longtime moonshine center up in the state's northwestern corner, did not host a secret organization. The groups began later than in Georgia, possibly in 1891 but most clearly by 1893. Less is known about the economic background of the members of the Alabama groups than of those in Georgia, but they too were mostly small farmers who were not outlaws until they began to strike out in defense of "a man's right to make a little licker."[21]

Alabama whitecaps do not seem to have attacked federal officers as directly as their brethren in Georgia, but they were not shy of killing them when necessary. Terrorists led by the Arrington brothers shot and wounded Brownston Forrester while he was plowing his field. Forrester was a frequent witness against moonshiners near the Beecham Settlement. When warrants were sworn out for the Arringtons and several others, the blockaders retreated to the mountains and built a fort where they hid during the day. Deputies Griggs and Lawrence went to their stronghold to arrest them, but when commanded to surrender, they opened fire. Griggs died, and

Will Arrington was mortally wounded; the others escaped farther into the mountains.[22]

Both Georgia and Alabama whitecaps were difficult to prosecute for familiar reasons: they effectively intimidated witnesses and jurors and sometimes included local officials in their ranks. State authorities attempted to prosecute and convict them but were successful only in Georgia's Pickens County, where they managed to suppress nightriding as early as 1890. They had learned the names of members of the Honest Man's Friend and Protector from a captured whitecap and were able to remove sympathizers from the juries. Their success was unusual, and whitecapping was broken up only by federal officials who moved slowly at first but eventually obtained convictions in major cases. Lacking jurisdiction over assault or murder, district attorneys framed indictments based on Reconstruction-era conspiracy statutes. They charged whitecaps with conspiring to violate the civil rights of witnesses to testify in federal court, attacking the reincarnation of the Klan with laws aimed at the original. Many whitecaps were convicted by 1895, although the Supreme Court threw out a major Alabama conviction on a technicality and the attorney general suspended prosecution of pending cases. Unlike the original Klan, respectable citizens often opposed whitecap terrorism although they did not do much about it. They began to support prosecution publicly when they learned of the nature of the terrorists' crimes and worried about the reputation and economic stability of their counties. Although the government followed a course similar to the earlier Ku Klux prosecutions, crackdown followed by abandonment, this time it worked, for whitecapping was effectively over in Georgia and Alabama at the end of 1895.[23]

Whitecapping was the most spectacular form of moonshiner resistance, but in most areas during the nineties it took the familiar form of confrontations between distillers and raiding parties. Three revenuers died in 1893, the highest number since 1882; two died in 1898 and 1901. Except for these years, deaths had never exceeded one since 1882. The largest number of wounded was five in 1898 and four in 1901, with three each in 1895–97. These figures were still small compared to the late seventies, but they clearly revealed increased violence. One reporter in 1896 described moonshiners as still engaging in "little more than passive resistance" because "the most ignorant of the mountaineers knows that a single officer has the authority and resources of the government at his back," but many were not so respectful of authority. Apparently there were local variations in moonshiners' response to raids: Georgia blockaders ran away; in Arkansas they were prone to ambush; Kentuckians faced the enemy and fought openly. Three episodes in 1897 indicated the hazards revenuers faced. In Arkansas, Joseph Dodson, a deputy marshal who had been "a terror to moonshiners for years," died along with another deputy in an ambush while they were approaching a still. Two other men, Arkansas deputy sheriffs, were missing. In Kentucky, Deputy Marshal Byrd was killed while taking an arrested moonshiner to a commissioner for hearing. After making supposedly the "biggest moonshine raid that ever took place in the South," Tennessee revenuers found the entire district aroused against them and several times were shot at by mountaineers concealed in brush by the roadside. It was obvious that revenuers required "courage, prudence and acquaintance with the neighborhood for any degree of success," for they battled with an enemy who was often hidden.[24]

Moonshiners resorted to familiar tactics of evasion as well as confrontation. Kentucky blockaders constantly moved their stills about to avoid detection; their Mississippi counterparts hid their stills while the federal court was in session because they knew that was a favorite time for raids. Tennesseeans developed the opposite strategy, going to work during court sessions because they knew the marshals and revenuers would be tied up giving testimony. Tennessee moonshiners also sent false reports to the deputy collector, who dispatched posses to spots where stills had never been located. Kentucky moonshiners attempted the old, though now much less frequent, tactic of charging revenuers with crimes in state courts. A posse ambushed by blockaders had returned the fire, killing Wilson Scott. Friends and relatives of Scott secured indictments in the state court, but the district attorney thought they did not really want a trial but the opportunity to get the men into the neighborhood and kill them. He was able to convince the state judge of this plot, and the case was transferred to federal court. In North Carolina, W. H. Chapman and four others were arrested by state authorities who prevented them from detaining a reluctant witness against moonshiners. Chapman averted "a close encounter with pistols by seizing hold of [a] Constables pistol and urging that no shooting be done." Chapman, who had been an agent since Raum's time, seems to have experienced almost everything a revenuer could live to describe, including being wounded and this arrest.[25]

Despite the obstacles of resistance, evasion, and harassment, some revenuers gained reputations for courage and ability. Agent David H. Gates, "the pride of the revenue service," was an "immense man, five or six inches more than six feet tall, with shoulders a yard across, a grim, clean shaven face, steely blue eyes, and a general 'don't tread on me' air." Although he was "as soft spoken as a woman," whenever he set out to capture a still, he was successful. On a raid in eastern Kentucky, a blockader fusillade clipped a chunk from the bridge of Gates's nose and knocked him from his horse. Ordering his men to charge, he followed on foot. After a twenty-minute gunfight, the moonshiners fled with the raiders in pursuit. The revenuers stumbled "plump into the largest still they had seen in that part of the country." They destroyed it, which allowed the distillers to escape, but the raiders later destroyed four more stills.[26]

John Burris of Arkansas was a dedicated and effective revenuer; moonshiners complained "now we have a man after us that never sleeps, . . . and we know that he has no sympathy for our business and cannot be bought." He was credited with destroying over 150 stills in his career. In February 1898, Burris accompanied two deputy marshals and a posse to Cleburne County, where they destroyed three stills and arrested five blockaders. On their return they were followed by sixteen armed men, who seized the Little Red River ferryboat, forcing the possemen to swim the river. They did not fire or attempt to rescue the prisoners. The marshal received letters and telegrams from citizens of Cleburne warning that the moonshiners were preparing to punish the people they suspected of informing. He immediately sent another posse to the area, which did not capture stills or arrest anybody but had more important results. The moonshiners understood that "the Government was determined to protect the law abiding citizens, suppress illicit distilling and bring to justice those engaged in this unlawful business." Realizing the officials' determination, they sent an emissary to arrange with the district attorney to surrender themselves and their stills in return for suspended sentences. Some forty-three people, about three-fourths of the inhabitants of the moonshine district including "constables, preachers, millmen, merchants, farmers, old men and boys," gave themselves up. They came into the town of Hiram in wagons loaded with copper stills and men. The marshal was convinced that this success was due to "the display of force on the part of the Government."[27]

Although all concerned were pleased with suspended sentences in Arkansas, the practice set off a controversy in North Carolina that simmered through the nineties. At the heart of the problem was the opposition of both the revenue commissioner and the attorney general to District Attorney R. B. Glenn's and federal judge R. P. Dick's routine suspension of sentences in minor cases, usually retailing. Dick had served many years as district judge, undoubtedly remembered Raum's use of suspended sentences, and was known for his "kindly temper" when hearing revenue cases. However, Raum had emphasized suspension as selective and temporary, not favoring it as a routine policy. Since 1882 or 1883 the district attorney recommended and Judge Dick normally suspended sentences for petty revenue violators, mostly sellers rather than distillers, who paid reduced fines averaging about $20 instead of the minimum of $100 and a thirty-day jail term prescribed by law. Between 1885 and 1888, under the Democrats, suspensions ranged from 44 percent in 1885 to a high of 60 percent of convictions in 1887. When the Republicans came into power, the suspensions ranged from an all-time high of 84 percent in 1889 to a low of 50 percent the next year, 1890. In the Republicans' last full year, 1892, which witnessed the beginning of the depression, suspensions rose to 75 percent of the highest number of convictions up to that time, 442. The first year of Democrat Glenn's term, 1893, saw suspensions rise to 87 percent of a smaller number of convictions. In 1894 they dropped to 81 percent and in 1895 to 62 percent. During these two years the pressure was on the district attorney to stop his practice, which was clearly not his innovation, although during Glenn's term western North Carolina led the moonshine districts in number of suspended sentences.

In 1893 the solicitor of internal revenue complained to the attorney general that the practice was "seriously interfering with the work of this Bureau" and that revenue violations were "constantly" increasing when sentences were routinely suspended. The commissioner of internal revenue normally had the power to compromise cases if the defendants petitioned him for a settlement. In every case he " 'tempers Justice with mercy,' " but no requests were coming from districts where sentences were suspended. The district attorney and the judge were claiming a power of clemency that belonged to the commissioner. District Attorney Glenn's reply justifying his policy inaugurated a long fight that arrayed Commissioner Joseph Miller, Attorney General Richard Olney, and even President Cleveland against him. The president chastised Glenn for continuing his leniency after the attorney general directed him to stop. Cleveland told Olney to instruct his subordinate that "he is expected in the future to do his full share towards the execution of the criminal law as he finds it, leaving the consideration of clemency to those entrusted with that duty."[28]

With such a presidential rebuke, one would expect Glenn to take the hint. He did not, for in early 1896 he acknowledged what he thought was a letter from the attorney general authorizing him "to continue the present practice, now in vogue in my District, until further orders." He promised that he would not "abuse the confidence that you place in my discretion, but . . . will look solely to what I conceive is for the best interest of the government." He should have read the letter more carefully, for what the attorney general had really authorized was suspension of sentences only in pending cases, requiring that he stop the practice in all new cases. Glenn read the attorney general's reply with "deep regret," marshaling all of his familiar arguments to justify himself.[29]

He apparently still did not give up, for when the Republicans came into office in 1897, they complained about Glenn's compromises, and the attorney general ordered him to stop in April. This time he obeyed but argued that the effect was that "first, a great many defendants ran away, and secondly, the Jury acquitted more than they *ever did* at any other Court." He lapsed once more, though, for in May, W. H. Chapman complained that revenue violations were increasing and extending into new areas of North Carolina. The revenuers were "zealous in the faithful performance of their duties" and "willing to do their whole duty to the Government," but they were hampered by the clemency policy. Acting Commissioner Wilson charged that "this mistaken leniency" was "undermining and corrupting the morals of a section that is otherwise as naturally law-abiding as any other." He warned that violations would spread "until the revenues of the Government are seriously endangered."[30]

The records of the North Carolina controversy end with Glenn's replacement by a Republican, but the commissioner of internal revenue was complaining of suspended sentences as a more general problem in 1898. He reported that revenuers worked well with other federal officers and it was not difficult to make arrests. However, "the ends of justice are frequently defeated" by suspended sentences that allow convicted violators to "escape punishment." He urged that "these crimes against the internal-revenue laws should be regarded as . . . serious offenses . . . and punished accordingly." Had the revenue bureau now repudiated Green B. Raum's use of suspended sentences to mollify opposition? Probably Raum would have agreed with his successor in this case, for the suspensions were out of the commissioner's control. Raum had always resisted local federal officials' initiatives in this matter. The lesson from the controversy was a reminder of how much freedom local subordinates had to interpret the law and develop their own methods of dealing with offenders. Even the attorney general seems to have been unable to rein in Glenn, who was absolutely convinced he was doing the right thing. The last word regarding suspended sentences is that whether in response to the revenue commissioner's criticisms or for other reasons, the number of suspensions declined during the McKinley administration, 1,861 between 1898 and 1901 compared with 2,851 between 1893 and 1897.[31]

Variation among different jurisdictions was also the rule in coping with the related problem of controlling the issue of warrants for the sake of making fees. Glenn had been legitimately concerned with the multiplication of cases brought against small retailers, and he believed that suspending their sentences was an effective and inexpensive way of dealing with them. He also hoped to check the efforts of marshals and commissioners to make fees off the trivial cases. Glenn found that newly appointed Democratic deputies were eager to go to work and make money and that among the 100 U.S. commissioners in his district, he found "some very corrupt and many incompetent." He went to work, first with a circular reminding them of their duties and that multiplication of small cases on dubious evidence was an abuse of their office. He also visited their hearings and gave private lectures about the need to reduce the number of trivial prosecutions. They did not respond, and he persuaded the federal circuit and district judges to fire all the commissioners and appoint only one in each county who was recommended by Glenn himself. This move reduced the number to forty-four, whom the district attorney described as "the very best men, irrespective of party," that he could persuade to take the position. He also drew up a set of rules, adopted by the federal courts, which carefully regulated the issue of warrants in revenue cases. They required that all warrants sworn by informers or deputy marshals had to be endorsed by the district attorney or by revenue officers who either had personal knowledge of the offense or had received the information themselves. This requirement could be suspended only in a sudden emergency, when the district attorney would review the warrant after it had been served. In any case, no fees would be paid until he had approved the warrant. He would not accept warrants sworn by one defendant against another, an effort to block the moonshiners' schemes to collect witness fees. In no case would a warrant be allowed for a single sale of untaxed liquor. Glenn, recognizing the source of the problem in the system of fee payment, had recommended that commissioners receive small salaries.[32]

The North Carolina rules were tough, but they did not cover all the possibilities deputies developed for increasing their income. Revenue deputies often cooperated with marshals and commissioners. Commissioner Thornley of South Carolina, whom investigators had praised earlier, seems to have relaxed his standards of evidence out of carelessness rather than corruption. By the late nineties he routinely filled out charges on information given by deputy marshals or informers, certified that the case was legitimate, and mailed the form to a deputy revenue collector for signing. This procedure rendered the required verification meaningless, but Thornley was merely conforming to the usual practice of all the commissioners in his district.[33]

Even with a revenuer nearby, verification could be suspiciously casual. A Kentucky commissioner heard 127 cases during the year 1894–95, with only 32 convictions. The same witnesses appeared over and over again, who had been "engaged in the business of working up frivolous cases for this commissioner for a number of years." The deputy revenue collector was supposed to check all of these warrants, but his office was next door to the commissioner's and he signed the forms without investigating the charges. The community surrounding the commissioner's office was "a hot-bed of professional witnesses." The collector defended his deputy, arguing that he was the "best deputy in the field" and could not possibly have colluded with the commissioner because the two men were of different political parties. The commissioner, though, resigned at the district judge's request. As part of his general effort to control the fee racket, the district judge explicitly prohibited deputy marshals from initiating revenue prosecutions. If there were proof that the marshals did begin the prosecution, the defendant would be discharged. Nevertheless, in 1898 deputies found ways around that limitation. The marshal himself noticed that in areas where deputies were local people, many revenue cases were "rather suspicious" because most of the witnesses were relatives of the deputy marshal or the commissioner.[34]

West Virginia Republicans charged that Democratic deputies were arresting McDowell County blacks on frivolous revenue charges. This was soon before the election of 1896, and the deputies boasted that they would jail 200 to 300 black Republicans before November. The witnesses were "low down colored men and women" testifying against "reliable industrious colored men" to earn the witness fees. Attorney General Harmon took the complaint seriously and ordered revocation of the local deputy marshal's commission. The Republican district attorney did battle with a different form of the witness racket in McDowell and Mercer County mining districts in 1897. "Professional witnesses" relied on the constant migration in the area to prevent officials from knowing "who, nor what kind of men" they were. They expected that their trumped-up cases would be absorbed in the general heavy load of the courts. The district attorney developed perjury cases against several of the informers and, when sufficient evidence for a charge was lacking, sometimes refused to allow witness fees. He also required that all revenue cases come to trial, forcing the witnesses to prepare depositions that could be checked for accuracy. The district attorney praised Deputy Marshal Elliott "to whose conscientious and intelligent zeal in the performance of his official duty, very much, of what has been accomplished is justly due." Honest officials had to battle not only the moonshiners but the dishonest and exploitative officers and citizens as well.[35]

The fee problem continued to generate abuses, even in Georgia where strict rules resembling Glenn's had been in effect for years. A Georgian called fee payment and reliance on informers for evidence "a relic of the dark ages." He joined the chorus, led by the attorney general himself, calling for salaries. In 1896 there was finally some progress: district attorneys, the marshals, and the office deputies who worked with them were placed on salary. Commissioners were salaried in 1897. This reform followed recommendations made by attorneys general since the 1870s. However, marshals' field deputies, scattered throughout each state and serving intermittently but most actively in revenue enforcement, remained under the fee system. Not until 1920, after the field deputies had been eliminated, were all members of the marshal's staff on salary.[36]

When the Republicans returned to office in 1897, they inherited the moonshining crisis and its problems of how to control resistance and check official misconduct. Their first actions did not bode well for the future of revenue enforcement, for they stripped several collectors of some of their deputies. At the same time the acting commissioner lectured the collectors, "There is no duty connected with the internal revenue service that is more important than assisting in the suppression of illicit distillation, and . . . it is expected that Collectors will promptly furnish Agents with the assistance of all the deputies that can be spared." Soon, though, Congress took a major step to relieve the crisis, providing for forty-four revenue agents, with twenty-one "assisting agents" in charge of divisions and on various special duties. This significant reinforcement undid the Republicans' original reduction of these spearheads of the war on moonshiners. The commissioner believed that increased forces discouraged moonshining. He implied that more revenuers prevented illicit distilling, which showed up in the decline of seizures and arrests first visible in 1899. Seizures reached a high of 2,400 in 1898 and dropped to 1,300 in 1901; arrests declined from 857 in 1898 to 585 in 1900, though they rose to 603 in 1901. Between 1901 and 1906 the revenuers almost bagged a moonshiner for every still they seized. Possibly because there were more revenuers, they were able to capture more fleeing blockaders. Moonshiners were still resisting the revenuers though, for total deaths between 1897 and 1901 (seven) exceeded those of the Cleveland administration (four), as did total wounded officers (twelve and six, respectively). Perhaps the increased revenue force was now encountering the most recalcitrant blockaders who had held out the longest.[37]

The number of revenue cases plummeted during 1896–97, the year of political transition, dropping to their lowest level since 1887 (from 7,078 to 3,992). This could also suggest reduced incidence of moonshining, as the commissioner believed was revealed by lower seizures and arrests. Cases rose slightly until 1901, when they slid steadily downward until 1909. Conviction rates, averaging 60 percent, were similar to those under the Democrats. In 1897–98, accounting for 59 percent of the nation's revenue cases, the prosecutors in moonshine districts secured convictions in 57 percent of their cases, compared with 43 percent in other areas. The battle was not over, and in many ways its contours were less under control of the revenue officials than in Raum's day.[38]

Commissioner Nathan Scott, a Kentuckian, recommended decreasing the liquor tax to reduce moonshining.[39] However, the needs of the Spanish-American War called for new taxes and increases of existing excises. Congress raised the beer tax but wisely left the whiskey tax at its 1894 level.

The conflict over alcohol was going beyond taxation by 1900. Local and county prohibition had expanded greatly, and soon states were going dry. By 1916 Alabama (which had passed prohibition in 1908, then repealed it and finally restored it), Arkansas, Georgia, Mississippi, North and South Carolina, Tennessee, Virginia, and West Virginia were dry. The moonshiner and his jug were more and more in demand in an expanding market of drinkers in dry areas.

Horace Kephart reported that moonshining was "turning from a little business to a big business." Blockaders were joined by bootleggers, who proved to be "one of the hard propositions to solve" by a limited number of revenuers who could not keep up with their movements. Prohibition encouraged moonshiners both where it was effectively enforced and where it was weakly supported. Effective prohibition drove up the price of illicit liquor, and moonshining grew most rapidly in areas that were truly dry. Congress, expecting that local officials would enforce prohibition, drastically cut appropriations for raiding activity. Where local officers did not do their job, the inadequate force of federal deputies could not control increased moonshining. The revenuers in the field were busy, seizing between 1911 and 1915 more stills than they had ever captured (3,382 in 1915 compared with the earlier record of 2,391 in 1898). There was also a greater disparity between seizures and arrests than during the nineties: revenuers were capturing the stills, but moonshiners were getting away. They also were shooting: three revenuers were killed in 1915, the highest number since 1893. In 1917 Congress dropped payment of rewards to informers and possemen, destroying many people's inducement for aiding revenuers. World War I led to tax increases to $8 per gallon, and later national wartime prohibition. Moonshining was in the Mason jar era, with illegal liquor selling for $4 per quart. The military camps established throughout the South, all of which were officially "dry," opened a new market for moonshine, and some of the bootleggers were soldiers themselves. To combat them, Commissioner Roper in 1918 organized a "flying squad" of revenuers, partly recruited from county sheriffs and their deputies, which grew to about 100 strong. "The Internal Revenue man [led] a busy life and was never busier" than just before national prohibition went into effect. The battle in the mountains was no longer simply over taxation and foreshadowed the difficulties of enforcing national prohibition in the twenties.[40]

At the turn of the century the revenuer represented a government whose reach into the lives of ordinary citizens slowly extended after the Civil War. Ironically, national prohibition represented both the triumph and the defeat of a bureaucratic state. The failure of national prohibition during the twenties revealed the inevitable problems arising when the state tried to regulate the lives of too many citizens, when its intrusion became moral instead of merely fiscal. Revenuers had always argued against state prohibition laws, partly because they were allied with the liquor industry, but also because they understood how prohibition encouraged moonshining. Even state prohibition threatened federal tax collection because of the increased demand for liquor in dry areas; drying up of counties and then states increasingly made the revenuers' job more difficult. The excise tax had always been at the outer margin of many Americans' tolerance for centralized government; prohibition was a giant step too far.

Before the lessons of prohibition had become clear, the revenuers had fought for and won their place in the mountains and would continue to do so after repeal of national prohibition. Their presence would always be resented and contested, and sometimes they filled their place honorably and bravely and at other times dishonestly and incompetently. Most revenuers were engaged in routine, sometimes dangerous police work. General Raum's campaign had occupied and held the ground; his successors had to keep up an army of occupation that usually dealt with individual moonshiner resistance but also was able to confront organized violence during the nineties. Revenuers were ensconced in the mountains to stay as the advance agents of a growing national state whose contours, however modest, were visible in 1900. Politicians of the Reconstruction era had hoped to build a powerful state around protection of citizens' rights. They failed, but a bureaucratic state was taking shape around the government's need for money and its ability to collect it in taxes.

Notes

. . . .

CHAPTER 1

1. M. L. White, "A History of the Life of Amos Owens, the Noted Blockader, of Cherry Mountain, N.C." (Shelby, N.C.: Cleveland Star Job Print, 1901). For more on Owens, see chap. 3 of this book.

2. This definition of the national state is in Stephen Skowronek, *Building a New American State: The Expansion of National Administrative Capacities, 1877–1920* (New York: Cambridge University Press, 1982), p. 20.

3. James G. Blaine, *Twenty Years of Congress, 1861–1881*, 2 vols. (Norwich, Conn.: Henry Bill, 1884, 1886) 2:160 (quotation); Harold M. Hyman, *A More Perfect Union: The Impact of the Civil War and Reconstruction on the Constitution* (New York: Knopf, 1973), esp. p. 548; Morton Keller, *Affairs of State: Public Life in Late Nineteenth-Century America* (Cambridge, Mass.: Harvard University Press, 1977), p. 2.

4. Keller, *Affairs of State*, p. 35; Wallace D. Farnham, " 'The Weakened Spring of Government': A Study in Nineteenth-Century American History," *American Historical Review* 68 (Apr. 1963): 662–80; Hyman, *More Perfect Union*; Skowronek, *New American State*. Since Homer Cummings and Carl McFarland's *Federal Justice: Chapters in the History of Justice and the Federal Executive* (New York: Macmillan, 1937), historians have not paid attention to federal law enforcement activities as part of the story of expanding national power. David R. Johnson, in a series of conference papers (e.g., "Police Powers of Federal Detectives: The Secret Service and Counterfeiting" [Social Science History Association Conference, Chicago, Oct. 1984], and "Island Communities, Federal Power: The Development of Federal Policing in Late 19th Century America" [Social Science History Association Conference, Washington, D.C., Oct. 1989]), and Stephen Cresswell, "Resistance and Enforcement: The U.S. Department of Justice, 1870–1893" (Ph.D. dissertation, University of Virginia, 1986), and "Signal Victories, Middling Successes and Stinging Failures: The Department of Justice and the Enforcement of Federal Criminal Laws in the Late 19th Century" (paper presented at the Social Science History Association Conference, Washington, D.C., Oct. 1989), are working in this area. Both Johnson and Cresswell have books in progress.

5. Historians have only recently devoted some attention to moonshiners. See William F. Holmes, "Moonshiners and Whitecaps in Alabama, 1893," *Alabama Review* 24 (Jan. 1981): 31–49, and "Moonshining and Collective Violence: Georgia, 1889–1895," *Journal of American History* 67 (Dec. 1980): 589–611; Edward Ayers, *Vengeance and Justice: Crime and Punishment in the 19th-Century American South* (New York: Oxford University Press, 1984), pp. 261–64; and Cresswell, "Resistance and Enforcement," chap. 4, on East Tennessee moonshining. Historians of taxation have had little to say about moonshining: Sidney Ratner, *Taxation and Democracy* (New

York: Macmillan, 1967), and Leonard D. White, *The Republican Era: A Study in Administrative History* (New York: Macmillan, 1958) are both almost silent about the internal revenue system. Tun Yuan Hu, *The Liquor Tax in the United States, 1791–1947: A History of the Internal Revenue Taxes Imposed on Distilled Spirits by the Federal Government* (New York: Graduate School of Business, Columbia University, 1950), is largely an economic analysis of excise taxation. Amy H. Mittleman, "The Politics of Alcohol Production: The Liquor Industry and the Federal Government, 1862–1900" (Ph.D. dissertation, Columbia University, 1986) analyzes the regulatory aspects of liquor taxation and industry lobbying and consolidation. It is the first discussion of this form of early industrial regulation but mentions moonshining in literally a single sentence. A detailed early history and analysis of the tax and its effects is in Frederic C. Howe, *Taxation and Taxes in the United States under the Internal Revenue System, 1791–1895* (New York: T. Y. Crowell, 1896), but Howe has only a few references to moonshiners, whom he does not consider very significant. David A. Wells, *The Theory and Practice of Taxation* (New York: D. Appleton, 1900), is an important work but does not discuss moonshining in depth. Popular writers have paid more attention to the confrontation of moonshiners and revenuers: see Jess Carr, *The Second Oldest Profession: An Informal History of Moonshining in America* (Englewood Cliffs, N.J.: Prentice-Hall, 1972), esp. chaps. 4–6; Joseph Earl Dabney, *Mountain Spirits: A Chronicle of Corn Whiskey from King James' Ulster Plantation to America's Appalachians and the Moonshine Life* (New York: Scribners, 1974), chap. 6; Esther Kellner, *Moonshine: Its History and Folklore* (Indianapolis: Bobbs-Merrill, 1971), chaps. 5–6; Gerald Carson, *The Social History of Bourbon: An Unhurried Account of Our Star-Spangled American Drink* (New York: Dodd, Mead, 1963), chap. 1.

6. In addition to Hyman, *More Perfect Union*, and Keller, *Affairs of State*, the discussion of the failure of Reconstruction in this chapter draws from the following studies: William Gillette, *Retreat from Reconstruction, 1869–1879* (Baton Rouge: Louisiana State University Press, 1979); Eric Foner, *Reconstruction: America's Unfinished Revolution, 1863–1877* (New York: Harper and Row, 1988); Robert Kaczorowski, *The Politics of Judicial Interpretation: The Federal Courts, Department of Justice and Civil Rights, 1866–1876* (New York: Oceana, 1985); and George C. Rable, *But There Was No Peace: The Role of Violence in the Politics of Reconstruction* (Athens: University of Georgia Press, 1984).

7. *CG*, 41st Cong., 3d sess. (1871), pt. 1, p. 574 (Wilson).

8. Hyman, *More Perfect Union*, 477. Comparisons to Ireland include Blaine, *Twenty Years of Congress*, 2:486–88; Rep. D. W. Vorhees (D-Ind.), *CG*, 41st Cong., 3d sess. (1871), appendix, p. 127; Rep. J. W. Storm (D-Pa.), *CG*, 42d Cong., 1st sess. (1871), appendix, p. 88; Rep. E. H. Roberts (R-N.Y.), ibid., p. 414; Sen. J. W.

Johnson (D-Va.), ibid., appendix, pp. 214–15; Sen. C. W. Jones (D-Fla.), *CR*, 46th Cong., 1st sess. (1879), p. 731. The attack on Republicans as the state is from Rep. J. S. Davis (D-N.C.), *CR*, 46th Cong., 1st sess. (1879), p. 793.

9. Skowronek, *New American State*, p. 30. Max Weber defined a bureaucracy as an "administrative apparatus with imperatives of its own": see Reinhard Bendix, *Nation Building and Citizenship: Studies of Our Changing Social Order* (New York: Vintage, 1969), p. 34.

10. For a similar discussion of the dilemma of force and restraint, see Bendix, *Nation Building and Citizenship*, pp. 25–26.

11. Injunctions to prosecute vigorously and impartially are found throughout the attorney general's letters, e.g., Amos Akerman to J. A. Minnis, Dist. Atty., Ala., Nov. 11, 1871, I, bk. C, p. 23; Benjamin Brewster to D. Saunders, Asst. Dist. Atty., S.C., Mar. 29, 1882, I, bk. L, p. 427. For enforcement problems, see Rable, *But There Was No Peace*; Foner, *Reconstruction*, chap. 9; Gillette, *Retreat*, chap. 2; Kaczorowski, *Politics*, chaps. 4–5; James E. Sefton, *The United States Army and Reconstruction, 1865–1877* (Baton Rouge: Louisiana State University Press, 1967).

12. Skowronek, *New American State*, pp. 39–46; William E. Nelson, *The Roots of American Bureaucracy, 1830–1900* (Cambridge, Mass.: Harvard University Press, 1982), p. 2. The bureau did not fit Nelson's remaining criteria. Although its employees were salaried, they did not make a career of government service nor enforce standards set by professional groups instead of the general public. Long service or formal education was not necessarily the route to promotion within an agency still dominated by the spoils system. One exception was the revenue agents, who became genuine professionals with long careers.

CHAPTER 2

1. Henry D. Shapiro, *Appalachia on Our Mind: The Southern Mountains and Mountaineers in the American Consciousness, 1870–1920* (Chapel Hill: University of North Carolina Press, 1978), pp. 104–5; E. J. Hobsbawm, *Primitive Rebels: Studies in Archaic Forms of Social Movement in the 19th and 20th Centuries* (New York: W. W. Norton, 1959), chaps. 1–2; for application of Hobsbawm's and other social scientists' theories to moonshiner resistance, see William F. Holmes, "Moonshining and Collective Violence: Georgia, 1889–1905," *Journal of American History* 67 (Dec. 1980), 589–611. Amos Akerman to E. Pierrepont, Atty. Gen., Feb. 22, 1876, SC, Ga.

2. Internal revenue records report moonshining in Utah, Indiana, Illinois, Ohio, Pennsylvania, Florida, Texas, New Hampshire, and the cities of Chicago, New Orleans, Brooklyn, Troy, and Poughkeepsie, New York.

3. *Annual Report, Commissioner of Internal Revenue*, 1891, *HED* 4, 52d Cong., 1st sess., pp. 44–46 (table).

4. Two of the many portraits of mountaineers as archaic survivors are William G. Frost, "Our Contemporary Ancestors in the Southern Mountains," *Atlantic Monthly* 83 (Mar. 1899): 311–19; and Rollin L. Hartt, "The Mountaineers: Our Own Lost Tribes," *Century Magazine* 95 (Jan. 1918): 395–404. For a critique of the stereotype and description of changing conditions, see Ronald D. Eller, *Miners, Millhands, and Mountaineers: The Industrialization of the Appalachian South, 1880–1930* (Knoxville: University of Tennessee Press, 1982). For social change as it affected politics, see Gordon B. McKinney, *Southern Mountain Republicans, 1865–1900: Politics and the Appalachian Community* (Chapel Hill: University of North Carolina Press, 1978). For changes in the Tug Valley along the Kentucky–West Virginia border (seat of the Hatfield-McCoy feud) see Altina L. Waller, *Feud: Hatfields, McCoys, and Social Change in Appalachia, 1860–1900* (Chapel Hill: University of North Carolina Press, 1988), chap. 2. Examples of the more complex view of preindustrial Appalachia include Durwood Dunn, *Cades Cove: The Life and Death of a Southern Appalachian Community, 1818–1937* (Knoxville: University of Tennessee Press, 1988), chaps. 2–3; and Gordon B. McKinney, "Preindustrial Jackson County and Economic Development in Jackson County [North Carolina]"; David Hsuing, "The Social World of Upper East Tennessee, 1780–1835," all papers delivered at the Appalachian Studies Conference, West Virginia University, Mar. 1989; and John C. Inscoe, *Mountain Masters, Slavery, and the Sectional Crisis in Western North Carolina* (Knoxville: University of Tennessee Press, 1989).

5. Ronald Eller is careful to note the unevenness of change and persistence of old ways in some areas (pp. 235–36), as do Jacquelyn D. Hall, James Leloudis, Robert Korstad, Mary Murphy, Lu Ann Jones, and Christopher B. Daly in *Like a Family: The Making of a Southern Cotton Mill World* (Chapel Hill: University of North Carolina Press, 1987), p. 10. For the two West Virginia counties, see Barbara Rasmussen, "Monroe County, W.Va.: Life and Work Where There Is No Coal" (Paper delivered at the Appalachian Studies Conference, West Virginia University, Mar. 1989).

6. Dunn, *Cades Cove*, pp. 184–85, 207, 225; Semple quoted in Mary Beth Pudup, "The Limits of Subsistence: Agriculture and Industry in Central Appalachia" (Paper delivered at the Appalachian Studies Conference, West Virginia University, Mar. 1989), p. 18.

7. Eller, *Miners, Millhands, and Mountaineers*, pp. 235–37; Hall et al., *Like a Family*, chap. 3.

8. Dunn, *Cades Cove*, pp. 183–84, chap. 5; Waller, *Feud*, p. 40.

9. Data on Tallulah and Whitewater are from U.S. Census, 1880, Rabun County, Ga., and Oconee County, S.C., microfilm rolls T9-162, and T9-1236. See also

Watson and Adams' New Topographical, Township and Railroad Map of South Carolina (New York, 1888) and *Watson and Adams' Topographical, County and Railroad Map of Georgia* (New York, 1890), Map Room, New York Public Library; and Moses King, ed., *King's Handbook of the United States* (Buffalo: Moses King, 1891), p. 470. For the existence of frame houses in the mountains, see Eller, *Miners, Millhands, and Mountaineers*, pp. 26–27; and Dunn, *Cades Cove*, pp. 38–40. Illiteracy as used here combines the proportion of those unable to write and those unable to both read and write (the enumerator did not record the information for Whitewater). For general information on Rabun County, including population growth rates, see Andrew Jackson Ritchie, *Sketches of Rabun County History* (Foote and Davies, [1948]), pp. 282–94, 305, 425.

10. Eller, *Miners, Millhands, and Mountaineers*, pp. 6–22. Sumac was used in tanning leather; ginseng was exported to China, where it was valued as an aphrodisiac. For hog raising, see "Testimony Before the Senate Special Committee to Investigate the Administration of the Collection of Internal Revenue in the Sixth District of North Carolina," *Senate Miscellaneous Documents* 116, 47th Cong., 1st sess. (1882), testimony of W. M. Walker, Deputy Collector of Internal Revenue, p. 161, and A. C. Avery, attorney, pp. 451–52.

11. The general discussion of settlement patterns is from Eller, *Miners, Millhands, and Mountaineers*, chap. 1; and Horace Kephart, *Our Southern Highlanders* (New York: Outing, 1913), chap. 2. Distances are from Samuel H. Thompson, *The Highlanders of the South* (New York: Eaton and Mains, 1910), pp. 52–53.

12. Eller, *Miners, Millhands, and Mountaineers*, pp. 16, 33–38; Wilbur G. Zeigler and Ben Grosscup, *The Heart of the Alleghenies; or, Western North Carolina . . .* (Raleigh: A. Williams, 1883), p. 90 (Nantahala).

13. On family patterns generally, Eller, *Miners, Millhands, and Mountaineers*, pp. 28–32; for a discussion of "family" as larger than kin, see Waller, *Feud*, pp. 77–85. Tallulah and Whitewater data are from U.S. Manuscript Census, 1880 and 1900, Rabun County and Oconee County. All percentage calculations are my own. I assume that people with the same surname are related, probably not always true. Many of the names in both Tallulah and Whitewater are very common throughout the entire border region of Georgia and the Carolinas. Probably, though, those living near each other regarded themselves as "family" even if distantly related. Of course, sharing a name is only a partial indicator of kinship, as it does not account for collateral relatives living in the community. Occasionally these connections can be made from the census, as when the old couple Hugh and Lucinda Mahaffey lived with their granddaughter Alma Shepherd, or nine year old Lillie Whitmire, a cousin, lived with Joseph and Alice Holden.

14. Forty-four of 207 Tallulah families had 7 or more children; in Whitewater, 28

of 149 (respectively, 21 percent and 19 percent). Family size information for 1880 is unreliable because the census taker recorded only the children at home at the time; in 1900 he reported the full number of children, including those not at home. He also indicated those who died; over 1 in 4 [28 percent] Whitewater families had experienced the death of 1 or more children. Deceased children are left out of my calculation of family sizes, except in the comparison to Cades Cove (Dunn, *Cades Cove*, pp. 79, 182).

15. Data from census manuscripts as cited above. In mountainous Pike County, Kentucky, in 1900, over two-thirds of the households had neighbors with the same surname. One-fifth of the households had three such neighbors; another fifth had four same-surname neighbors (Thomas A. Arcury and Julia D. Porter, "Households and Families in Eastern Kentucky in 1900," in *The Many Faces of Appalachia: Exploring a Region's Diversity*, ed. Sam Gray [Boone, N.C.: Appalachian Consortium Press, 1985], pp. 54–55).

16. For a detailed study of kin networks in the Durham–Chapel Hill area of North Carolina, well east of the mountains, see Robert C. Kenzer, *Kinship and Neighborhood in a Southern Community: Orange County, North Carolina, 1849–1881* (Knoxville: University of Tennessee Press, 1987). For kinship networks similar to those of the mountains, but in the urban northeast among European immigrants, see Judith E. Smith, *Family Connections: A History of Italian and Jewish Immigrant Lives in Providence, Rhode Island, 1900–1940* (Albany: State University of New York Press, 1985).

17. Dunn, *Cades Cove*, p. 179; Eller, *Miners, Millhands, and Mountaineers*, pp. 28–32.

18. Eller, *Miners, Millhands, and Mountaineers*, pp. 11–12; Inscoe, *Mountain Masters*.

19. Dunn, *Cades Cove*, chap. 5; Phillip S. Paludan, *Victims: A True Story of the Civil War* (Knoxville: University of Tennessee Press, 1981), pp. 7–8; 24 (quotation); chaps. 2–5.

20. Dunn, *Cades Cove*, pp. 196–98; and see chap. 3 of this study for some of the "kings."

21. Eller, *Miners, Millhands, and Mountaineers*, p. 236; Hall et al., *Like a Family*, p. 140.

22. John Gaventa, *Power and Powerlessness: Quiescence and Rebellion in an Appalachian Valley* (Urbana: University of Illinois Press, 1980), pp. 53–55. An example of resistance to surveyors is described by Dean Herrin, "Traditionalism and Industrialization" (Paper delivered at the Social Science History Association Conference, Washington, D.C., Oct. 1989).

23. Eller, *Miners, Millhands, and Mountaineers*, pp. 88–89; Waller, *Feud*, chap. 2.

24. Eller, *Miners, Millhands, and Mountaineers*, pp. 92–127.

25. Ibid., chaps. 4–6; Dean Herrin, "Impact of the Company Town on Traditional Life," in *The Impact of Institutions in Appalachia*, ed. Jim Lloyd and Anne G. Campbell (Boone, N.C.: Appalachian Consortium Press, 1986), pp. 166–74.

26. Hall et al., *Like a Family*, pp. 36–39, chaps. 2–3; I. A. Newby, *Plain Folk in the New South: Social Change and Cultural Persistence, 1880–1915* (Baton Rouge: Louisiana State University Press, 1989), chaps. 8, 10–13.

27. Cratis D. Williams, "The Southern Mountaineer in Fact and Fiction" (Ph.D. dissertation, New York University, 1961), pp. 137, 145, 163; Dunn, *Cades Cove*, p. 69; northern Georgia data from U.S. Census Office, *Report on the Productions of Agriculture as Returned at the Tenth Census (June 1, 1880)* (Washington, D.C.: Government Printing Office, 1883), pp. 40–44; U.S. Census Office, *Report on the Statistics of Agriculture in the United States at the Eleventh Census: 1890* (Washington, D.C.: Government Printing Office, 1895), pp. 130–32; U.S. Census Office, *Twelfth Census of the United States, Taken in the Year 1900 . . . : Agriculture, Part I* (Washington, D.C.: U.S. Census Office, 1902), pp. 68–71; Pike and Logan from Waller, *Feud*, pp. 37–38, 204.

28. Waller, *Feud*, pp. 37–38, 204; Whitewater and Tallulah economic information from 1880 and 1900 census, percentage calculations my own; northern Georgia tenantry data from Agricultural Census, 1880–1900, cited in note 27 above, percentage calculations my own; Dunn, *Cades Cove*, p. 180; James L. Allen, "Mountain Passes of the Cumberland," *Harper's New Monthly Magazine* 81 (Sept. 1890): 575–76.

29. Edward King, "The Great South: Among the Mountains of Western North Carolina," *Scribner's Monthly* 7 (Mar. 1874): 536–37; Frost, "Ancestors," p. 312; James L. Allen, "Through Cumberland Gap on Horseback," *Harper's New Monthly Magazine* 73 (June 1886): 58; Charles D. Warner, "Comments on Kentucky," *Harper's New Monthly Magazine* 78 (Jan. 1889): 269 (my italics); Waller, *Feud*, pp. 43–44 (an example of increasing land values).

30. Young E. Allison, "Moonshine Men," *Southern Bivouac* 5 (Feb. 1887): 531–32; *Atlanta Constitution*, May 19, 1880 (Union County), Aug. 31, 1890, and Feb. 12, 1893 (hogs and turkeys); *Morganton Star*, Sept. 18, 1885 (Burke); M. L. White, "A History of the Life of Amos Owens, the Noted Blockader, of Cherry Mountain, N.C." (Shelby, N.C.: Cleveland Star Job Print, 1901), p. 10.

31. William L. Downward, *Dictionary of the History of the American Brewing and Distilling Industry* (Westport, Conn.: Greenwood, 1980), p. xxi; Henry M. Wiltse, *The Moonshiners* (Chattanooga, Tenn.: Times Publishing Co., 1895), pp. 208–9.

32. "Testimony . . . Revenue in the Sixth District of N.C.," testimony of A. H. Brooks, Revenue Agent, p. 136; George Wesley Atkinson, *After the Moonshiners, by*

One of the Raiders (Wheeling, W.Va.: Frew and Campbell, 1881), pp. 24, 14–15; Samuel G. Blythe, "Raiding Moonshiners," *Munsey's Magazine* 25 (June 1901): 420.

33. Dunn, *Cades Cove*, p. 233.

34. Daniel Tompkins to Hal, Aug. 12, 1883, Tompkins Papers, photocopy courtesy Duke University Library; Francis Lynde, "The Moonshiners of Fact," *Lippincott's Magazine* 57 (Jan. 1896): 70; Atkinson, *After the Moonshiners*, p. 15; Kephart, *Highlanders*, p. 121 (all on taxes); *Atlanta Constitution*, Aug. 10, 1896; Rebecca Harding Davis, "By-Paths in the Mountains, III," *Harper's New Monthly Magazine* 61 (Sept. 1880), 535. Since dialect has been quoted here for the first time, a comment on its use in this book is appropriate. Nineteenth-century writers used dialect to heighten the impression of mountaineers' quaintness and isolation. Some of the dialect may be accurate transcription; other quotations are what journalists thought mountaineers should sound like. Since I am neither a native of the mountain South nor an expert in American speech pattern, my safest course is simply to record all the spellings as they appeared in the original source.

35. *Atlanta Constitution*, Dec. 18, 1896; on social status of moonshiners generally, see Williams, "Mountaineer in Fact," p. 113, drawing from a study conducted during the prohibition era. Though prohibition made moonshine a bigger business, I think that many nineteenth-century moonshiners could also be described as substantial citizens. For Crawford, see Records of the U.S. District Court, Northern Georgia, Record Group 21, National Archives, Atlanta Branch, box 94, case no. 4496 (March Term 1881), and no. 38 in the 1880 census; Cantrell was in box 208, case no. 8755 (March Term 1890) and no. 60 in the 1900 census; Tilley, box 97, case no. 4588 (March Term 1881), and no. 57 in the 1880 census. For Blalock information, see District Court Records, box 98, case no. 4650 (March Term 1881); Ritchie, *Sketches of Rabun Co.*, p. 300, and 1900 census (where he is household number one). The Blalock family had a small settlement named after them in northwestern Rabun County.

36. Kephart, *Highlanders*, pp. 187–89; Gaventa, *Power and Powerlessness*, p. 56; Eller, *Miners, Millhands, and Mountaineers*, pp. 101, 186–87, 234–35; Hall et al., *Like a Family*, pp. 164–65, 132; McKinney, *Southern Mountain Republicans*, p. 129. For discussion of impact of prohibition, see chaps. 7 and 8 of this book.

37. Kephart, *Highlanders*, p. 140; T. N. Cooper, Coll., N.C., to Raum, Feb. 15, 1883, LR, box 894 (portable stills).

38. *New York Times*, Sept. 29, 1882 (Folias); Jan. 7, 1895 (underwater); O. H. Blocken, Rev. Agt., to Raum, Aug. 4, 1880, LR, box 911 (blacksmith); *New York Times*, Apr. 14, 1895 (minister).

39. Kephart, *Highlanders*, pp. 128, 132–36; Esther Kellner, *Moonshine: Its History and Folklore* (Indianapolis: Bobbs-Merrill, 1971), pp. 56–60. The methods de-

scribed here are the simplest and most traditional. Refinements introduced in the twentieth century included a "thump keg" or doubler located between the still and worm through which the hot vapor passed with great buildup of heat, amounting to a second distillation. This saved the step of doubling in the original still. Another timesaving step was use of sugar instead of sprouted corn to begin fermentation. Real old-timers scoffed at such corner cutting, which did not produce true corn juice. For details on newer methods, see Jess Carr, *The Second Oldest Profession: An Informal History of Moonshining in America* (Englewood Cliffs, N.J.: Prentice-Hall, 1972), pp. 98–104.

40. J. Olney, Rev. Agt., to Raum, May 14, 1877, LR, box 910; *New York Times*, May 17, 1888; Lynde, "Moonshiners of Fact," pp. 72–73; A. H. Guernsey, "Illicit Distillation of Liquors," *Harper's Weekly* 11 (Dec. 7, 1867): 773 (taste); Allison, "Moonshine Men," p. 534 (adulteration); Donald A. Baine, "Among The Moonshiners," *Dixie* 1 (Aug. 1885): 12–13 (effects). The arrival of state prohibition encouraged more widespread adulteration of moonshine (Kephart, *Highlanders*, pp. 188–89).

41. Kephart, *Highlanders*, p. 138 (quotation); Charles D. Warner, "On Horseback," *Atlantic Monthly* 56 (July–Oct. 1885): 99 (quotation); Lynde, "Moonshiners of Fact," p. 73. On condemnation of drinking, see Dunn, *Cades Cove*, pp. 193–94, 233. For young men, see Waller, *Feud*, pp. 94–97; on violent effects of whiskey drinking, see Williams, "Mountaineer in Fact," pp. 104, 352–56; William L. Montell, *Killings: Folk Justice in the Upper South* (Lexington: University Press of Kentucky, 1986), p. 158; *Morganton Star*, June 26, 1885; May 29, 1885; Sept. 25, 1885; Dahlonega *Mountain Signal*, Feb. 13, 1873; Aug. 29, 1874; Apr. 18, 1879; Warner, "Comments on Kentucky."

42. John C. Campbell, *The Southern Highlander and His Homeland* (New York: Russell Sage Foundation, 1921), p. 109; Margaret W. Morley, *The Carolina Mountains* (Boston: Houghton Mifflin, 1913), p. 216 (sales methods); Guernsey, "Illicit Distillation," p. 773 (sledges); Zeigler and Grosscup, *Heart of the Alleghenies*, pp. 362–64.

43. Kephart, *Highlanders*, p. 130 (markets); Rebecca Harding Davis, "By-Paths," p. 535; Morley, *Carolina Mountains*, p. 213 (vinegar); map drawn by Deputy Collector W. W. Colquitt, in W. H. Chapman, Rev. Agt., to Commissioner, Dec. 7, 1889, MLR, box 914.

44. J. W. Corsbie, Dep. Coll., N.C., in J. Wagner, Rev. Agt., to Raum, May 18, 1877, "Enforcement of Internal Revenue Laws: . . . Report of the Commissioner of Internal Revenue . . . to Explain the Necessity For Employment of Armed Men . . . ," *HED* 62, 46th Cong. 2d sess. (1880), p. 93 (describing a family settlement); Lieut. J. M. McDougall, 7th Cav., to Asst. Adj. Gen., Dept. South, Feb. 6, 1875,

831 AGO '75 (Ga. list); Lieut. J. Anderson, 18th Inf., to Cmdg. Officer, Feb. 21, Mar. 5, 1877, 1343, 1394 AGO '77 (two S.C. lists); J. F. Buckner, Coll., Ky., to Raum, Jan. 22, 1879, "Enforcement of Internal Revenue Laws," p. 78 (Ky. list); J. J. Mott, Coll., N.C., to Raum, Dec. 10, 1877, ibid., p. 102 (N.C. list); Isaac Stapleton, *Moonshiners in Arkansas* (Independence, Mo.: Zion's Printing and Publishing Co., 1948), p. 45 (Ramseys); Wiltse, *Moonshiners*, p. 121 (ten); Gerald Carson, *The Social History of Bourbon: An Unhurried Account of Our Star-Spangled American Drink* (New York: Dodd, Mead, 1963), pp. 110–11 (Gibsons).

45. Lt. W. S. Patten, 18th Inf., to Post Adj., June 21, 1876, 3629 AGO '76; D. J. Lewis, Dep. Marshal, to J. L. Lewis, Marshal, Feb. 2, 1879, in J. L. Lewis to Atty. Gen., Feb. 5, 1879, SC Va.; J. L. Black, Dep. Coll., S.C., to D. F. Bradley, Coll., Nov. 20, 1885, in Bradley to Commissioner, Dec. 1, 1885, LR, box 889; Dahlonega *Mountain Signal*, Aug. 14, 1875 (partners); *Atlanta Constitution*, Dec. 13, 1891; *Charlotte Observer*, Nov. 30, 1902 (black moonshiners); M. L. White, "Amos Owens," p. 10 (preacher); W. H. Brawley, Dist. Judge, S.C., to Atty. Gen., Apr. 3, 1895, DJ 1661 '94, box 74 (selling).

46. J. A. George, Dep. Coll., Ga., to Raum, Apr. 28, 1877, LR, box 897 (ignorance and warnings); J. A. Cooper, Coll., Tenn., to Raum, July 6, 1877, "Enforcement of Internal Revenue Laws," p. 111 (unreliable information); W. O. H. Shepard, Dep. Coll., to A. Clark, Coll., Ga., Apr. 9, 1880, in Clark to Raum, Apr. 15, 1880, LR, box 891 (cursing) (original italics); H. H. Jillson, Dep. Coll., to E. M. Brayton, Coll., S.C., Aug. 23, 1877, "Enforcement of Internal Revenue Laws," p. 183 (shout); Wiltse, *Moonshiners*, pp. 120–21 (fists); Olive D. Campbell Diary, Nov. 20, 1908, p. 37, typescript, Southern Historical Collection, University of North Carolina (wife).

47. Atkinson, *After the Moonshiners*, pp. 158–59 (Van Meter).

48. *New York Times*, Oct. 15, 1891 (McClure); *Cincinnati Enquirer*, n.d., quoted in *Internal Revenue Record and Customs Journal*, June 4, 1894, p. 175 (Miller); Wiltse, *Moonshiners*, pp. 65–68; Joseph E. Dabney, *Mountain Spirits: A Chronicle of Corn Whiskey from King James' Ulster Plantation to America's Appalachians and the Moonshine Life* (New York: Scribners, 1974), pp. 137–39 (Betsy), 128–29 (Henderson); *New York Times*, Mar. 18, 1893 (Turner); Waller, *Feud*, p. 241 (Phillips); Jasper, Ga., *Piedmont Republican*, Sept. 19, 1891, copied from *Arkansaw Traveler* (*sic*) (Smith; courtesy of Robert S. Davis, Jr.).

49. McKinney, *Southern Mountain Republicans*, p. 126.

50. Ibid., chap. 7, on modernization as increasing the level of violence in the mountains.

CHAPTER 3

1. William M. Robinson, "Prohibition in the Confederacy," *American Historical Review* 37 (Oct. 1931): 50–58; Henry D. Scomp, *King Alcohol in the Realm of King Cotton: A History of the Liquor Traffic and of the Temperance Movement in Georgia from 1733 to 1887* ([Atlanta]: Blakeley, 1888), p. 668; *New York Times*, Apr. 14, 1895 (Confederacy); *Atlanta Constitution*, May 19, 1880 (ignorance).

2. *Atlanta Constitution*, Jan. 13, 1895 (attitude); George Wesley Atkinson, *After the Moonshiners, by One of the Raiders* (Wheeling, W.Va.: Frew and Campbell, 1881), pp. 13–14 (Republic); *Atlanta Constitution*, May 19, 1880 (Stephens); Wilbur Zeigler and Ben Grosscup, *In the Heart of the Alleghenies; or, Western North Carolina . . .* (Raleigh: A. Williams and Co., [1883]), p. 142; *New York Tribune*, Aug. 20, 1878 (Akerman); Raleigh *Daily Standard*, Feb. 3, 1870 (representation); *Morganton Star* (N.C.), Oct. 16, 1885 (spies).

3. *Atlanta Constitution*, May 11, 1880 (Fannin Co.); Dahlonega *Mountain Signal*, Mar. 3, 1876 (White Co.). For discussions of the wartime conflicts in two areas that later contained enclaves of moonshiners, see Durwood Dunn, *Cades Cove: The Life and Death of a Southern Appalachian Community, 1818–1937* (Knoxville: University of Tennessee Press, 1988), on part of Blount County, Tennessee; and Phillip S. Paludan, *Victims: A True Story of the Civil War* (Knoxville: University of Tennessee Press, 1981), on part of Madison County, North Carolina.

4. Charleston *News and Courier*, Jan. 27, 1877, in D. T. Corbin, U.S. Senator, to C. Devens, Atty. Gen., Dec. 3, 1877, SC S.C. (Yankee oppression); *New York Times*, Apr. 14, 1880 (Hampton); July 15, 1878 (Redmond); R. M. Wallace, Dep. Coll., S.C., to C. Delano, Commissioner, Jan. 15, 1870, 79S AGO '70 (with 112 I) (raid); S. A. Darnell, Asst. Dist. Atty., to C. Devens, Atty. Gen., July 29, 1880, SC Ga.; Atkinson, *After the Moonshiners*, p. 14 (rebellion).

5. "Testimony Before the Senate Special Committee to Investigate the Administration of the Collection of Internal Revenue in the Sixth District of North Carolina," *Senate Miscellaneous Documents* 116, 47th Cong., 1st sess. (1882), testimony of Green B. Raum, p. 311; Paul E. Isaac, *Prohibition and Politics: Turbulent Decades in Tennessee, 1885–1920* (Knoxville: University of Tennessee Press, 1965), pp. 55–56; "Enforcement of Internal Revenue Laws: . . . Report of the Commissioner of Internal Revenue . . . to Explain the Necessity for Employment of Armed Men . . . ," *HED* 62, 46th Cong., 2d sess. (1880), pp. 111–55 (Tenn. counties); *Atlanta Constitution*, May 15, 1880; "Testimony . . . Revenue in the Sixth District of N.C.," testimony of M. G. Campbell, Dep. Coll., p. 118, and Tyre Glenn, Dep. Coll., p. 125 (Wilkes and Burke); L. C. Northrop, Dist. Atty., to C. Devens, Atty. Gen., Jan. 5, 1878, SC S.C. (strange); Lee Meriweather, *The Tramp at Home* (New York:

Harper, 1889), p. 95; Francis Lynde, "The Moonshiners of Fact," *Lippincott's Magazine* 57 (Jan. 1896), 69; A. H. Pettibone, Asst. Dist. Atty., Tenn., to Raum, Dec. 24, 1879, "Enforcement of Internal Revenue Laws," p. 118 (loyalists).

6. Olive H. Shadgett, *The Republican Party in Georgia: From Reconstruction through 1900* (Athens: University of Georgia Press, 1964), pp. 41, 339–41; *Atlanta Constitution*, Dec. 31, 1881; "Speech of Hon. Joseph E. Brown, of Georgia, delivered in the Senate of the United States . . . June 26, 1884," Pamphlet, Georgia Collection, University of Georgia, p. 5; Rep. C. H. Porter (R-Va.), *CG*, 42d Cong., 1st sess. (1871), appendix, p. 317; Rep. W. P. Price (D-Ga.), ibid., pt. 1, p. 440; Rep. H. Persons (D-Ga.), *CR*, 46th Cong., 2d sess. (1880), p. 2882 (alienation); Stephen Cresswell, "Resistance and Enforcement: The U.S. Department of Justice, 1870–1893" (Ph.D. dissertation, University of Virginia, 1986), p. 202 (Houk).

7. Daniel J. Whitener, *Prohibition in North Carolina, 1715–1945*, James Sprunt Studies in History and Political Science (Chapel Hill: University of North Carolina Press, 1946), 27 (no. 1): 52, 79; Raleigh *Daily Standard*, Apr. 22, 1870; O. H. Dockery to Carl Schurz, Nov. 22, 1877, in James A. Padgett, ed., "Reconstruction Letters from North Carolina," *North Carolina Historical Review* 19 (July 1942): 299; "Testimony . . . Revenue in the Sixth District of N.C.," testimony of M. G. Campbell, p. 117 (Mr. Bryan).

8. *New York Tribune*, June 20, 1882; Gordon B. McKinney, *Southern Mountain Republicans 1865–1900: Politics and the Appalachian Community* (Chapel Hill: University of North Carolina Press, 1978), pp. 59, 71, 103–4 (Va.), 122, 192 (W.Va.), 48–49, 63, 96–98, 159 (N.C.); Shadgett, *Republican Party in Georgia*, esp. chap. 7; Mason to J. B. Eaves, Coll., N.C., July 3, 1889; to A. H. Brooks, Rev. Agt., Nov. 29, 1889, Mason Papers, West Virginia Collection, West Virginia University, series II, box 2; to L. C. Houck and A. A. Taylor, May 23, 1890, ibid.; to D. N. Comingore, Coll., Ky., Mar. 12, 1892, ibid., box 4; to B. F. Morton, Dec. 9, 1889, ibid., box 2. Mason's personal correspondence, five boxes of letterbooks, is an interesting revelation of how much time and effort management of the patronage network consumed. He tried to stay out of many fights but did get involved in efforts to settle others, mostly in his home state of West Virginia.

9. R. P. Dick, Dist. Judge, to G. Williams, Atty. Gen., Feb. 5, 1874, SC N.C.; Maj. C. H. Morgan, 4th Artillery, Report, June 9, 1871, 1723 AGO '71; *New York Times*, July 21, 1878; *Atlanta Constitution*, Mar. 26, 1879; May 13, 1880; May 19, 1880 (Fitzsimmons); G. B. Raum quotation from "Enforcement of Internal Revenue Laws," p. 29.

10. Horace Kephart, *Our Southern Highlanders* (New York: Outing, 1913), p. 127; S. Ball, Asst. Dist. Atty., N.C., to C. Devens, Atty. Gen., Feb. 23, 1878, SC N.C. (Snider); D. B. Booth, Dep. Coll., Ala., to Raum, July 5, 1878, LR, box 887

(ringleaders); G. W. Emery, Supervisor of Int. Rev., Tenn., to C. Delano, Commissioner, Apr. 30, 1870, MLR, box 909; Lieut. W. A. Miller, 18th Inf., to Post Adj., Apr. 26, 1877, 2494 AGO '77 (troops); *Atlanta Constitution*, Dec. 23, 1894 (Tankersley); J. A. George, Dep. Coll., Ga., to H. C. Rogers, Actg. Commissioner, Apr. 28, May 15, 1877, LR, box 897 (possemen); J. H. Duval, Coll., W.Va., to Raum, Mar. 16, 1880, LR, box 895 (mailman); Capt. J. Stewart, 18th Inf., to HQ, Dept. South, July 9, 1875, 3658 AGO '75 (horses).

11. W. S. Ball, Asst. Dist. Atty., to C. Devens, Atty. Gen., Feb. 23, 1878, SC N.C. (Snider); *New York Tribune*, July 9, 1899; Paludan, *Victims* (Sheltons); *Greenville Daily News*, June 30, 1935, reprinting article from May 30, 1894, photocopy courtesy Greenville County Library; V. S. Lusk, Dist. Atty., to Devens, Mar. 1, 1878, SC N.C. (Dark Corner); Dunn, *Cades Cove*, pp. 196–98.

12. *Knoxville Daily Chronicle*, Aug. 11, 1878, in J. A. Clark, Coll., to Raum, Aug. 11, 1878, LR, box 891; S. W. Melton, Dist. Atty., S.C., to Raum, Nov. 23, 1881, LR, box 900 (Amerine).

13. J. H. Rogers, Dist. Judge, to Atty. Gen., Nov. 8, 1898, DJ 12956 '97, box 987.

14. *New York Times*, July 15, 1878; *Morganton Star*, Mar. 12, 1886 (The *Star* says that Duckworth was killed in 1879, but the other sources have Redmond already in South Carolina by that year).

15. L. C. Carpenter, Coll., S.C., to Raum, Jan. 17, 22, 1877, "Enforcement of Internal Revenue Laws," pp. 175–77 (Barton).

16. E. M. Brayton, Coll., S.C., to Raum, Apr. 20, 1878, "Enforcment of Internal Revenue Laws," pp. 189–90; Raum to J. Sherman, Secy. of Treasury, July 18, 1878, R. B. Hayes Papers, photocopy courtesy Hayes Presidential Center, Fremont, Ohio (both on jailbreak); E. H. Hoffman, special Dep. Coll., to E. M. Brayton, Coll., S.C., Mar. 29, 1878, LR, box 887 (jury); *New York Tribune*, July 28, Aug. 20, 1878.

17. *New York Times*, Sept. 1, 1881 (which has him sent for life to the penitentiary at Columbus, Ohio); Records of the U.S. District Court, Western South Carolina, Record Group 21, National Archives, Atlanta Branch, box 11, case nos. 1261, 1264–68, 1284–85, (the sentences); S. W. Melton, Dist. Atty., to Atty. Gen., Mar. 24, 1884, SC S.C. (WCTU); *New York Times*, Mar. 14, 1900. The account of Redmond's revival is corroborated by reference to him as a licensed distiller in Joseph Miller, Commissioner, to S. A. Townes, Coll., S.C., Dec. 28, 1895, LC, bk. 599, p. 586. Neither man mentioned his past.

18. M. L. White, "A History of the Life of Amos Owens, the Noted Blockader, of Cherry Mountain, N.C." (Shelby, N.C.: Cleveland Star Job Print, 1901); Joseph E. Dabney, *Mountain Spirits: A Chronicle of Corn Whiskey from King James' Ulster Plantation to America's Appalachians and the Moonshine Life* (New York: Scribners, 1974), pp. 93–106.

19. J. A. George, Dep. Coll., Ga., to H. C. Rogers, Actg. Commissioner, Apr. 28, 1877, LR, box 897 (ignorance); G. W. Atkinson, Dep. Coll., W.Va., report in J. H. Duval, Coll., to Raum, May 18, 1877, LR, box 895 (toiling); G. S. Saylor, Dep. Coll., Tex., report in M. N. Brewster, Coll., to Raum, May 28, 1877, LR, box 895 (experiment).

20. H. Smyth, Marshal, to G. Williams, Atty. Gen., Feb. 14, 1873, SC Ga.; W. Stone, Asst. Dist. Atty., to D. Corbin, Dist. Atty., in Corbin to Williams, May 18, 1873, SC S.C.; E. H. Hoffman, Dep. Coll., to E. M. Brayton, Coll., S.C., Mar. 29, 1878, LC, box 887 (Redmond).

21. H. Smyth, Marshal, to G. Williams, Atty. Gen., Jan. 25, 1875, SC Ga.; R. M. Wallace, Marshal, to C. Devens, Atty. Gen., Apr. 22, 1878, SC S.C.; G. B. Raum, Commissioner, to A. L. Morgan, Coll., Ala., Nov. 20, 1880, LC 124, pp. 632–33 (blacks); *New York Times*, Aug. 25, 1880.

22. Clark to Raum, June 13, 1879, and Nov. 15, 1881, LR, box 891; E. C. Wade, Coll., Ga., to Raum, May 3, 1879, LR, box 908 (quotation); E. M. Brayton, Coll., S.C., to Raum, May 23, 1879, LR, box 890. Other examples of terrorism are in J. J. Mott, Coll., N.C., to Raum, Dec. 10, 1879, in "Enforcement of Internal Revenue Laws," pp. 108–9; D. B. Cliffe, Coll., Tenn., to Raum, Oct. 13, 1877, ibid., pp. 127–28; W. M. Woodcock, Coll., Tenn., to Raum, July 11, 1879, ibid., pp. 147–48; J. H. Rives, Coll., Va., to Raum, July 9, 1879, ibid., pp. 164–65; O. G. Scofield, Dep. Coll., to J. H. Duval, Coll., W.Va., June 25, 1877, ibid., pp. 168–69; L. C. Carpenter, Coll., S.C., to Raum, June 14, 1877, ibid., pp. 180–81.

23. P. W. Perry, Supervisor, Int. Rev., to J. W. Douglass, Commissioner, Feb. 24, 1873, MLR, box 909; *New York Times*, Jan. 14, 1876 (link of moonshine and Klan regions in Ga. and S.C., respectively); P. Rollins, Coll., N.C., to P. W. Perry, Apr. 26, 1871, 1723 AGO '71 (protectorship); "M. F. T. Comman'g" to R. J. Donaldson & Co., May 4, 1871, ibid. (KKK letter); L. Murdoch, Coll., Mo., to A. Pleasonton, Commissioner, May 8, 1871, ibid. (disguise); L. A. Guild, Dep. Coll., Ga., to G. Williams, Atty. Gen., Oct. 9, 1874, SC Ga. (buggy); "To Henry Martin US Martial," Nov. 4, 1875, in Lt. J. Anderson, 18th Inf., to Capt. J. Stewart, Nov. 15, 1875, 5912 AGO '75, (Kuclucks); G. C. Wharton, Dist. Atty., to Atty. Gen., Aug. 28, 1874, SC Ky., (Owen Co.). For several incidents of Klan activity in behalf of moonshiners, see Allen W. Trelease, *White Terror: The Ku Klux Klan Conspiracy and Southern Reconstruction* (New York: Harper Torchbooks, 1972), pp. xlviii, 185, 239, 282, 305, 331, 341.

24. *New York Times*, Nov. 20, 1878 (Black Hawks); H. H. Dotson, Dep. Coll., to J. H. Rives, Coll., Va., Nov. 2, 1879, "Enforcement of Internal Revenue Laws," p. 165 ("clan"); L. B. Penington, Dep. Coll., to I. J. Young, Coll., N.C., Aug. 25, 1879, ibid., p. 90 (secret lodges); Tracie-Raum, May 4, 1881, ibid., p. 7 (Va.); J. S. James,

Dist. Atty., Ga., to Atty. Gen., May 2, Dec. 15, 1894, DJ 7112 '86, box 271 (whitecaps).

25. J. S. James, Dist. Atty., Ga., to AG, Dec. 15, 1894, DJ 7112 '86, box 271; Henry M. Wiltse, *The Moonshiners* (Chattanooga, Tenn.: Times Printing Co., 1895), pp. 144–49. For full accounts of moonshiners and whitecapping, see William F. Holmes, "Moonshining and Collective Violence: Georgia, 1889–1895," *Journal of American History* 67 (Dec. 1980): 589–611 (pp. 606–7 on Worley); and "Moonshiners and Whitecaps in Alabama, 1893," *Alabama Review* 24 (Jan. 1981): 31–49.

26. W. J. Landrum, Coll., Ky., to Raum, Aug. 2, 1877, LR, box 899; S. J. Young, Coll., N.C., to Raum, Nov. 11, 1881, LR, box 907 (quotation); Dunn, *Cades Cove*, pp. 193–94.

27. A. Clark, Coll., Ga., to Raum, Dec. 29, 1877, "Enforcement of Internal Revenue Laws," p. 32 ($5); J. A. George, Dep. Coll., to H. C. Rogers, Actg. Commissioner, May 15, 1877, LR, box 897; J. Olney, Rev. Agt., to Raum, June 9, 1877, MLR, box 910; *New York Times*, Feb. 2, 1880; Kephart, *Highlanders*, p. 171; Margaret W. Morley, *The Carolina Mountains* (Boston: Houghton Mifflin, 1913), p. 207; Emil O. Peterson, "A Glimpse of the Moonshiners," *Chautauquan* 26 (Nov. 1897): 179 (motivations).

28. Atkinson, *After the Moonshiners*, p. 111 (Berongs); Wiltse, *Moonshiners*, pp. 115–17 (Sallie); James W. Raine, *The Land of Saddlebags* (New York: Council of Women for Home Missions and Missionary Education Movement, 1924), p. 135; Isaac Stapleton, *Moonshiners in Arkansas* (Independence, Mo.: Zion's Printing and Publishing Co., 1948), pp. 5–6; Dunn, *Cades Cove*, p. 234; G. B. Raum, interview in *New York Herald*, Feb. 5, 1881, in *Internal Revenue Record and Customs Journal*, Feb. 14, 1881, p. 49; Wiltse, *Moonshiners*, p. 97.

29. *New York Times*, Aug. 23, 1894 (Smith); Records of the U.S. District Court, Northern Georgia, Record Group 21, National Archives, Atlanta Branch, box 96, case nos. 4539–40; Stapleton, *Moonshiners in Arkansas*, pp. 53–54, 56 (Foster). For the importance of family loyalty see Ronald D. Eller, *Miners, Millhands, and Mountaineers: Industrialization of the Appalachian South, 1880–1930* (Knoxville: University of Tennessee Press, 1982), pp. 28–38; Dunn, *Cades Cove*, p. 179. Exceptions to this view include Altina Waller's reminder that, in the case of the Hatfields, family loyalty included unrelated people obligated to the patriarch, who were viewed as kin by other members of the community (*Feud: Hatfields, McCoys, and Social Change in Appalachia, 1860–1900* [Chapel Hill: University of North Carolina Press, 1988], pp. 77–85), and William L. Montell's argument that in the Kentucky-Tennessee border area he studied, "individuals rather than families constituted the basic units of society" (*Killings: Folk Justice in the Upper South* [Lexington: University Press of Kentucky, 1986], p. 155). Montell's conclusion rests on the absence of family feuds and lack of common expressions of kinship, such as "blood tells."

30. Leonidas Hubbard, Jr., "The Moonshiner at Home," *Atlantic Monthly* 90 (Aug. 1902): 234–35 (Payne); Glasgow, Ky., *Times*, quoted by *Internal Revenue Record and Customs Journal*, Oct. 6, 1879, p. 310; *New York Times*, Aug. 23, 1894 (Ashford); G. D. H. Floyd, 18th Infantry, to Post Adjutant, May 6, 1877, 2724 AGO '77. A writer of 1876 asserted that competitiveness among moonshiners prompted some of them to become deputy marshals (Dahlonega *Mountain Signal*, Mar. 31, 1876).

31. V. S. Lusk, Dist. Atty., to C. Devens, Atty. Gen., Mar. 1, 1878, SC N.C.; *New York Times*, Nov. 12, 1885 (N.C. band, Pyle); Atkinson, *After the Moonshiners*, pp. 107–11; S. M. Nealon, Dep. Coll., to Raum, Feb. 12, 1880, "Enforcement of Internal Revenue Laws," p. 43.

32. Mountain people usually preferred going to the law over violence in resolving personal disputes, and invoking the revenue laws could be another form of this choice: see Waller, *Feud*, pp. 85–93; Dunn, *Cades Cove*, pp. 207–12. The story is in Otis K. Rice, *The Hatfields and the McCoys* (Lexington: University Press of Kentucky, 1982), pp. 107–8; *Wheeling Intelligencer*, Nov. 23, 1889; Waller, *Feud*, p. 3. For Mississippi, see G. M. Buchanan, Dep. Coll., to W. H. Knisely, Rev. Agent, Jan. 26, 1891, MLR, box 915.

33. Holmes, "Moonshining and Collective Violence," pp. 590–91. "Reactionary violence" is originally Charles Tilly's phrase.

CHAPTER 4

1. George Wesley Atkinson, *After the Moonshiners, by One of the Raiders* (Wheeling, W.Va.: Frew and Campbell, 1881), p. 56.

2. Amy H. Mittleman, "The Politics of Alcohol Production: The Liquor Industry and the Federal Government, 1862–1900" (Ph.D. dissertation, Columbia University, 1986), pp. 3, 22–29.

3. For the administrative history of the revenue bureau, see Laurence F. Schmeckebier and Francis X. Eble, *The Bureau of Internal Revenue: Its History, Activities and Organization* (Baltimore: Johns Hopkins University Press, 1923), pp. 7–27.

4. Mittleman, "Politics of Alcohol Production," pp. 66–71; "Report from the Select Committee on Internal Revenue Frauds," *House Reports* 24, 39th Cong., 2d sess. (1867), pp. 6, 3, 4. A second report, from the House Committee on Retrenchment, is based on the evidence of the first but is only a shrill denunciation of Johnson and his minions—ex-convicts or ex-rebels milking the government for revenge—and unscrupulous distillers, "Jews for the most part" (*House Reports* 24, 40th Cong., 2d sess. [1868], esp. p. 6). *New York Times*, Oct. 12, 1869; *Atlanta Constitution*, May 19, 1880; David A. Wells, *The Theory and Practice of Taxation*

(New York: D. Appleton, 1900), p. 45; Frederick C. Howe, *Taxation and Taxes in the United States under the Internal Revenue System* (New York: T. Y. Crowell, 1896), p. 43.

5. Atkinson, *After the Moonshiners*, pp. 73–77. The Brooklyn raids occurred in 1869 through 1873, involving 200 or more soldiers, far larger than any actions in the South. See Wilbur R. Miller, "Moonshiners in Brooklyn: Federal Authority Confronts Urban Culture, 1869–1880," *Long Island Historical Journal* 2 (Spring 1990): 232–50.

6. William S. McFeely, *Grant: A Biography* (New York: Norton, 1981), p. 405.

7. *Annual Report, Commissioner of Internal Revenue*, 1875, *HED* 4, 44th Cong., 1st sess., pp. xv–xviii.

8. In 1871, before the depression, the government lost $9 million from the previous year's collections. This was the height of the whiskey ring. In 1872, revenues began to recover, aided by an increase of the tax to 70 cents per gallon. The increase concealed how much was still being siphoned off by the ring. Whiskey revenues rose above the 1870 level in 1873 and continued to rise slowly, aided by a tax increase to 90 cents per gallon in 1875. These tax increases were most likely to recoup losses from other sources, principally customs duties, during the depression. The tax increases raised revenues but did not realize their full potential. Yearly figures of revenue from "spirits distilled from materials other than apples, peaches or grapes" (mostly whiskies) are in the *Annual Report, Commissioner of Internal Revenue, HED*, for the appropriate years.

9. Ross A. Webb, *Benjamin Helm Bristow, Border State Politician* (Lexington: University Press of Kentucky, 1969), chap. 8; Mittleman, "Politics of Alcohol Production," pp. 76–100; *Annual Report, Commissioner of Internal Revenue*, 1876, *HED* 4, 44th Cong., 2d sess., pp. xvii–xviii.

10. Schmeckebier and Eble, *Bureau of Internal Revenue*, pp. 7–27.

11. *New York Tribune*, Apr. 2, 1877; *New York Times*, Nov. 10, 1879.

12. "Testimony Before the Senate Special Committee to Investigate the Administration of the Collection of Internal Revenue in the Sixth District of North Carolina," *Senate Miscellaneous Documents* 116, 47th Cong., 1st sess. (1882), testimony of W. G. Bogle, Storekeeper, p. 2; A. H. Kestler, Storekeeper, pp. 77–78; and Green B. Raum, Comm. of Int. Rev., pp. 296–97 (quotation), 311.

13. John M. Mason to H. G. Ewart, Oct. 9, 1889; to C. W. Payne, Jan. 23, 1890; to J. B. Eaves, Dec. 27, 1889; to J. A. Dean, Jan. 21, 1890, Mason Papers, West Virginia Collection, West Virginia University, series II, box 2.

14. C. C. Vest, Dep. Coll., to P. Rollins, Coll., N.C., Apr. 10, 1871, 1723 AGO '71 (Ga.); R. P. Dick, Dist. Judge, to Atty. Gen., Feb. 5, 1874, SC N.C.

15. Dick to Atty. Gen., Feb. 5, 1874, SC N.C.; H. Alderman to A. S. Gray, Marshal, Dec. 22, 1873, SC Va. (quotation).

. . . .

16. A. B. Fall, Chief Clerk, to A. B. Newcomb, Secret Service, Dec. 12, 1874, L, bk. K, p. 579; R. M. Douglas, Marshal, to Atty. Gen., Apr. 14, 1874, SC N.C.; R. M. Wallace, Marshal, to Atty. Gen., June 8, 1872, SC S.C. (deaths of deputies); E. Latham, Coll., Ala., to Commissioner, Mar. 30, 1875, LR, box 899; J. M. Edgar, Dep. Marshal, to E. L. Latham, Coll., Ala., June 3, 1875, "Enforcement of Internal Revenue Laws: . . . Report of the Commissioner of Internal Revenue . . . to Explain the Necessity for Employment of Armed Men . . . ," HED 62, 46th Cong., 2d sess. (1880), p. 47; C. Mayer, Dist. Atty., to Atty. Gen., Aug. 12, 1878, SC Ala., box 126; C. Devens, Atty. Gen., to Mayer, Aug. 30, 1878, I, bk. H, p. 267; Mayer to Devens, Sept. 9, 1878, SC Ala., box 131 (Leatherwood).

17. McDonald to Commissioner, May 5, 1870, MLR, box 909; H. C. Whitley, *In It* (Cambridge, Mass.: Riverside Press, 1894), p. 94.

18. *New York Times*, May 19, 1875 (agents); W. A. Gavett, Rev. Detective, to Commissioner, Oct. 25, 1871, MLR, box 903; F. S. Sewell, Supervisor, Int. Rev., to Commissioner, Aug. 18, 1875, MLR, box 909 (coordination); *New York Times*, Dec. 24, 1875, and Jan. 17, 1876 (Wagner); Feb. 24, Apr. 28, June 23, July 9, Sept. 17, 1875 (raids in Ala., S.C., N.C., Va., Ga.).

19. Evarts to A. Magruder, Marshal, Fla., Aug. 20, 1868, I, bk. A, pp. 95–96. A copy of this letter also went to the marshal in Kentucky: J. H. Ashton, Actg. Atty. Gen., to W. A. Meriweather, Marshal, Ky., Sept. 13, 1868, I, bk. A, p. 106.

20. J. Holt, Judge Advocate General, memorandum, Feb. 20, 1870, 79S AGO '70 (with 112 I); Sherman, note on jacket of this file, Jan. 29, 1870.

21. General Orders no. 75, Dept. South, Oct. 20, 1874, in 4788 AGO '76 (quotation); Capt. C. E. Morse, 16th Inf., to Sgt. D. Kellier, Feb. 8, 1876, and Sgt. P. Sowers, May 1, 1876, 1042 AGO '76, and 3068 AGO '76; Lieut. A. L. Howell, 2d Artillery, to Capt. E. A. Williston, Oct. 5, 1874, 4269 AGO '74 (Ky. and N.C. detachment orders).

22. Report of Halleck in *Annual Report of the Secretary of War*, 1870, HED, 41st Cong., 2d sess. (1869–70), 2:78; ibid., 1871, HED, 41st Cong., 3d sess. (1870–71), 2:38.

23. Jacket summaries, notes, 2619 AGO '71 (Pope); [John Esten Cooke], "Moonshiners," *Harper's New Monthly Magazine* 58 (Feb. 1879): 380–90.

24. C. McKeever, Asst. Adj. Gen., Dept. South, to Capt. J. K. Hyer, Jan. 11, 1876, 338 AGO '76.

25. Report, Maj. Gen. Irvin McDowell, Commanding Div. of South, Oct. 19, 1875, Annual Reports, AGO '75 (stats. 1875); Register of Letters Received, AGO, (reports for 1870–77). James E. Sefton, *The United States Army and Reconstruction, 1865–1877* (Baton Rouge: Louisiana State University Press, 1967), chap. 10, treats the army and moonshiners very briefly.

26. S. H. Wilery, Coll., N.C., to P. W. Perry, Supervisor, May 24, 1869, 3381

AGO '76; P. W. Perry to Commissioner, Feb. 12, 1873, 800 AGO '73; J. Inman, Spec. Dep. Coll., to W. J. Landram, Coll., Ky., Feb. 1, 1878, "Enforcement of Internal Revenue Laws," p. 83; A. C. Sharpe, Coll., Tenn., to Commissioner, Jan. 28, 1875, 842 AGO '75; L. C. Carpenter, Coll., S.C., to Maj. Gen. Irvin McDowell, Mar. 18, 1876, 1659 AGO '76; F. D. Sewall, Supervisor, to Commissioner, Aug. 18, 1875, LR, box 909; G. B. Chamberlain, Rev. Agt., to Raum, Mar. 6, 1877, LR, box 910 (2d Infantry) (all praise for troops); Brig. Gen. A. H. Terry, Ann. Rpt., Dept. South, Oct. 10, 1870, AGO.

27. S. H. Wilery, Coll., N.C., to P. W. Perry, Supervisor, May 24, 1869, 4788 AGO '76; Perry to Commissioner, June 21, 1871, 2377 AGO '71; Perry to Commissioner, Feb. 12, 1873, 800 AGO '73; J. M. Douglass, Commissioner, to Secy. of War, Feb. 4, 1875, 842 AGO '75; L. C. Carpenter, Coll., S.C., to Maj. Gen. I. McDowell, Mar. 18, 1876, 1659 AGO '76; John Olney, Rev. Agt., to Raum, June 9, 1877, LR, box 910; D. B. Booth, Coll., Ala., to Raum, June 2, 1877, LR, box 887 (all on nonresistance to troops). Lt. J. Anderson, 18th Inf., to Cmdg. Officer, Greenville, Feb. 21, 1877, 1343 AGO '77; Capt. W. Falck, 2d Inf., to Asst. Adj. Gen., Dept. South, Mar. 11, 1877, 1560 AGO '77; Report, Capt. C. E. Morse, 16th Inf., June 20, 1873, 2783 AGO '73, (effectiveness); J. J. Mott, Coll., N.C., to Secy. of War, Sept. 7, 1876, 3681 AGO '76; *Atlanta Constitution*, May 8, 1877 (conciliation).

28. V. S. Lusk, Dist. Atty., to Atty. Gen., Dec. 23, 1873, SC N.C.; J. J. Mott, Coll., N.C., to Raum, Dec. 3, 1877, LR, box 900.

29. Lt. A. Haines, 2d Inf., to Post Adj., Atlanta, Mar. 25, 1876, 1812 AGO '76; Atty. Gen. to H. P. Farrow, Dist. Atty., Ga., May 23, 1876, I, bk. E, p. 489. For the version of the story told by John Emory's wife and friends, see Robert S. Davis, Jr., "The North Georgia Moonshine War of 1876–1877," *North Georgia Journal* 6 (Autumn 1989): 43. Mr. Davis has also supplied me with a copy of the original trial testimony, including that of the county coroner, from Gilmer County Miscellaneous Court Records, RG 161-12-11, box 23, Georgia Department of Archives and History.

30. Summary of papers in 1225 AGO '76.

31. Summary of papers in 1738 AGO '72 (court martial: unfortunately the sentence is illegible).

32. Lt. W. T. Howard, 2d Artillery, to Asst. Adj. Gen., Dept. South, Feb. 27, 1877, 1345 AGO '77; J. Holt, Judge Advocate General, memorandum, Feb. 20, 1870, 79S AGO '70 (with 112 I) (wounding of soldiers).

33. Capt. H. C. Clark, 2d Inf., to Asst. Adj. Gen., Dept. South, Feb. 12, 1877; Maj. Gen. F. Wharton, 2d Inf., to Adj. Gen., Feb. 14, 1877, both 1015 AGO '77; Atty. Gen. to H. P. Farrow, Dist. Atty., Ga., Sept. 19, 1878, I, bk. H, p. 285; O. P. Fitzsimmons, Marshal, to Atty. Gen., Apr. 3, 1879, SC Ga.; *Atlanta Constitution*,

May 8, 1877, and Apr. 4, 1879; Robert S. Davis, "North Georgia Moonshine War," pp. 43–45.

34. Reports, affidavits, Sept. 8, 1871, in 3130 AGO '71.

35. Lt. C. W. Williams, 18th Inf., to Cmdg. Officer, Morgantown, May 19, 1877, 3112 AGO '77; Lt. J. Anderson, 18th Inf., to Capt. J. Stewart, Greenville, Nov. 15, 1875, 5912 AGO '75; Cpl. O. Marius, 16th Inf., to Capt. C. Morse, Apr. 19, 1876, 2206 AGO '76; Capt. J. Stewart, 18th Inf., to Asst. Adj. Gen., Dept. South, July 9, 1875, 3658 AGO '75; L. C. Carpenter, Coll., S.C., to Secy. of War, July 17, 1875, ibid. (conditions on raids); Lt. H. Adams, 18th Inf., to Asst. Adj. Gen., Dept. South, Feb. 9, 19, 1877, 940, 1346 AGO '77; Lt. W. Miller, 18th Inf., to Capt. J. Stewart, Mar. 2, 1877, 1348 AGO '77 (carbines and horses).

36. G. W. Emery, Supervisor, to Commissioner, Apr. 30, 1870, LR, box 909; Lt. W. A. Miller, 18th Inf., to Cmdg. Officer, Greenville, Mar. 11, 1876, 1502 AGO '76; Miller to Cmdg. Officer, Apr. 26, 1877, 2494 AGO '77; (warnings); Lt. C. Harkins, 2d Inf., to Post Adjutant, Atlanta, Mar. 3, 1876, 1364 AGO '76; Lt. J. Anderson, 18th Inf., to Cmdg. Officer, Greenville, Mar. 30, 1877, 1894 AGO '77 (guides); Andrew Jackson Ritchie, *Sketches of Rabun County History* (Foote and Davies, [1948]), p. 284.

37. Reports, letters, jacket notes, Apr. 2–July 1, 1875, 842 AGO '75 (original italics).

38. Lt. L. S. Ames, report, Jan. 5, 1875, 3579 AGO '75, (missing: in Register, p. 12) (drink); Capt. J. K. Hyer, 18th Inf., to Asst. Adj. Gen., Dept. South, Jan. 6, 1876, 338 AGO '76 (Rachel); Lieut. C. W. Williams, 18th Inf., to Post Adj., Atlanta, Feb. 14, 1876, 1017 AGO '76 (language); Lieut. H. Catley, 2d Inf., to Post Adj., Huntsville, Ala., Apr. 4, 1875, 1916 AGO '75 (Leatherwood); Lt. H. H. Adams, 18th Inf., to Asst. Adj. Gen., Dept. South, Feb. 19, 1877, 1346 AGO '77 (escape).

39. Atkinson, *After the Moonshiners*, p. 56.

40. A. S. Sharpe, Coll., Tenn., note on letter from McIntyre, May 22, 1876, in Sharpe to H. C. Rogers, Dep. Commissioner, Mar. 30, 1876 (McIntyre); S. H. Wiley, Coll., N.C., to Commissioner, July 16, 1869, LR, box 907; Rpt. Maj. J. C. Morgan, 4th Artillery, June 9, 1871, 1723 AGO '71; *New York Times*, Dec. 24, 1875 (Wagner); I. T. Whitlock, Coll., Va., to Commissioner, Nov. 20, 1869, LR, box 907 (Va.); R. P. Dick, Dist. Judge, to Atty. Gen., Feb. 5, 1874, SC N.C.; *Internal Revenue Record and Customs Journal*, Feb. 14, 1881, p. 49 (Raum).

41. L. C. Carpenter, Coll., S.C., to Secy. of War, Nov. 18, 1876, 3681 AGO '76; Secy. of War to Secy. of Treasury, Aug. 8, 1876; Secy. of Treasury to Secy. of War, Aug. 10, 1876, 2861 AGO '76.

42. Raum to Secy. of Treasury, Jan. 18, 1877, 3681 AGO '76; Dahlonega *Signal and Advertiser*, Mar. 23, 1877 (Raum's directive).

43. *New York Tribune*, July 30, 1878, p. 4; *CR*, 45th Cong., 2d sess. (1878), vol. 7,

pt. 5, p. 4241 (Blaine); ibid., pt. 4, p. 3848 (Rep. H. C. Burchard, R-Ill.); ibid., p. 3849 (Rep. W. Aldrich, R-Ill.); Devens to W. E. Earle, Spec. Asst. Dist. Atty., July 27, 1878, I, bk. H, pp. 212–17.

CHAPTER 5

1. Dumas Malone, ed., *Dictionary of American Biography* (New York: Scribners, 1935), 15:391–92 (quotation); Rossiter Johnson, ed., *The Twentieth Century Biographical Dictionary of Notable Americans* (Boston: Biographical Society, 1904), 14: n.p.; *New York Times*, Apr. 29, 1883 (quotations).

2. *National Cyclopaedia of American Biography* (New York: James T. White, 1920), 13:588–89 (photo); *New York Tribune*, Aug. 3, 1876 (telegram); Sherman quoted in Robert Marcus, *Grand Old Party: Political Structure in the Gilded Age, 1880–1896* (New York: Oxford University Press, 1971), p. 30.

3. Raum quoted in Leonard D. White, *The Republican Era: A Study in Administrative History* (New York: Macmillan, 1958), pp. 316–17 (objections to civil service); "Testimony Before the Senate Special Committee to Investigate the Administration of the Collection of Internal Revenue in the Sixth District of North Carolina," *Senate Miscellaneous Documents* 116, 47th Cong., 1st sess. (1882), testimony of Raum, p. 312.

4. "Testimony . . . Revenue in the Sixth District of N.C.," testimony of Raum, p. 312; W. H. Chapman to R. B. Hayes, Dec. 28, 1880, R. B. Hayes Papers, photocopy courtesy R. B. Hayes Presidential Center, Fremont, Ohio; Raum to C. Devens, Atty. Gen., July 19, 1880, ibid.; H. P. Farrow Affidavit, Jan. 14, 1881, ibid. (charges and countercharges regarding Fitzsimmons and Farrow).

5. *New York Tribune*, Aug. 6, 1881 (efficiency), and Oct. 18, 1883 (defense); "Testimony . . . Revenue in the Sixth District of N.C.," testimony of Raum, p. 312 (party work); *New York Times*, Apr. 29, 1883 (honesty).

6. Raum to Senator L. M. Morrill, Jan. 18, 1877, 3681 AGO '76; *New York Tribune*, Jan. 20, 1877, p. 1; *Annual Report, Commissioner of Internal Revenue*, 1877, *HED* 4, 45th Cong., 2d sess., p. xxx; ibid., 1878, *HED* 4, 45th Cong., 3d sess., quoted in Horace Kephart, *Our Southern Highlanders* (New York: Outing, 1913), p. 180.

7. *Annual Report, Commissioner of Internal Revenue*, 1879, *HED* 4, 46th Cong., 2d sess., p. iv; ibid., 1882, *HED* 4, 47th Cong., 2d sess., p. xv; ibid., 1883, HED 4, 48th Cong., 1st sess., p. xvi; Raum to E. M. Brayton, Coll., S.C., May 1, 1879 (and other Colls.), LC, bk. 75, pp. 474, 476, 489, 136.

8. *Annual Report, Commissioner of Internal Revenue*, 1879, *HED* 4, 46th Cong., 2d

sess., p. iv; interview with Raum, *New York Herald*, Feb. 5, 1881, in *Internal Revenue Record and Customs Journal*, Feb. 14, 1881, p. 49.

9. Raum to J. F. Buckner, Coll., Ky., July 2, 1879, LC, bk. 81, p. 217 (praise); Raum to W. A. Stuart, Coll., Ky., Nov. 21, 1879, LC, bk. 91, p. 722; Raum to W. J. Landrum, Coll., Ky., June 18, 1879, LC, bk. 79, p. 826 (nudging); Raum to S. R. Crumbaugh, Coll., Ky., Jan. 30, 1883, LC, bk. 186, p. 423 (criticism); Raum to A. Clark, Coll., Ga. (and other Colls.), Aug. 24, 1878, LC, bk. 52, pp. 144–46.

10. For the Wellborns and Holcomb, see Records of the U.S. District Court, Northern Georgia, Record Group 21, National Archives, Atlanta Branch, Sept. Term 1881, box 98, case nos. 4643, 4650 (the Wellborns and Holcomb actually put up bail for some men they had not arrested themselves: Mar. Term 1882, box 99, case nos. 4663, with John Wellborn as surety for Joseph Carnes, and 4672, with J. Wellborn and T. J. Holcomb as sureties for Irve Dickerson); H. B. Whitefield, Dep. Coll., Miss., to Raum, Mar. 10, 1877, LR, box 907 (quotation, original emphasis); E. M. Brown, Rev. Agt., to John M. Mason, Commissioner, Apr. 25, 1889, MLR, box 914 (quotation).

11. George W. Atkinson, *After the Moonshiners, by One of the Raiders* (Wheeling, W.Va.: Frew and Campbell, 1881), pp. 89–91.

12. *Tennessee v. Davis*, 100 U.S. Reports 257 (Oct. Term 1879).

13. Henry M. Wiltse, *The Moonshiners* (Chattanooga, Tenn.: Times Printing Co., 1895), pp. 60–64; *Internal Revenue Record and Customs Journal*, Mar. 20, 1882, p. 90, and Dec. 18, 1882, p. 402.

14. Ruling of Judge Hugh Bond in *Internal Revenue Record and Customs Journal*, Nov. 14, 1878, p. 350; Atkinson, *After the Moonshiners*, pp. 39–41, 165; Raum to E. M. Brayton, Coll., S.C., Dec. 16, 1878, LC, bk. 61, pp. 365–66; Raum to A. Clark, Coll., Ga., Mar. 6, 1879, "Enforcement of Internal Revenue Laws: . . . Report of the Commissioner of Internal Revenue . . . to Explain the Necessity for Employment of Armed Men . . . ," HED 64, 46 Cong., 2d sess. (1880), pp. 38–40 (seizures).

15. Joseph E. Dabney, *Mountain Spirits: A Chronicle of Corn Whiskey from King James' Ulster Plantation to America's Appalachians and the Moonshine Life* (New York: Scribners, 1974), p. 79; Atkinson, *After the Moonshiners*, pp. 33–35.

16. Raum to R. C. Powers, Coll., Miss., Dec. 28, 1877, LC, bk. 31, pp. 801–2; to W. A. Stuart, Coll., Ky., Jan. 24, 1880, LC, bk. 97, pp. 308–9; to A. Clark, Coll., Ga., Jan. 26, 1880 (and other Colls.), LC, bk. 97, pp. 723–24, 765–67, 770–71.

17. W. A. Gavett, Rev. Detective, to J. W. Douglass, Commissioner, Oct. 25, 1871, MLR, box 903; F. S. Sewall, Superintendent of Int. Rev., to D. D. Pratt, Commissioner, Aug. 18, 1875, MLR, box 909 (early coordination); Raum to W. J. Landrum, Coll., Ky., and I. H. Duval, Coll., W.Va., Dec. 26, 1878, LC, bk. 60, pp. 542–43, 527–28; to J. H. Rives, Coll., Va., Dec. 27, 1878, ibid., pp. 347–50; Raum

to E. M. Brayton, Coll., S.C., A. Clark, Coll., Ga., J. J. Mott, Coll., N.C., Jan. 10, 1880, LC, bk. 96, pp. 294–96, 310–12, 350–52; Raum to R. F. Patterson, Coll., Tenn., Jan. 29, 1878, LC, bk. 34, pp. 844–45 (all details of coordinated raids; quotations in 1880 letters); Raum to J. A. Cooper, Coll., Tenn., Dec. 4, 1878, "Enforcement of Internal Revenue Laws," pp. 113–14; Raum to W. J. Landrum, Dec. 6, 24, 1878, LC, bks. 60, p. 542, and 61, p. 231; W. O. H. Shepard, Dep. Coll., to A. Clark, Coll., Ga., Apr. 9, 1880, in Clark to Raum, Apr. 15, 1880, LR, box 891; *Internal Revenue Record and Customs Journal*, Feb. 12, 1877, p. 45; Jan. 21, 1878, p. 17; Feb. 25, 1878, p. 57 (no rewards).

18. Capt. C. B. Williston, 2d Artillery, to Asst. Adj. Gen., Dept. South, Mar. 16, 1876, 1885 AGO '76; J. H. Duval, Coll., W.Va., to Raum, May 18, 1877, LR, box 895.

19. R. M. Wallace, Marshal, to Atty. Gen., Dec. 31, 1877, Apr. 22, 1878, SC S.C. (dangers); E. M. Brayton, Coll., S.C., to Raum, Apr. 20, 1878, "Enforcement of Internal Revenue Laws," p. 193 (Springs); F. J. B. to editor, *Journal of Commerce*, quoted in *Internal Revenue Record and Customs Journal*, May 21, 1877, p. 171; *Annual Report, Commissioner of Internal Revenue*, 1879, HED 4, 46th Cong., 2d sess., p. xiv; ibid., 1883, HED 4, 48th Cong., 1st sess., p. xviii (statistics).

20. Atkinson, *After the Moonshiners*, p. 62; S. D. Mather, Dep. Coll., to W. M. Woodcock, Coll., Tenn., Oct. 5, 1878, "Enforcement of Internal Revenue Laws," p. 138; H. H. Dotson, Dep. Coll., to J. H. Rives, Coll., Va., May 15, 1879, ibid., pp. 161–62; *New York Times*, Mar. 13, 1881 (cannon); *Annual Report of the Attorney General*, 1890, HED 7, 51st Cong., 2d sess., pp. 13–14, 368 (West).

21. Homer Cummings and Carl McFarland, *Federal Justice: Chapters in the History of Justice and the Federal Executive* (New York: Macmillan, 1937), pp. 481–82; Raum letter in *New York Tribune*, Nov. 25, 1878; E. A. Angier, Asst. Dist. Atty., Ga., to Atty. Gen., Dec. 19, 1890, DJ 7112 '86, box 271; W. H. Chapman, Rev. Agt., to J. M. Mason, Commissioner, Dec. 19, 1890, MLR, box 914; Mason to Sen. W. B. Allison, May 29, 1890, Mason Papers, West Virginia Collection, West Virginia University, series II, box 3; to Rep. B. H. Bunn, Apr. 4, 1892, ibid., box 4; to E. A. Webster, Coll., S.C., Jan. 20, 1890, ibid., box 2; to W. O. Bradley, Coll., Ky., Nov. 23, 1892, ibid., box 5.

22. "Testimony . . . Revenue in the Sixth District of N.C.," testimony of W. M. Walker, and question of Z. B. Vance (quoted words), p. 176.

23. Clark to Raum, Apr. 30, 1880, LR, box 891, original emphasis.

24. Table in "Enforcement of Internal Revenue Laws," p. 208; R. M. Wallace, Marshal, to Atty. Gen., Sept. 13, 1877, SC S.C.

25. D. T. Corbin, Dist. Atty., to Atty. Gen., Dec. 16, 1874; A. Mattison to Atty. Gen., Dec. 28, 1874; Corbin to Atty. Gen., Dec. 30, 1875, all SC S.C.

26. J. J. Mott, Coll., N.C., to S. M. Phillips, Solicitor Gen., Nov. 30, 1877, SC N.C.; R. M. Douglas, Marshal, to Atty. Gen., Dec. 14, 1877, ibid.; R. P. Dick, Dist. Judge, to Atty. Gen., Jan. 22, 1881, ibid. For the *Davis* decision, see 100 U.S. Reports 257 (1879). Two justices dissented, arguing that there was no authority for treating murder as a federal offense, so Davis could not be tried in federal court.

27. *Atlanta Constitution*, May 11, 1880; Joseph G. De Roulhac Hamilton, *North Carolina Since 1860* in *History of North Carolina*, 3 vols. (Chicago: Lewis, 1919), 3:194–95, and "Testimony . . . Internal Revenue in the Sixth District of N.C.," testimony of G. B. Everitt, Coll., Int. Rev., p. 196 (all on criticisms of removal); Devens to G. Turner, Marshal, Ala., June 15, 1878, I, bk. H, p. 147; Devens to L. C. Northrop, Dist. Atty., S.C., July 13, 1878, I, bk. H, p. 187.

28. H. P. Kane to E. M. Brayton, Coll., S.C., June 10, 1878; J. Wagner to Raum, June 13, 1878, "Enforcement of Internal Revenue Laws," pp. 194–95.

29. Brayton to Raum, June 10, 1878, LR, box 887; Earle to Devens, June 15, 1878, SC S.C.; L. C. Northrop, Dist. Atty., to Devens, Aug. 14, 1878, SC S.C. The "bad character" charges, repeated during the deputies' trial, had originally come up in an earlier case, in which the only testimony against citizens who seized contraband whiskey from revenue men was provided by Kane, Moose, and Durham. Frank Moses was a Reconstruction governor of South Carolina, admittedly corrupt.

30. Devens to Earle, July 27, 1878, I, bk. H, pp. 212–17; Devens to Earle, Aug. 8, 1878, ibid., p. 241; *New York Tribune*, July 30, 1878.

31. Northrop to Devens, Sept. 30, 1878, SC S.C.; Devens to Earle, Oct. 18, 1878, I, bk. H, p. 333; Devens to Northrop, Nov. 13, 1878, I, bk. H, p. 375.

32. Court Proceedings, Dec. 7, 1881, SC S.C.; Brayton to Raum, Aug. 27, 1881, LR, box 890; *New York Tribune*, Aug. 20, 1878; Earle to Atty. Gen., Apr. 4, 1882 (telegram), SC S.C.

33. Brayton to Raum, Aug. 27, 1881, LR, box 890; Earle to Pres. R. B. Hayes, clipping, n.d., in Northrop to Devens, July 19, 1878, SC S.C. Mr. Earle was strictly impartial, for he defended moonshiners in general and Lewis Redmond himself while the case of Kane and the others was pending.

34. *Charleston News and Courier*, June 27, 1878, in L. C. Northrop, Dist. Atty., to Atty. Gen., June 27, 1878, SC S.C.

35. *Atlanta Constitution*, May 8, 1877; Dahlonega *Signal and Advertiser*, Mar. 30, 1877; for ties to moonshiners, see also *Atlanta Constitution*, May 8, 1877; Dahlonega *Signal and Advertiser*, Mar. 9, 1877; Raum to Secy. of Treasury, Dec. 30, 1876, 3681 AGO '76; C. S. Winstead, Coll., N.C., to Raum, Jan. 16, 1877, LR, box 907; E. C. Wade, Coll., S.C., to Raum, May 3, 1879, LR, box 908; A. H. Holt, Chief Clerk, Bureau of Int. Rev., to E. M. Brayton, Coll., S.C., Jan. 21, 1880, LC, bk. 97, pp. 206–7. Other charges are in *Atlanta Constitution*, May 12, 13, 15, 19, 1880; for

Alabama, *Opelika Weekly Times*, Jan. 31, 1879, with C. Mayer, Dist. Atty., to Atty. Gen., Dec. 13, 1878, SC Ala.

36. *Opelika Weekly Times*, Jan. 31, 1879, with C. Mayer, Dist. Atty., to Atty. Gen., Dec. 13, 1878, SC Ala. (memorial); E. Speer (D-Ga.), *CR*, 46th Cong., 2d sess. (1880), appendix, p. 6.

37. N.C. resolution, 1881, quoted in Hamilton, *North Carolina Since 1860*, p. 196; Vance quoted in Daniel J. Whitener, *Prohibition in North Carolina, 1715–1945*, James Sprunt Studies in History and Political Science (Chapel Hill: University of North Carolina Press, 1946), 27 (no. 1): 79.

38. Sen. Zebulon Vance, 1884, and Rep. W. R. Cox, 1882, cited in Whitener, *Prohibition in North Carolina*, p. 79; "Testimony. . . Revenue in the Sixth District of N.C.," esp. testimony of W. G. Bogle, Storekeeper, pp. 12–14, and W. H. Kestler, Gauger, pp. 49–57, 73–78; *Atlanta Constitution*, Jan. 2, 1879, (partisanship). Georgia's Senator John Gordon proposed to reform the revenue system by placing all officials under strict civil service rules in 1876 (*New York Tribune*, July 26, 1876).

39. J. Olney to Raum, May 10, 1877, LR, box 910; Wiltse, *Moonshiners*, pp. 49–50; O. P. Fitzsimmons to Atty. Gen., May 27, 1880, SC Ga.; Dahlonega *Mountain Signal*, Apr. 21, 1876; Northrop to Atty. Gen., June 18, 1878, SC S.C. (original italics).

40. Raum to W. M. Woodcock, Coll., Tenn., Apr. 11, 1878, "Enforcement of Internal Revenue Laws," p. 131; Raum to Brayton, Jan. 21, 1878, ibid., p. 187.

41. *Annual Report, Commissioner of Internal Revenue*, 1881, *HED* 4, 47th Cong., 1st sess., p. ix; Records of the District Court, Northern Georgia, Record Group 21, National Archives, Atlanta Branch, box 100, case no. 4689, William Green, Mar. Term 1882; Dahlonega *Signal and Advertiser*, Mar. 16, 1877; "Joint Memorial to the Congress of the United States . . . ," *Opelika Weekly Times*, Jan. 31, 1879, with C. Mayer, Dist. Atty., to Atty. Gen., Dec. 13, 1878, SC Ala.; *Martinsville Herald* quoted by Rep. G. C. Cabell (D-Va.), *CR*, 46th Cong., 2d sess. (1880), appendix, p. 301 (quotation).

42. W. L. Fernald, Coll., Va., to Raum, May 23, 1878, LR, box 896.

43. J. A. Holzclaw, Rev. Agt., to Atty. Gen., Oct. 1, 1873; W. Somerville, Rev. Agt., to Raum, May 14, 1879; E. Wade to Raum, June 8, 1879, all in SC Ga. For a similar ring in North Carolina, see R. P. Dick, Dist. Judge, to Atty. Gen., Dec. 24, 1874, SC N.C.

44. A. Clark, Coll., Ga., to Raum, May 20, 1880, LR, box 891; "Testimony. . . Revenue in the Sixth District of N.C.," testimony of G. B. Everitt, attorney, p. 196 (moiety).

45. *Annual Report, Attorney General*, 1874, *HED* 7, 43d Cong., 2d sess., p. 17; *Internal Revenue Record and Customs Journal*, Nov. 15, 1875, p. 361 (Pratt's order);

. . . .

Annual Report, Commissioner of Internal Revenue, 1879, *HED* 4, 46th Cong., 2d sess., p. xii; *Atlanta Constitution,* Jan. 4, 1878.

46. B. Brewster to Raum, Mar. 13, 1882, L, bk. K, p. 290; R. P. Dick, Dist. Judge, to C. Devens, Atty. Gen., Feb. 19, 1881, SC N.C.; Brewster to Rep. Wm. Springer, May 19, 1884, L, bk. N, pp. 591–94. For solution of fee problem, salaries for marshals and office deputies, and fees for field deputies, see chap. 8.

47. Raum to T. Stevenson, Jan. 22, 1880, LC, bk. 97, pp. 418–22; *Annual Report, Commissioner of Internal Revenue,* 1880, *HED* 4, 46th Cong., 3d sess., p. xii; Devens to all marshals, Jan. 30, 1878, I, bk. G, p. 98.

48. Andrews, "Instruction to U.S. Commissioners," cited by Stephen Cresswell, "Resistance and Enforcement: The U.S. Department of Justice, 1870–1893" (Ph.D. dissertation, University of Virginia, 1986), p. 232. Other examples: South Carolina: Raum to E. M. Brayton, Coll., July 21, 1882, LC, bk. 173, pp. 434–35; Alabama: C. Mayer, Dist. Atty., to Atty. Gen., Mar. 14, 1879, SC Ala.; Kentucky: B. Ballard, Dist. Judge, to Atty. Gen., July 14, 1876, SC Ky.

49. Cresswell, "Resistance and Enforcement," pp. 211–12, 230–31, 216–17.

50. Dick to Atty. Gen., Dec. 22, 1873, Nov. 21, Dec. 24, 1874, July 24, 1876, with newspaper clipping of "Rules of Court"; Dick to Atty. Gen., Feb. 5, 1874; R. M. Douglas, Marshal, to Atty. Gen., Feb. 9, 1874, SC N.C.

51. Dick to Atty. Gen., Nov. 21, 1874, SC N.C.; see W. S. Surty, Dist. Atty., to Atty. Gen., Dec. 29, 1880, SC Va., for a similar complaint.

52. C. Devens, Atty. Gen., to J. E. Boyd, Dist. Atty., N.C., Jan. 18, 1881, I, bk. K, p. 387; J. W. Albertson, Dist. Atty., to MacVeagh, Aug. 29, Oct. 3, 1881, SC N.C.; for draft of proposed court order, see *Annual Report, Attorney General* 1881, *Senate Executive Documents* 4, 47th Cong., 1st sess., pp. 12–13; T. N. Cooper, Coll., N.C., to Raum, Feb. 12, 1883, LR, box 894.

53. B. Brewster, Atty. Gen., to Raum, July 15, 1882, L, bk. L, pp. 72–73; Raum to Brayton, July 21, 1882, LC, bk. 173, pp. 434–35.

54. Farrow to Atty. Gen., Dec. 14, 1875, Mar. 8, 25, 1878, SC Ga.; *Atlanta Constitution,* June 1, 1877.

55. Clark to Raum, July 3, 1877, LR, box 891.

56. Farrow to Atty. Gen., June 10, 1878, Jan. 4, Mar. 19, 1879, with newspaper clippings, Mar. 28, 1879, SC Ga.; *Atlanta Constitution,* Mar. 25, 26, 1879; Farrow to Atty. Gen., June 10, 1878, Jan. 4, Mar. 19, 1878, with newspaper clippings, Mar. 28, 1879, SC Ga.; *Atlanta Constitution,* Mar. 25, 26, 1879; Somerville to Raum, Apr. 30, 1879; Farrow to Atty. Gen., June 7, 1879; Raum to Farrow, July 10, 1879, in Farrow to Atty. Gen., Sept. 4, 1879, SC Ga.; Devens to Farrow, Oct. 4, 1879, H. P. Farrow Papers, box 2, folder 14, Special Collections, University of Georgia. Biographical and political material on Farrow is in Farrow to Atty. Gen., July 1, 1875, SC Ga.

57. Farrow to Atty. Gen., June 10, 1878, Jan. 4, Mar. 19, Mar. 28, 1879, SC Ga.; *Atlanta Constitution*, Mar. 25, (quotation), 26, 1879; Farrow to Atty. Gen., June 7, 1879; Raum to Farrow, July 10, 1879, in Farrow to Atty. Gen., Sept. 4, 1879, SC Ga.; Devens to Farrow, Oct. 4, 1879, Farrow Papers, box 2, folder 14. For later court orders, see W. H. Brawley, Dist. Judge, to Atty. Gen., Apr. 3, 1895, DJ 1661 '94, box 746 (S.C.); A. M. Tillman, Dist. Atty., to Atty. Gen., Mar. 13, 1899, DJ 12935 '98, box 1102 (Tenn.).

58. *Atlanta Constitution*, May 23, June 1, 1880; note by Raum on jacket of papers to Secy. of Treasury, in Farrow Papers, box 2, folder 16 (Farrow's note to this says that Raum did not remove him, as he served out his full term; nevertheless correspondence with the attorney general in 1880 indicates that he desperately sought reappointment). Longstreet to Atty. Gen., Aug. 30, 1881; Mollin to Atty. Gen., Sept. 1, 1881; Speer to Atty. Gen., June 4, June 26, 1883, SC Ga.

59. "Rules relating to Commissioners of the Circuit Court of the United States and Commissioners' warrants, 1886," in O. E. Mitchell, Chief Dep. Marshal, Ga., to Atty. Gen., June 26, 1896, DJ 6525, box 699; J. S. James, Dist. Atty., Ga., to Atty. Gen., Jan. 7, 1897, DJ 14997, box 868.

CHAPTER 6

1. "Enforcement of Internal Revenue Laws: . . . Report of the Commissioner of Internal Revenue . . . to Explain the Necessity for Employment of Armed Men . . . ," *HED* 62, 46th Cong., 2d sess. (1880), esp. p. 1. This report contains many letters not found in the manuscript files.

2. Clark to Raum, Jan. 8, 15, 1877, "Enforcement of Internal Revenue Laws," pp. 25–26.

3. The legislature's report is in *Atlanta Constitution*, May 8, 1877.

4. Chamberlin to Raum, Feb. 10, 12, Mar. 6, 8, 1877, "Enforcement of Internal Revenue Laws," pp. 26–28.

5. Raum's narrative, "Enforcement of Internal Revenue Laws," pp. 29–30. For convictions, see the *Annual Report of the Attorney General, HED* for appropriate years, which publish each year's results of criminal prosecutions for various offenses, including revenue violations. The proportion of guilty pleas was not recorded by the Justice Department until 1908; between 1908 and 1919 in Georgia they comprised from 56 percent to 72 percent of all convictions without a special amnesty arrangement.

6. Clark to Raum, Dec. 28, 1877, "Enforcement of Internal Revenue Laws," p. 31; Farrow to Grant, Mar. 3, 1877, H. P. Farrow Papers, Special Collections, University of Georgia, box 2, folder 6.

7. Clark to Raum, Jan. 27, 1878, "Enforcement of Internal Revenue Laws," pp. 32–33.

8. Clark to Raum correspondence, "Enforcement of Internal Revenue Laws," pp. 33–38; Raum to Clark, Mar. 6, 1879, ibid., pp. 38–39.

9. Hendrix to Clark, Nov. 27, 1879, "Enforcement of Internal Revenue Laws," pp. 5–6, original emphasis.

10. Shepard to Clark, Nov. 29, 1879, and Clark to Raum, Dec. 2, 1879, "Enforcement of Internal Revenue Laws," pp. 8–9, original emphasis.

11. Raum to Clark, Dec. 2, 1879, and Clark to Raum, Dec. 3, 16, 1879, "Enforcement of Internal Revenue Laws," pp. 6–7, 9–10.

12. Clark to Raum, Dec. 19, 23, 1879, "Enforcement of Internal Revenue Laws," pp. 10–11.

13. Raum to Clark, Jan. 10, 1880, and Clark to Raum, Jan. 21, Feb. 1, 1880, "Enforcement of Internal Revenue Laws," pp. 14, 17–20.

14. Clark to Raum, Feb. 17, 1880, "Enforcement of Internal Revenue Laws," pp. 21–24.

15. George W. Atkinson, *After the Moonshiners, by One of the Raiders* (Wheeling, W.Va.: Frew and Campbell, 1881), pp. 108–11. In 1890 a William Berong, whether the old man or a namesake kinsman is not clear, turned up in court on a charge of working in an illegal distillery and received a one-month jail sentence. See Records of the U.S. District Court, Northern Georgia, Record Group 21, National Archives, Atlanta Branch, box 208, case no. 8736.

16. Hendrix to Clark, June 21, May 29, 1880, and Clark to Raum, June 1880, LR, box 891; Conviction rates, *Annual Report, Commissioner of Internal Revenue, HED* 4 (usually) for appropriate years.

17. *Atlanta Constitution*, Apr. 3, 1879, May 12, 13, 19, 1880 (Farrow and Fitzsimmons); Dahlonega *Mountain Signal*, Mar. 1, 1878 (circular to law abiding citizens); "Enforcement of Internal Revenue Laws," p. 29; Raum to C. Devens, Atty. Gen., July 19, 1880, R. B. Hayes Papers, photocopy courtesy Hayes Presidential Center, Fremont, Ohio (Raum's charges); Henry D. Scomp, *King Alcohol in the Realm of King Cotton: A History of the Liquor Traffic and of the Temperance Movement in Georgia from 1733 to 1887* ([Atlanta]: Blakeley, 1888), pp. 655–56, 659 (legislature).

18. *New York Times*, Dec. 10, 1883 (sentence); Raum's narrative, "Enforcement of Internal Revenue Laws," p. 43; Raum to Xen. Wheeler, Dist. Atty., Tenn., Feb. 9, 1880, ibid., p. 207.

19. R. M. Wallace, Marshal, to Atty. Gen., Apr. 22, Aug. 7, 1878, SC S.C. (see also *New York Times*, Aug. 28, 1878); L. C. Northrop, Dist. Atty., to Atty. Gen., June 19, 1880, SC S.C.; Fannin to Raum, May 23, 1877, LR, box 896; Clark to H. P. Farrow, Dist. Atty., Ga., Sept. 4, 1879, in Farrow to Atty. Gen., Oct. 23, 1879, SC Ga.; *Internal Revenue Record and Customs Journal*, Mar. 11, 1878, p. 75 (Rives).

20. L. E. Parsons, Dist. Atty., to Atty. Gen., Oct. 8, 1877, SC Ala.; "Testimony Before the Senate Special Committee to Investigate the Administration of the Collection of Internal Revenue in the Sixth District of North Carolina," *Senate Miscellaneous Documents* 116, 47th Cong., 1st sess. (1882), testimony of Raum, p. 291 ("wall"); Raum's narrative, "Enforcement of Internal Revenue Laws," pp. 206–7; *New York Tribune*, Aug. 12, 1878. Information on number of suspended sentences in each state each year is in the revenue commissioner's annual reports, usually table I. Moonshiners could avoid payment of costs by swearing an oath that they were too poor. In the May 1879 term of the district court at Asheville, N.C., virtually every moonshiner who appeared was allowed to plead guilty and receive a suspended sentence, and only one of the cases was recorded as "costs paid." See Records of U.S. District Courts, Western North Carolina, Trial Docket Book, vol. 2, in Record Group 21, National Archives, Atlanta Branch.

21. C. Devens, Atty. Gen., to C. E. Mayer, Dist. Atty., Ala., Dec. 9, 23, 1878, I, bk. H, pp. 428, 464 (describing Raum's recommendation); Devens to V. S. Lusk, Dist. Atty., N.C., Oct. 25, 1878, I, bk. H, p. 348; Raum's note on jacket, Lusk to Atty. Gen., Dec. 3, 1878, SC N.C.; J. MacVeagh, Atty. Gen., to J. S. Bigby, Dist. Atty., Ga., Mar. 24, 1881, I, bk. K, p. 484; Devens to X. Wheeler, Dist. Atty., Tenn., Aug. 28, 1880, I, bk. K (all conveying Raum's denial of suspension to resisters); Devens to W. S. Bell, Asst. Dist. Atty., N.C., Nov. 29, 1878, I, bk. H, p. 412; S. M. Phillips, Actg. Atty. Gen., to J. D. White, May 25, 1883, L, bk. M, pp. 264–65; Raum to W. W. Murray, Dist. Atty., Tenn., Dec. 12, 1877, "Enforcement of Internal Revenue Laws," p. 154.

22. Raum to Farrow, Dec. 11, 1879, Farrow Papers, box 2, folder 14; R. M. Wallace, Marshal, to Atty. Gen., Aug. 7, 1878, and L. C. Northrop to Atty. Gen., Aug. 8, 1878, SC S.C.; Atty. Gen. to Northrop, Aug. 7, 1878, I, bk. H, p. 231; *New York Times*, Nov. 23, 1878 (S.C. confusion); Northrop to Atty. Gen., June 19, 1880, SC S.C.; Raum to J. Sherman, Secy. of Treasury, Apr. 16, 1879, "Enforcement of Internal Revenue Laws," p. 144; V. S. Lusk, Dist. Atty., to Atty. Gen., Dec. 13, 1878, SC N.C.

23. Henry M. Wiltse, *The Moonshiners* (Chattanooga, Tenn.: Times Printing Co., 1895), pp. 37, 207–8, 130–31 (quotation); Francis Lynde, "The Moonshiners of Fact," *Lippincott's Magazine* 57 (Jan. 1896): 72 (promise).

24. R. M. Wallace, Marshal, to Atty. Gen., Aug. 9, 1878, SC S.C.; L. C. Northrop, Dist. Atty., to Atty. Gen., n.d., ibid.; *Speight's Spartanburg Daily*, Sept. 1878, clipping in E. M. Brayton, Coll., to Raum, Nov. 8, 1878, LR, box 887; V. S. Lusk, Dist. Atty., to Atty. Gen., Dec. 3, 1878, SC N.C.; R. P. Dick, Dist. Judge, to Atty. Gen., Jan. 22, 1881, ibid.; "Testimony . . . Revenue in the Sixth District of N.C.," testimony of W. M. Walker, Dep. Coll., pp. 158–60.

25. For early promoting of legal distillation, see Collector J. A. Holtzclaw's statement, Dahlonega *Mountain Signal*, Sept. 12, 1873. For Raum's efforts, Raum to E. C. Wade and other Collectors, July 24, 1878, and narrative, "Enforcement of Internal Revenue Laws," pp. 208–9. For effects, "Testimony . . . Revenue in the Sixth District of N.C.," testimony of J. J. Mott, Coll., p. 367; Question of Zebulon Vance to Tyre Glenn, Dep. Coll., ibid., p. 130; testimony of Glenn, ibid., pp. 123, 126; D. C. Pearson, Storekeeper, ibid., p. 322; A. H. Brooks, Rev. Agt., ibid., p. 136. See also T. C. Tracie, Rev. Agt., to Raum, Nov. 21, 1882, LR, box 911; *New York Times*, July 7, 1880 (Brayton); R. M. Douglas, Marshal, to Atty. Gen., Feb. 9, 1874, SC N.C.; *New York Times*, Mar. 8, 1876, Nov. 10, 1879; H. B. Whitfield, Dep. Coll., Miss., to Raum, Mar. 10, 1877, LR, box 907 (problems of small distillers); Cox, Hill, and Thompson, Jno. M Hill & Co., et al. to Raum, Feb. 27, 1879, "Enforcement of Internal Revenue Laws," p. 201. For the problem, collusion of storekeepers and distillers, see chap. 4.

26. Raum to J. H. Rives, Coll., Va., Dec. 28, 1877, LC, bk. 31, p. 803; Raum to Rives, May 29, 1877, and Rives to Raum, June 11, 1877, "Enforcement of Internal Revenue Laws," pp. 157–59; *New York Times*, May 30, 1877 (Va.); B. H. Hollowell, Dep. Coll., Ark., to E. Wheeler, Coll., Oct. 26, Nov. 1, 1878, in Wheeler to Raum, Nov. 1, LR, box 908; D. B. Booth, Coll., Ala., to Raum, June 2, 1877, Jan. 14, Mar. 20, 1878, LR, box 887.

27. Dahlonega *Mountain Signal*, Sept. 27, 1878, Feb. 21, 1879; clipping from a Gainesville, Ga., paper, May 1877, in Clark to Raum, July 3, 1877; D. B. Booth, Coll., Ala., to Raum, June 2, 1877, Jan. 14, Mar. 20, 1878, both in LR, box 887.

28. *New York Times*, Aug. 29, 1877; R. F. Patterson, Coll., Tenn., to Raum, Aug. 29, 1877, "Enforcement of Internal Revenue Laws," p. 153; C. Devens, Atty. Gen., to J. Waldron, Marshal, Tenn., Aug. 2, 1877, I, bk. G, p. 419; *New York Times*, Dec. 22, 1878 (informers).

29. Northrop to Atty. Gen., Aug. 30, 1878, SC S.C.; E. M. Brayton, Coll., S.C., to Raum, in *New York Times*, Dec. 25, 1878.

30. W. H. Chapman, Rev. Agt., to Raum, May 18, 31, 1880, LR, box 891; J. E. Hendrix, Dep. Coll., to A. Clark, Coll., Ga., Jan. 31, 1880, in J. Wagner, Rev. Agt., to Raum, Feb. 17, 1880, LR, box 911; *Atlanta Constitution*, May 19, 1880.

31. Charleston, S.C., *News*, Aug. 3, 1881, quoted *New York Times*, Aug. 6, 1881; Greenville, S.C., *News*, July 21, 1881, quoted *New York Times*, July 24, 1881; E. M. Brayton, Coll., S.C., to Raum, June 7, 1882, LR, box 890.

32. W. W. Woodcock, Coll., Tenn., report in *New York Times*, July 7, 1880; G. B. Everitt, Coll., N.C., to Raum, Nov. 10, 1881, LR, box 896; P. M. Penndrucker, Dep. Coll., to J. M. Buckner, Coll., Ky., Feb. 12, 1881, in Buckner to Raum, Feb. 16, 1881, LR, box 890; J. E. Blaine, Coll., Ky., to Raum, June 12, 1882, LR, box 890;

H. M. Cooper, Coll., Ark., to Raum, June 3, 1882, LR, box 894; *Montgomery Advertiser and Mail*, May 25, 1883, in Report of J. W. Bowman and T. W. Nightingale, examiners, to Atty. Gen., Aug. 11, 1883, DJ 1457 '83.

33. The attorney general and the commissioner of internal revenue both provided statistics of the outcomes of revenue cases in their annual reports (usually *HED* 7 and *HED* 4, respectively, for each year). The two sets are organized according to different categories, but generally the total number of cases and proportion of convictions for each state agree, with a few exceptions each year. Except for the 1877–78 figures from the revenue commissioners' report, those in the text are from the attorney general's report (which has 1877–78 convictions in moonshine districts at 56 percent).

34. These figures must be used as only a rough guide to success or failure in coping with moonshining. They report *all* revenue violations, from licensed distillers to people selling glasses of whiskey in their homes. In tobacco areas, they included tobacco tax violators as well as liquor violators. The commissioner of internal revenue did not distinguish among types of revenue prosecutions in his statistics, except in 1891 and 1892. Those figures reveal that distilling cases made up at most 31 percent of revenue prosecutions (northern Georgia) and minimally 3 percent in West Virginia (1891); the next year the high was 51 percent (western North Carolina) and the low, 1 percent (northern Mississippi). In the moonshine districts covered, though, they can serve as a guide to trends in prosecution of blockaders because most distillers sold their product and it was easier to prosecute and convict them on retailing charges. Tobacco violations were very few in 1891. See *Annual Report, Commissioner of Internal Revenue*, 1891, *HED* 4, 52d Cong., 1st sess., table, pp. 44–46; ibid., 1892, *HED* 4, 52d Cong., 2d sess., table, pp. 45–46. Conviction figures for Ku Klux cases are from William Gillette, *Retreat from Reconstruction, 1869–1879* (Baton Rouge: Louisiana State University Press, 1979), table, p. 43.

35. Attorney general's annual report, *HED* 7 (usually), table I for each year.

36. "Testimony... Revenue in the Sixth District of N.C.," testimony of Raum, p. 300, and J. J. Mott, Coll., pp. 364–65.

37. Guilty pleas made up a high proportion of revenue convictions. This information is unfortunately not recorded in the attorney general's report until 1908, but there is little reason to assume marked variation in earlier years. The low year was 1909, with only 39 percent of convictions because of guilty pleas in the moonshine judicial districts; in 1912 the proportion was 60 percent, and for all other years between 1908 and 1918 the proportion of guilty pleas was above 70 percent overall.

38. Stephen Cresswell, a close student of moonshining and revenue enforcement in eastern Tennessee (which, as noted above, had consistently the highest proportion of convictions in revenue cases), argues that jurors, mostly Methodists and

Baptists from outside the mountain districts, were inclined to convict moonshiners because of the jurors' attitudes toward liquor. The argument is suggestive but the question of convictions is more complicated. Cresswell himself notes the district's two federal judges' leniency toward revenue violators. Jurors are usually more prone to convict even minor offenders when they know the sentence will be lenient. However, leniency is not sufficient to explain the conviction rates either. Judge Key was lenient, but conviction rates plummeted from over 85 percent in 1884 to 56 percent in 1887. They rose and dropped before his term was over in 1894. His successor, C. D. Clark, was much tougher, and his conviction rates were consistently higher than Key's. Guilty pleas probably also contributed to a high conviction rate, in 1908–18 ranging from 62 percent to 90 percent in eastern Tennessee revenue cases. See Cresswell, "Resistance and Enforcement: The U.S. Department of Justice, 1870–1893" (Ph.D. dissertation, University of Virginia, 1986), pp. 199, 211–15. For Clark's toughness, see Wiltse, *Moonshiners*, p. 124.

39. *Mobile Daily Advertiser*, Jan. 13, 1878, quoting *Jasper* [Walker Co.] *Eagle*, in Booth to Raum, Jan. 14, LR, box 887.

40. *Chattanooga Times*, copied by *Atlanta Post*, May 1880, in A. Clark, Coll., Ga., to Raum, May 12, 1880, LR, box 891; *Knoxville Chronicle*, quoted in Atkinson, *After the Moonshiners*, p. 31; "Testimony . . . Revenue in the Sixth District of N.C.," testimony of J. J. Mott, p. 367.

41. *Annual Report, Commissioner of Internal Revenue*, 1882, *HED* 4, 47th Cong., 2d sess., p. xv; ibid., 1883, *HED* 4, 48th Cong., 1st sess., p. xvi.

42. T. S. Tracie to Raum, Sept. 18, 1882, MLR, box 911.

CHAPTER 7

1. Evans was also a Union veteran and was elected to the Kentucky state legislature in 1871 and the state Senate in 1873. He won a seat in the U.S. House in 1894, where he was a strong and influential protectionist. Appointed U.S. district judge in Kentucky in 1899, he rendered a decision that protected collectors of internal revenue against state use of their records to enforce prohibition (see chap. 8). *National Cyclopaedia of American Biography* (New York: James T. White, 1920) 17:112; *Internal Revenue Record and Customs Journal*, May 25, 1883, p. 169.

2. *Annual Report, Commissioner of Internal Revenue*, 1886–87, *HED* 4, 50th Cong., 1st sess., p. xii (arrests and seizures).

3. Attorney general's annual report (usually *HED* 7) for each year (convictions, etc.: percentages are my calculation); revenue commissioner's annual reports (usually *HED* 4), table I (suspended sentence information).

4. James D. Richardson, comp., *Messages and Papers of the Presidents* (New York:

Bureau of National Literature, [1917]), 11:4722; Tun Yuan Hu, *The Liquor Tax in the United States, 1791–1947: A History of the Internal Revenue Taxes Imposed on Distilled Spirits by the Federal Government* (New York: Graduate School of Business, Columbia University, 1950), table in appendix (statistics).

5. John D. Long, ed., *The Republican Party, Its History, Principles, and Policies* (New York: M. W. Hazen, 1888), pp. 351–52 (platform); *New York Tribune*, Aug. 8, 1885 (reductions); *Internal Revenue Record and Customs Journal*, June 23, 1884, pp. 189–92, quotation at 191.

6. Leonard D. White, *The Republican Era: A Study in Administrative History* (New York: Macmillan, 1958), p. 319; *Internal Revenue Record and Customs Journal*, Dec. 24, 1894, p. 405; *New York Tribune*, Nov. 28, 1897 (civil service: Republicans weakened the civil service requirements in 1897, allowing collectors to replace their predecessors' appointments with candidates from the list of those who had passed the civil service exam). Long, *Republican Party*, pp. 237–39; *Morganton Star*, May 1, 1885.

7. *Internal Revenue Record and Customs Journal*, Mar. 30, 1885, p. 93, and Apr. 4, 1894, p. 101; *Wheeling Intelligencer*, Mar. 17, 1885; *Wheeling Register*, Mar. 17, 1885 (Miller); Miller quoted in *New York Tribune*, Aug. 8, 1885; *Statesville Landmark*, quoted by *Morganton Star*, Aug. 28, 1885; ibid., Oct. 16, 1885; Henry M. Wiltse, *The Moonshiners* (Chattanooga, Tenn.: Times Printing Co., 1895), pp. 209–10 (Cleveland).

8. Statistics from revenue commissioner's and attorney general's annual reports (usually *HED* 4 and 7, respectively). Among various states, three districts (western Arkansas and both in Missouri) reported over 60 percent convictions throughout the four years of Democratic administration. In contrast, the district attorney in northern Georgia seems to have had a jury revolt on his hands, for convictions plunged from 82 percent in 1884–85 to 47 percent the next year, remaining in that vicinity through 1888–89. It was acquittals rather than discontinuance of cases that accounted for the tremendous drop in convictions. The whitecap vigilante movement was growing in the later eighties and may have manifested itself in moonshiners' unwillingness to plead guilty, jurors' refusal to convict, and witnesses' fear of coming forward. Local factors remained important influences on the effectiveness of revenue enforcement.

9. *Annual Report, Commissioner of Internal Revenue*, 1884–85, *HED* 4, 49th Cong., 1st sess., p. xiv; *New York Times*, quoted in *Internal Revenue Record and Customs Journal*, May 31, 1886, p. 166; *Morganton Star*, Nov. 6, 1885 (agents).

10. J. Lofland, Rev. Agt., to Miller, Sept. 10, 1886, Apr. 3, 1886, Apr. 17, 1886, MLR, box 913.

11. W. Lay, Rev. Agt., to Miller, July 27, 1885, MLR, box 913 (Ky.); *New York*

· ·

Times, Nov. 7, 12, 1885 (Pyle); G. B. Clark, Rev. Agt., to Miller, Feb. 2, 1888, MLR, box 913 (Dark Corner); N. Gregg, Coll., to Miller, Mar. 2, 1887, LR, box 897 (Tenn.); W. M. Nixon, Marshal, Tenn., to Atty. Gen., Dec. 17, 1888, DJ 9960 '88, box 385 (Goodson).

12. C. Dowd, Coll., to Miller, Dec. 11, 1886, LR, box 895 (foxes); J. S. Battle, Rev. Agt., to Miller, May 22, 1888, MLR, box 913; W. H. Chapman, Rev. Agt., to Miller, Jan. 13, 1888, MLR, box 913; T. C. Crenshaw, Coll., Ga., to Miller, Nov. 30, 1885, LR, box 891 (N.C., Ga.); J. W. Nelms, Marshal, Ga., to Atty. Gen., Mar. 17, 1888, DJ 7112 '86, box 271 (no. of raids in Ga.: this records only raids in which *no* arrests were made, so there were probably more); G. B. Clark, Rev. Agt., to Miller, Mar. 23, 1888, MLR, box 913 (raiding deputies).

13. T. C. Crenshaw, Coll., Ga., to Miller, Dec. 9, 1885, LR, box 891; Dahlonega *Mountain Signal*, June 12, 1885 (Speer); *New York Times*, May 17, 1888.

14. J. H. Hurlburt, Rev. Agt., to Miller, Feb. 27, 1888, and W. H. Chapman, Rev. Agt., to Miller, Jan. 2, 1888, MLR, box 913.

15. W. H. Chapman, Rev. Agt., to Miller, Oct. 19, 1886, July 19, 1887; J. W. Nelms, Marshal, Ga., to Atty. Gen., June 20, 1887; Chapman to Miller, July 30, 1887; J. L. Clay, Dep. Coll., to Chapman, in Chapman to Miller, Aug. 12, 1887, all in DJ 7112 '86, box 271.

16. G. B. Clark, Rev. Agt., to Miller, Aug. 12, 1887, DJ 7112 '86, box 271; Chapman to Miller, Jan. 2, 1888, MLR, box 913; J. M. Mason, Commissioner, to W. W. Rollins, Coll., N.C., Oct. 28, 1891, Zeb V. Walser Papers, Southern Historical Collection, University of North Carolina, letterbook 15.

17. *Annual Report of the Attorney General*, 1885, *HED* 7, 49th Cong., 1st sess., p. 12.

18. G. B. Clark, Rev. Agt., to Miller, Feb. 2, 1888, MLR, box 913; *U.S. Revenue Journal*, Feb. 5, 1896, p. 49. Drying up of the appropriation for revenue raids in 1887 temporarily added to the confusion between revenuers and marshals because raids had to be financed from judicial appropriations, with revenuers specially commissioned as deputy marshals (*Annual Report, Attorney General*, 1887, HED 7, 50th Cong., 1st sess., p. xx.

19. W. W. Colquitt, Dep. Coll., Ala., to W. H. Chapman, Rev. Agt., Nov. 12, 1887, in W. E. Henderson, Actg. Commissioner, to Atty. Gen., Nov. 30, 1887, DJ 7112 '86, box 271; original emphasis.

20. Wiltse, *Moonshiners*, pp. 26–28; Young E. Allison, "Moonshine Men," *Southern Bivouac* 5 (Feb. 1887): 534; Stephen Cresswell, "Resistance and Enforcement: The U.S. Department of Justice, 1870–1893" (Ph.D. dissertation, University of Virginia, 1986), p. 217.

21. *Internal Revenue Record and Customs Journal*, Feb. 7, Oct. 8, 22, 1888; for

continued reliance on testimony of deputy marshals, who "are not deemed disinterested parties," see W. W. Rollins, Coll., N.C., to Z. V. Walser, Dep. Coll., Sept. 15, 1891, Walser Papers, letterbook 15; *New York Times*, Mar. 4, 1900.

22. *New York Times*, Nov. 5, 1885; J. L. Black, Dep. Coll., S.C., to D. F. Bradley, Coll., in Bradley to Miller, Dec. 1, 1885, LR, box 889.

23. Frederic C. Howe, *Taxation and Taxes in the United States under the Internal Revenue System, 1791–1895* (New York: T. Y. Crowell, 1896), pp. 5–6; Richardson, *Messages*, 12: 5474; *Internal Revenue Record and Customs Journal*, Apr. 21, 1890, p. 117, Mar. 9, 1891, p. 69.

24. *Internal Revenue Record and Customs Journal*, Mar. 25, 1889, p. 86; *Wheeling Intelligencer*, Mar. 19, 1889, and Apr. 17, 1893 (biographical information).

25. Mason to W. W. Colquitt, Jan. 1, 1893, John M. Mason Papers, West Virginia Collection, West Virginia University, series II, box 5; Mason to Rev. J. H. Flanagan, Apr. 3, 1889, ibid., box 1; to Flanagan, Apr. 16, 1889, and to C. W. Wisner, Apr. 16, 1889, ibid., box 1; to Agt. Thrasher, June 6, 1889, to Agt. E. M. Brown, Aug. 2, 1889, to A. B. White, Coll., W.Va., Aug. 10, 1889, ibid., box 2 (A. B. Mason); to M. T. Levall and to Louis Kitzwieller, Apr. 3, 1889, box 1.

26. J. M. Mason to E. A. Webster, Coll., S.C., Jan. 20, 1890, ibid., box 2; to W. H. Chapman, Mar. 10, 1892, ibid., box 4.

27. *Atlanta Constitution*, Dec. 13, 1891 (quotation); statistics, same sources as n. 2. Among the individual states under the Democrats, seven prosecutors had reported conviction rates of over 50 percent during the four years. Now only five were able to sustain that proportion of convictions. Another five were at the opposite extreme, reporting 50 percent or better convictions in only one year.

28. Mason to W. O. Bradley, July 8, 1889, Mason Papers, series II, box 1; W. H. Chapman to Mason, Dec. 7, 1889, MLR, box 914 (inexperience); E. M. Brown, Rev. Agt., to Mason, Apr. 25, 1889, MLR, box 914 (fees); *Atlanta Constitution*, Dec. 31, 1891 (nature of raids and arrests).

29. Records of the U.S. District Court, Northern Georgia, Record Group 21, National Archives, Atlanta Branch, box 208, case no. 8742 (Bowen); *Atlanta Constitution*, Dec. 31, 1891, p. 5; Dahlonega *Signal and Advertiser*, Jan. 15, 1894, (jail); for a similar description of comfortable quarters and "plain but nutritious food, which is an epicure's feast compared to his own table," see Allison, "Moonshine Men," p. 534. The federal prison in Atlanta was not open until the turn of the century.

30. G. B. Clark, Rev. Agt., to Mason, Dec. 5, 1889, MLR, box 914 (Ark.); E. M. Brown, Rev. Agt., to Mason, Mar. 30, 1889, ibid.; G. W. Jolly, Dist. Atty., to Atty. Gen., Aug. 30, 1889, Mar. 25, 1892, DJ 2816 '89, box 398 (Ky.); W. H. Chapman, Rev. Agt., to Mason, Feb. 15, Dec. 7, 1889, MLR, box 914 (Ala.); L. E. Parsons, Dist. Atty., Ala., to AG, Feb. 14, Dec. 31, 1891, DJ 7112 '86, box 271 (wounding).

· ·

31. *Internal Revenue Record and Customs Journal*, Sept. 19, 1887, p. 293, actually referring to a case in northern New York; E. M. Brown, Rev. Agt., to Mason, Apr. 25, 1889, MLR, box 914.

32. Cresswell, "Resistance and Enforcement," pp. 217–19.

33. W. H. Chapman, Rev. Agt., to Mason, May 17, 1890; Mason to D. B. Smith, B. K. Collier, June 2, 1890; R. A. Mosely, Coll., Ala., June 4, 1890, all in Mason Papers, series II, box 3.

34. J. E. Hilton to Benjamin Harrison, July 31, 1890, MLR, box 914; *New York Times*, July 25, 1890, p. 2; W. W. Rollins, Coll., to Z. V. Walser, Dep. Coll., Dec. 31, 1891 (quoting Commissioner's circular), Sept. 23, 1891, Walser Papers, letterbook 15.

35. J. E. Kercheval, examiner, to Atty. Gen., May 29, 1891, and W. R. Hazen, examiner, to Atty. Gen., Mar. 27, 1893, DJ 5465 '91, box 574.

36. Olive H. Shadgett, *The Republican Party in Georgia: From Reconstruction through 1900* (Athens: University of Georgia Press, 1964), p. 94 (Pleasant); A. M. Swope, Coll., Ky., to Raum, Jan. 23, 1882; LR, box 906; W. L. Fernald, Coll., Va., to Raum, May 11, 1881, LR, box 896; W. A. Knisely, Rev. Agt., to Mason, Jan. 2, 1891, MLR, box 915 (Miss.); W. H. Chapman, Rev. Agt., to Mason, 1889, MLR, box 915; A. Brady to G. Wilson, Dep. Commissioner, Int. Rev., Feb. 22, 1893, MLR, box 915; Mason to W. W. Rollins, Coll., N.C., Mar. 30, 1892, Mason Papers, series II, box 4; Gordon B. McKinney, *Southern Mountain Republicans 1865–1900: Politics and the Appalachian Community* (Chapel Hill: University of North Carolina Press, 1978) pp. 9–10, 138–39.

37. *New York Times*, July 25, 1890; *Atlanta Constitution*, Dec. 23, 1894.

CHAPTER 8

1. *Annual Report, Commissioner of Internal Revenue*, usually *HED* 4 for appropriate years; Frederick C. Howe, *Taxation and Taxes in the United States under the Internal Revenue System, 1791–1895* (New York: T. Y. Crowell, 1896), p. 151, quoting Wells's "Special Letter to Secretary of Treasury John G. Carlisle," July 1893, and pp. 252–53; *New York Tribune*, Jan. 25, 1896 (estimate); *New York Times*, Apr. 14, 1895.

2. Mason to L. Mallonee, Mar. 14, 1893, John M. Mason Papers, West Virginia Collection, West Virginia University, series II, box 5; *Wheeling Intelligencer*, Apr. 17, 18, 1893.

3. Seizure and arrest figures, revenue commissioners' annual reports.

4. Conviction rates, *Annual Report of the Attorney General*, usually *HED* 7 for appropriate years; comparisons with national conviction rates, revenue commission-

er's report; all percentages my calculation. There are variations between the two sets of figures, usually only one or two percentage points different in the averages, in the eight-year period, making the attorney general's average 60 percent, the commissioner's 61 percent. Both reports were based on the district attorneys' statistical data; it is possible that those of the attorney general were more up to date, but only by a few weeks at most. State variations continued as in other years, but certain patterns were fixed: eastern Tennessee still had the strongest conviction rates, above 70 percent in seven of eight years between 1893 and 1901; neighboring middle Tennessee was above 60 percent in all eight. West Virginia continued to be the place where blockaders most likely got off, remaining under 50 percent during the whole period, mainly because the district attorney dropped large numbers of cases without trial. Northern Mississippi closely followed, with convictions at 50 percent only in 1894–95. Acquittals by juries accounted for moonshiners getting off more than in West Virginia.

5. *Annual Report, Commissioner of Internal Revenue*, 1897–98, *HED* 11, 55th Cong., 3d sess., p. 30; *Atlanta Constitution*, June 28, 1894; J. S. James, Dist. Atty., to Atty. Gen., Feb. 19, 1897, DJ 3721 '97, box 932; *Annual Report, Commissioner of Internal Revenue*, 1896–97, *HED* 11, 55th Cong., 2d sess., p. 24; *Atlanta Constitution*, Mar. 25, 1896.

6. *Annual Report, Commissioner of Internal Revenue*, 1897–98, *HED* 11, 55th Cong., 3d sess., p. 31; ibid., 1901, *HED* 11, 57th Cong., 1st sess., p. 24; William L. Downward, *Dictionary of the History of the American Brewing and Distilling Industries* (Westport, Conn.: Greenwood, 1980), pp. xxiii, 213–14.

7. This discussion summarizes the various state studies, representing the common theme of which there were local variations: Thomas H. Appleton, " 'Like Banquo's Ghost': The Emergence of the Prohibition Issue in Kentucky Politics" (Ph.D. dissertation, University of Kentucky, 1981); Paul E. Isaac, *Prohibition and Politics: Turbulent Decades in Tennessee, 1885–1920* (Knoxville: University of Tennessee Press, 1965); C. C. Pearson and J. Edwin Hendricks, *Liquor and Anti-Liquor in Virginia, 1619–1919* (Durham, N.C.: Duke University Press, 1967); Henry D. Scomp, *King Alcohol in the Realm of King Cotton: A History of the Liquor Traffic and of the Temperance Movement in Georgia from 1733 to 1887* ([Atlanta]: Blakeley, 1888); James Benson Sellers, *The Prohibition Movement in Alabama, 1702 to 1943*, James Sprunt Studies in History and Political Science, vol. 26, no. 1 (Chapel Hill: University of North Carolina Press, 1943); Daniel J. Whitener, *Prohibition in North Carolina, 1715–1945*, James Sprunt Studies in History and Political Science, vol. 27, no. 1 (Chapel Hill: University of North Carolina Press, 1946). Jess Carr, *The Second Oldest Profession: An Informal History of Moonshining in America* (Englewood Cliffs, N.J.: Prentice-Hall, 1972), pp. 84–91, offers a general summary.

8. Stephen Cresswell, "Resistance and Enforcement: The U.S. Department of Justice, 1870–1893" (Ph.D. dissertation, University of Virginia, 1986), pp. 224–25; W. S. Powell, ed., *Dictionary of North Carolina Biography* (Chapel Hill: University of North Carolina Press, 1971), 2:307 (Glenn); Whitener, *Prohibition in North Carolina*, pp. 71–78, 68 (newspaper quotation); Mott to Raum, July 1, 1881, LR, box 900; Gordon B. McKinney, *Southern Mountain Republicans 1865–1900: Politics and the Appalachian Community* (Chapel Hill: University of North Carolina Press, 1978), p. 117 (Kentucky).

9. *New York Graphic*, n.d., quoted in *Internal Revenue Record and Customs Journal*, Oct. 10, 1881, p. 317; *New York Evening Post*, Oct. 10, 1881, quoted in *Internal Revenue Record and Customs Journal*, Nov. 14, 1881, p. 358; A. Burwell, "Dramshops, Industry and Taxes: An Address to the People of Mississippi" (New York: National Temperance Society, 1874), p. 2; Mason to Mrs. S. D. LaFetra, Pres. W.C.T.U., Jan. 19, 1892, Mason Papers, series II, box 4 (Mason got into trouble with hometown prohibitionists when he wrote to a judge hoping he could find extenuating circumstances in sentencing an old family friend guilty of illegal liquor selling. The prohibitionists somehow learned of this personal correspondence and charged the commissioner with attempting to intimidate the judge: Mason to J. T. Hoke, and to Ellen McAvay, Apr. 3, 1892, and to E. I. Allen, June 14, 1892, Mason Papers, series II, box 4); Scomp, *King Alcohol*, pp. 668–69. For a full discussion of prohibitionist objections to the revenue system, with examples from throughout the country, see Richard Hamm, "Origins of the Eighteenth Amendment: Prohibition in the Federal System, 1880–1920" (Ph.D. dissertation, University of Virginia, 1987), chap. 4.

10. Hamm, "Origins of the Eighteenth Amendment," chap. 5, with quotations, discusses this controversy in full.

11. Whitener, *Prohibition in North Carolina*, p. 73; Leonard S. Blakey, *The Sale of Liquor in the South: The History of the Development of a Normal Social Restraint in Southern Commonwealths*, Columbia University Studies in History, Economics, and Public Law, 51, no. 127 (New York: Columbia University Press, 1912), plates 2 and 3; Isaac, *Prohibition and Politics*, pp. 55–56.

12. Margaret W. Morley, *The Carolina Mountains* (Boston: Houghton Mifflin, 1913), p. 203; Horace Kephart, *Our Southern Highlanders* (New York: Outing, 1913), pp. 188–89; *New York Times*, July 25, 1890; *Atlanta Constitution*, Dec. 23, 1894 ("jug"); *Bonfort's Wine and Spirit Circular*, quoted in *Internal Revenue Record and Customs Journal*, Feb. 28, 1887, p. 63.

13. McKinney, *Southern Mountain Republicans*, p. 129 (middle class); R. H. McNeill, letter in *Charlotte Observer*, Jan. 22, 1899; E. O. Stafford, in *Atlanta Constitution*, Jan. 2, 1895; Dahlonega *Signal and Advertiser*, Nov. 3, 1893, Jan. 12, 1894; "Enforcement of Internal Revenue Laws: . . . Report of the Commissioner of

Internal Revenue . . . to Explain the Necessity for Employment of Armed Men . . . ,"
HED 62, 46th Cong., 2d sess. (1880), p. 205 (criticisms quoted by Raum); Peyton
Jones et al. to Atty. Gen., Mar. 21, 1900, DJ 50601 '00, box 1204; John C.
Campbell, *The Southern Highlander and His Homeland* (New York: Russell Sage
Foundation, 1921), p. 106; William L. Montell, *Killings: Folk Justice in the Upper
South* (Lexington: University Press of Kentucky, 1986), pp. 38–39 (whiskey and
violence).

14. Charles Dudley Warner, "On Horseback," *Atlantic Monthly* 56 (Aug. 1885):
196, 200; Dahlonega *Mountain Signal*, Feb. 9, 1875, Jan. 18, 1878; *Morganton Star*,
May 29, June 26, 1885; J. Wesley Smith, *The Mountaineers; or, Bottled Sunshine for
Blue Mondays* (Nashville: Publishing House of the Methodist Episcopal Church,
South, 1902), chap. 11 (reforms); *New York Times*, Apr. 14, 1895; *New York Tribune*,
July 23, 1899; Dahlonega *Signal and Advertiser*, Nov. 10, 1893 (moonshining
churchmen); Montell, *Killings*, pp. 159–61.

15. *New York Tribune*, Jan. 5, 1895 (Ark.), and June 29, 1895 (S.C.); *Greenville
Daily News*, June 30, 1935, reprinting article from May 30, 1894, photocopy courtesy Greenville County Library (S.C.); Olive Campbell Diary, Dec. 25–30, 1908, p.
68, typescript, Southern Historical Collection, University of North Carolina.

16. Francis B. Simpkins, *Pitchfork Ben Tillman, South Carolinian* (Baton Rouge:
Louisiana State University Press, 1944), chaps. 16–17 (Darlington riot). The *New
York Tribune* almost literally cackled with glee over South Carolina's suppression of
local autonomy, considering all the trouble the state had caused in the past over that
issue (Mar. 31, 1894); Kephart, *Highlanders*, p. 187; Emil O. Peterson, "A Glimpse
of the Moonshiners," *Chautauquan* 26 (Nov. 1897): 180 (state punishment).

17. Edward Ayers, *Vengeance and Justice: Crime and Punishment in the 19th-Century
American South* (New York: Oxford University Press, 1984), chap. 7; Barton C.
Shaw, *The Wool-Hat Boys: Georgia's Populist Party* (Baton Rouge: Louisiana State
University Press, 1984), p. 104 (gins); McKinney, *Southern Mountain Republicans*,
chap. 5; William F. Holmes, "Moonshiners and Whitecaps in Alabama, 1893,"
Alabama Review 24 (Jan. 1981): 32, and "Moonshining and Collective Violence:
Georgia, 1889–1895," *Journal of American History* 67 (Dec. 1980): 592.

18. Holmes, "Moonshining and Collective Violence," pp. 596–98; Robert S.
Davis, Jr., "The Night Riders of Pickens County," *North Georgia Journal* 4 (June
1987): 22–24; Henry M. Wiltse, *The Moonshiners* (Chattanooga, Tenn.: Times
Printing Co., 1895), pp. 150–57. Data on tenancy and farm size are in U.S. Census
Office, *Report on the Productions of Agriculture as Returned at the Tenth Census (June 1,
1880)* (Washington, D.C.: Government Printing Office, 1883), pp. 40–44; U.S.
Census Office, *Report on the Statistics of Agriculture in the United States at the Eleventh
Census: 1890* (Washington, D.C.: Government Printing Office, 1895), pp. 130–32;

U.S. Census Office, *Twelfth Census of the United States, Taken in the Year 1900 . . . Agriculture, Part 1* (Washington, D.C.: Census Office, 1902), pp. 68–71.

19. Holmes, "Moonshining and Collective Violence," p. 600 n. 39 (Trammell); *Atlanta Constitution*, Jan. 31, 1895 (quotation); S. B. Sheibley, Examiner, to Atty. Gen., Mar. 2, 3, 4, 1895, Dec. 11, 1894, Jan. 23, Feb. 16, 1895, DJ 6525 '93, box 699 (all on corruption: also cited Holmes, "Moonshining and Collective Violence," p. 610 n. 72). By 1897 Marshal Dunlap's office received a favorable report; six deputies had been dismissed, one for drunkenness, by direction of the Justice Department, and no corruption problem was mentioned. J. Easby-Smith, Examiner, to Atty. Gen., Mar. 9, 1897, DJ 6525 '93, box 699. Mrs. W. H. Felton to Atty. Gen., Dec. 24, 1894, DJ 7112 '86 (original italics). Wright and other deputies may have been playing a complicated double game. According to District Attorney James, the deputy was himself a whitecapper, involved in the attempted hanging and later murder of Henry Worley, an informer. Three other deputies, discharged by the marshal, also seem to have been in league with the terrorists (James to Atty. Gen., Dec. 15, 1894, DJ 7112 '86, box 271).

20. J. S. James, Dist. Atty., to Atty. Gen., Dec. 15, 1894, DJ 7112 '86, box 271; Holmes, "Moonshining and Collective Violence," p. 601; *Atlanta Constitution*, Nov. 7, 29, 1893 (Lewis), and Mar. 17, 1894; James to Atty. Gen., May 2, 1894, (Goodson), and Dec. 15, 1894 (Goodson and Wright), both in DJ 7112 '86, box 271.

21. Holmes, "Moonshiners and Whitecaps in Alabama," pp. 36–37; Scomp, *King Alcohol*, pp. 790–98; Sellers, *Prohibition in Alabama*, p. 91.

22. B. W. Briggs, U.S. Commissioner, to W. H. Chapman, Rev. Agt., Aug. 17, 1893, and J. C. Musgrove, Marshal, to Atty. Gen., Sept. 1, 1893, DJ 3017 '93, box 664. Another Alabama deputy was killed by a man who mistakenly believed he was a whitecap coming to whip him. Holmes, "Moonshiners and Whitecaps in Alabama," p. 41.

23. Holmes, "Moonshining and Collective Violence," pp. 599, 604–7, and "Moonshiners and Whitecaps in Alabama," pp. 41–47. A draft of the indictment in the Worley case is in J. S. James, Dist. Atty., to Atty. Gen., Mar. 16, 1895, DJ 7112 '86, box 271.

24. Francis Lynde, "The Moonshiners of Fact," *Lippincott's Magazine* 57 (Jan. 1896): 72, 73; Samuel G. Blythe, "Raiding Moonshiners," *Munsey's Magazine* 25 (June 1901): 422 (variations); *New York Tribune*, Aug. 31, 1897 (Ark.); W. M. Smith, Dist. Atty., Ky., to Atty. Gen., Oct. 6, 1897, DJ 915 '97, box 923; *New York Tribune*, Nov. 20, 1897 (Tenn.); W. S. Forman, Commissioner, to Coll. of Int. Rev., Ky., Nov. 20, 1897, LC, bk. 659, p. 569.

25. R. A. Hancock, Dep. Coll., to J. F. Hazzard, Rev. Agt., Sept. 21, 1893; R.

Williams, Rev. Agt., to J. Miller, May 2, 1894 (hiding), both MLR, box 915; Cresswell, "Resistance and Enforcement," p. 184; L. A. Thrasher, Rev. Agt., to Miller, Aug. 7, 1893, MLR, box 915 (Tenn.); W. M. Smith, Dist. Atty., Ky., to Atty. Gen., Jan. 16, 1896, DJ 8416 '95, box 874; W. H. Chapman to Commissioner, telegram, June 7, 1897, DJ 8474 '97, box 954, with Commissioner to Atty. Gen., June 8, 1897.

26. Blythe, "Raiding Moonshiners," pp. 422–24.

27. Isaac Stapleton, *Moonshiners in Arkansas* (Independence, Mo.: Zion's Printing and Publishing Co., 1948), pp. 35–36, 17–18; H. M. Cooper, Marshal, to Atty. Gen., Mar. 2, 1898, DJ 12956 '98, box 987.

28. Powell, ed., *Dictionary*, 2:63 (Dick); R. T. Hough, Solicitor, Int. Rev., to Atty. Gen., Dec. 18, 28, 1893, and R. B. Glenn, Dist. Atty., to Atty. Gen., Dec. 21, 1893, DJ 12471 '93, box 731; Glenn to Atty. Gen., Jan. 22, 1897, DJ 1652 '95, box 870 (with Dick's endorsement, and with table of cases, convictions, suspensions, 1885–95, attached; overall number of suspensions from revenue commissioners' reports); Cleveland to Olney, personal, Dec. 21, 1895, DJ 12471 '93, box 731.

29. The controversy between Glenn and his superiors can be followed in a long paper trail: R. T. Hough, Solicitor, Int. Rev., to Atty. Gen., Dec. 28, 1893, Mar. 31, 1894, and J. Miller, Commissioner, to J. G. Carlisle, Sec. of Treas., Dec. 16, 1895, DJ 12471 '93, box 731; Glenn to Atty. Gen., Jan. 22, 1897; Glenn to Miller, Dec. 23, 1895; Glenn to Atty. Gen., Feb. 29, Apr. 14, 1896, DJ 16512 '95, box 870.

30. Secy. of Treas. to Atty. Gen., Apr. 5, 1897; G. W. Wilson, Actg. Commissioner, Int. Rev., to Secy. of Treas., Apr. 9, 1897; Glenn to Atty. Gen., Apr. 12, 1897; Chapman to W. S. Forman, Commissioner, May 17, 1897; G. W. Wilson, Actg. Commissioner, to Secy. of Treas., May 21, 1897, all in DJ 16512 '95, box 870.

31. *Annual Report, Commissioner of Internal Revenue*, 1898, *HED* 11, 55th Cong., 3d sess., pp. 30–31; statistics in annual reports for appropriate years.

32. Newspaper clipping of circular letter, in Glenn to Atty. Gen., Apr. 25, 1894, DJ 12471 '93, box 731; "New Rules of the United States Court" (1894), in Glenn to Atty. Gen., Jan. 22, DJ 1897 '95, and 16512 '95, box 870.

33. Unsigned examiners' report, Feb. 28, 1898, DJ 5465 '91, box 575.

34. J. S. Easby-Smith, Examiner, to Atty. Gen., Sept. 10, 1896; W. M. Shelby, Coll., Ky., to J. Miller, Oct. 7, 1896, both DJ 452 '95, box 816; C. D. Clark, Dist. Judge, to Atty. Gen., Aug. 5, 1898, DJ 12935 '98, box 1102 (Ky. prohibition); A. D. James, Marshal, Ky., to Atty. Gen., June 15, 1898, DJ 9840 '98, box 1088 (relatives).

35. W. M. O. Dawson, Chair, W.Va. Republican State Committee, to Atty. Gen., Oct. 21, 1896, and C. E. Wells, Marshal, W.Va., to Atty. Gen., Oct. 24, 1896, DJ 16299 '96, box 912; J. Gaines, Dist. Atty., W.Va., to Atty. Gen., Dec. 11, 1897, DJ 12379 '93, box 731.

36. *Atlanta Constitution*, Feb. 26, 1896. On salaries: *Annual Report, Attorney General*, 1895, *HED* 9, 54th Cong., 1st sess., pp. 5–6; ibid. 1896 *HED* 9, 54th Cong., 2d sess., pp. ix–xi; Frederick S. Calhoun, Historian, U.S. Marshals Service, letter to author June 30, 1986.

37. Various letters from commissioner to collectors in Va., Ky., Ala., Ga., Mar. 31, 1897, LC, bk. 639, pp. 199, 206, 239, 256, 267; G. Wilson, Actg. Comm., to B. Johnson, Coll., Ky., Mar. 30, 1897; W. M. Shelby, Coll., Ky., Apr. 1, 1897, LC, bk. 639, pp. 117, 338; *Annual Report, Commissioner of Internal Revenue*, 1900, *HED* 11, 56th Cong., 2d sess., p. 28 (effect of agents).

38. Number of cases, conviction rates, from attorney general's annual reports.

39. *Annual Report, Commissioner of Internal Revenue*, 1898, *HED* 11, 55th Cong., 3d sess., p. 31.

40. Horace Kephart, "Roving with Kephart: The Sport of Still Hunting (Moonshine Stills)," *All Outdoors* (Sept. 1919): 491 (clipping in North Carolina Collection, University of North Carolina Library); *Annual Report, Commissioner of Internal Revenue*, 1913, *HED* 513, 63d Cong., 2d sess., p. 21; seizure, arrest, casualty figures in commissioners' reports for each year; Carr, *Second Oldest Profession*, pp. 88–91; Theodore H. Price and Richard Spillane, "The Commissioner of Internal Revenue as a Policeman," *Outlook* 120 (Nov. 27, 1918): 498, 503, 505.

Selected Bibliography

. . . .

MANUSCRIPTS

Federal Government Records, National Archives, Washington, D.C.

Adjutant General's Office, Record Group 94
   Letters received by the adjutant general's office (microfilm)
Bureau of Internal Revenue, Record Group 58
   Letters from the commissioner of internal revenue to collectors
   Letters received by the commissioner of internal revenue from collectors and
      others
   Miscellaneous official letters received by the commissioner of internal
      revenue
Bureau of the Census
   U.S. Census, Population Schedules, Oconee County, S.C., and Rabun
      County, Ga., 1880, 1900 (microfilm)
Department of Justice, Record Group 60
   Department of Justice yearly letter files
   Instructions from attorney general to U.S. district attorneys and marshals
   Letters from attorney general to executive officers, members of Congress,
      and others
   Source Chronological Files: Letters received by the Department of Justice
      from each state (microfilm)
Department of Justice, Record Group 21, Atlanta Branch
   Records of United States district courts: South Carolina, northern Georgia,
      North Carolina, and Tennessee

Personal Papers

Southern Historical Collection, University of North Carolina
 John C. and Olive D. Campbell Papers, Ms. Diary and Photograph
 Collection
 Zeb V. Walser Papers, Letterbooks
Special Collections, University of Georgia
 Henry P. Farrow Papers
West Virginia Collection, West Virginia University
 John M. Mason Papers, Letterbooks, Series II

PUBLISHED GOVERNMENT DOCUMENTS

Congressional Globe
Congressional Record
Annual Report of the Attorney General (usually *HED* 7 for each year)
Annual Report of the Commissioner of Internal Revenue (usually *HED* 4 for
 each year)
"Enforcement of Internal Revenue Laws. . . . Report of the Commissioner of
 Internal Revenue to the Secretary of the Treasury, in Reply to House Resolution
 of February 10, 1880, Making Inquiry for Information Tending to Explain the
 Necessity for Employment of Armed Men in Enforcement of the Internal
 Revenue Laws": *HED* 62, 46th Cong., 2d sess. (1880)
"Testimony Before the Senate Special Committee to Investigate the
 Administration of the Collection of Internal Revenue in the Sixth District of
 North Carolina, Appointed April 21, 1882": *Senate Miscellaneous Documents* 116,
 47th Cong., 1st sess. (1882)

NEWSPAPERS

Atlanta Constitution
Dahlonega *Mountain Signal, Signal and Advertiser* (Ga.)
Internal Revenue Record and Customs Journal
Morganton Star (N.C.)
New York Times
New York Tribune
Raleigh *Daily Standard*
Wheeling Intelligencer

PUBLISHED OFFICIAL MEMOIRS

Atkinson, George Wesley. *After the Moonshiners, by One of the Raiders*. Wheeling, W.Va.: Frew and Campbell, 1881.
Stapleton, Isaac. *Moonshiners in Arkansas*. Independence, Mo.: Zion's Printing and Publishing Co., 1948.
Whitley, H. C. *In It*. Cambridge, Mass.: Riverside Press, 1894.
Wiltse, Henry M. *The Moonshiners*. Chattanooga, Tenn.: Times Printing Co., 1895.

BOOKS AND ARTICLES ON MOUNTAINEERS AND MOONSHINING BY NINETEENTH- AND EARLY-TWENTIETH-CENTURY WRITERS

Allen, James L. "Mountain Passes of the Cumberland." *Harper's New Monthly Magazine* 81 (Sept. 1890): 561–76.
———. "Through Cumberland Gap on Horseback." *Harper's New Monthly Magazine* 73 (June 1886): 50–66.
Allison, Young E. "Moonshine Men." *Southern Bivouac* 5 (Feb. 1887): 528–34.
Baine, Donald A. "Among the Moonshiners." *Dixie* 1 (Aug. 1885): 9–14.
Blythe, Samuel G. "Raiding Moonshiners." *Munsey's Magazine* 25 (June 1901): 418–24.
Campbell, John C. *The Southern Highlander and His Homeland*. New York: Russell Sage Foundation, 1921.
[Cooke, John Esten]. "Moonshiners." *Harper's New Monthly Magazine* 58 (Feb. 1879): 380–90.
Davis, Rebecca Harding. "By-Paths in the Mountains, III." *Harper's New Monthly Magazine* 61 (Sept. 1880): 532–47.
Frost, William G. "Our Contemporary Ancestors in the Southern Mountains." *Atlantic Monthly* 83 (Mar. 1899): 311–19.
Guernsey, A. H. "Hunting for Stills." *Harper's Weekly* 11 (Dec. 21, 1867): 811.
———. "Illicit Distillation of Liquors." *Harper's Weekly* 11 (Dec. 7, 1867): 773.
Hartt, Rollin Lynde. "The Mountaineers: Our Own Lost Tribes." *Century Magazine* 95 (Jan. 1918): 395–404.
Hubbard, Leonidas, Jr. "The Moonshiner at Home." *Atlantic Monthly* 90 (Aug. 1902): 234–41.
Kephart, Horace. *Our Southern Highlanders*. New York: Outing, 1913.
———. "Roving with Kephart: The Sport of Still Hunting (Moonshine Stills)." *All Outdoors* (Sept. 1919): 490–91.

King, Edward. "The Great South: Among the Mountains of Western North Carolina." *Scribner's Monthly* 7 (March 1874): 513–44.

Lynde, Francis. "The Moonshiners of Fact." *Lippincott's Magazine* 57 (Jan. 1896): 66–76.

Miles, Emma B. *The Spirit of the Mountains.* 1905. Reprint. Knoxville: University of Tennessee Press, 1975.

Morley, Margaret W. *The Carolina Mountains.* Boston: Houghton Mifflin, 1913.

Peterson, Emil O. "A Glimpse of the Moonshiners." *Chautauquan* 26 (Nov. 1897): 178–82.

Pierson, Mrs. D. L. "The Mountaineers of Madison County, North Carolina." *Missionary Review of the World* (Nov. 1897): 821–31.

Price, Theodore H., and Richard Spillane. "The Commissioner of Internal Revenue as a Policeman." *Outlook* 120 (Nov. 27, 1918): 498, 503–5.

Smith, J. Wesley. *The Mountaineers; or, Bottled Sunshine for Blue Mondays.* Nashville: Publishing House of the Methodist Episcopal Church, South, 1902.

Spalding, Arthur W. *Men of the Mountains.* Nashville: Southern Publishing Association, [1915].

Thompson, Samuel H. *The Highlanders of the South.* New York: Eaton and Mains, 1910.

Warner, Charles D. "Comments on Kentucky." *Harper's New Monthly Magazine* 78 (Jan. 1889): 255–71.

———. "On Horseback." *Atlantic Monthly* 56 (July–Oct. 1885): 88–100, 194–207, 388–98, 540–54.

White, M. L. "A History of the Life of Amos Owens, the Noted Blockader, of Cherry Mountain, N.C." Shelby, N.C.: Cleveland Star Job Print, 1901.

Wilson, Samuel T. *The Southern Mountaineers.* New York: Literature Department, Presbyterian Home Missions, 1906.

Zeigler, Wilbur G., and Ben Grosscup. *The Heart of the Alleghenies; or, Western North Carolina.* . . . Raleigh: A. Williams and Co., [1883].

SECONDARY SOURCES

Arcury, Thomas A., and Julia D. Porter. "Household Composition and Early Industrial Transformation: Eastern Kentucky 1880–1910." Paper delivered at the Appalachian Studies Conference, West Virginia University, Mar. 1989.

———. "Households and Families in Eastern Kentucky in 1900." In *The Many Faces of Appalachia: Exploring a Region's Diversity*, edited by Sam Gray. Boone, N.C.: Appalachian Consortium Press, 1985.

Ayers, Edward. *Vengeance and Justice: Crime and Punishment in the 19th-Century American South.* New York: Oxford University Press, 1984.

Blakey, Leonard S. *The Sale of Liquor in the South: The History of the Development of a Normal Social Restraint in Southern Commonwealths.* Columbia University Studies in History, Economics, and Public Law, 51 no. 127. New York: Columbia University Press, 1912.

Carr, Jess. *The Second Oldest Profession: An Informal History of Moonshining in America.* Englewood Cliffs, N.J.: Prentice-Hall, 1972.

Carson, Gerald. *The Social History of Bourbon: An Unhurried Account of Our Star-Spangled American Drink.* New York: Dodd, Mead, 1963.

Cresswell, Stephen. "Resistance and Enforcement: The U.S. Department of Justice, 1870–1893." Ph.D. dissertation, University of Virginia, 1986.

Cummings, Homer, and Carl McFarland. *Federal Justice: Chapters in the History of Justice and the Federal Executive.* New York: Macmillan, 1937.

Dabney, Joseph Earl. *More Mountain Spirits.* Asheville, N.C.: Bright Mountain Books, 1980.

―――. *Mountain Spirits: A Chronicle of Corn Whiskey from King James' Ulster Plantation to America's Appalachians and the Moonshine Life.* New York: Scribners, 1974.

Davis, Robert S., "The Night Riders of Pickens County." *North Georgia Journal* 4 (June 1987): 22–24.

―――. "The North Georgia Moonshine War of 1876–1877." *North Georgia Journal* 6 (Autumn 1989): 42–45.

Downward, William L. *Dictionary of the History of the American Brewing and Distilling Industries.* Westport, Conn.: Greenwood, 1980.

Dunn, Durwood. *Cades Cove: The Life and Death of a Southern Appalachian Community, 1818–1937.* Knoxville: University of Tennessee Press, 1988.

Eller, Ronald D. *Miners, Millhands, and Mountaineers: Industrialization of the Appalachian South, 1880–1930.* Knoxville: University of Tennessee Press, 1982.

Gillette, William. *Retreat from Reconstruction, 1869–1879.* Baton Rouge: Louisiana State University Press, 1979.

Hamilton, Joseph G. de Roulhac. *North Carolina Since 1860.* Vol. 3 of *History of North Carolina.* Chicago: Lewis, 1919.

Hamm, Richard. "Origins of the Eighteenth Amendment: Prohibition in the Federal System, 1880–1920." Ph.D. dissertation, University of Virginia, 1987.

Holmes, William F. "Moonshiners and Whitecaps in Alabama, 1893." *Alabama Review* 24 (Jan. 1981): 31–49.

―――. "Moonshining and Collective Violence: Georgia, 1889–1895." *Journal of American History* 67 (Dec. 1980): 589–611.

_____. "Whitecapping, Agrarian Violence in Mississippi, 1902–1906." *Journal of Southern History* 25 (May 1969): 165–85.

Howe, Frederic C. *Taxation and Taxes in the United States under the Internal Revenue System, 1791–1895.* New York: T. Y. Crowell, 1896.

Hsuing, David. "The Social World of Upper East Tennessee, 1780–1835." Paper delivered at the Appalachian Studies Conference, West Virginia University, Mar. 1989.

Hu, Tun Yuan. *The Liquor Tax in the United States, 1791–1947: A History of the Internal Revenue Taxes Imposed on Distilled Spirits by the Federal Government.* New York: Graduate School of Business, Columbia University, 1950.

Hyman, Harold M. *A More Perfect Union: The Impact of the Civil War and Reconstruction on the Constitution.* New York: Knopf, 1973.

Inscoe, John C. *Mountain Masters, Slavery, and the Sectional Crisis in Western North Carolina.* Knoxville: University of Tennessee Press, 1989.

Isaac, Paul E. *Prohibition and Politics: Turbulent Decades in Tennessee, 1885–1920.* Knoxville: University of Tennessee Press, 1965.

Kaczorowski, Robert. *The Politics of Judicial Interpretation: The Federal Courts, Department of Justice and Civil Rights, 1866–1876.* New York: Oceana, 1985.

Keller, Morton. *Affairs of State: Public Life in Late Nineteenth-Century America.* Cambridge, Mass.: Harvard University Press, 1977.

Kellner, Esther. *Moonshine: Its History and Folklore.* Indianapolis, Ind.: Bobbs-Merrill, 1971.

Long, John D., ed. *The Republican Party: Its History, Principles, and Policies.* New York: M. W. Hazen, 1888.

McKinney, Gordon B. "Preindustrial Jackson County and Economic Development in Jackson County." Paper delivered at the Appalachian Studies Conference, West Virginia University, Mar. 1989.

_____. *Southern Mountain Republicans 1865–1900: Politics and the Appalachian Community.* Chapel Hill: University of North Carolina Press, 1978.

Marcus, Robert. *Grand Old Party: Political Structure in the Gilded Age, 1880–1896.* New York: Oxford University Press, 1971.

Mittleman, Amy H. "The Politics of Alcohol Production: The Liquor Industry and the Federal Government, 1862–1900." Ph.D. dissertation, Columbia University, 1986.

Montell, William L. *Killings: Folk Justice in the Upper South.* Lexington: University Press of Kentucky, 1986.

Nelson, William E. *The Roots of American Bureaucracy, 1830–1900.* Cambridge, Mass.: Harvard University Press, 1982.

Paludan, Phillip S. *Victims: A True Story of the Civil War*. Knoxville: University of Tennessee Press, 1981.

Pearson, C. C., and J. Edwin Hendricks. *Liquor and Anti-Liquor in Virginia, 1619–1919*. Durham, N.C.: Duke University Press, 1967.

Pudup, Mary Beth. "Beyond the Traditional Mountain Subculture: A New Look at Pre-industrial Appalachia." In *The Impact of Institutions in Appalachia*, edited by Jim Lloyd and Ann Campbell, pp. 114–27. Boone, N.C.: Appalachian Consortium Press, 1986.

———. "The Limits of Subsistence: Agriculture and Industry in Central Appalachia." Paper presented at the Appalachian Studies Conference, West Virginia University, Mar. 1989.

Rable, George C. *But There Was No Peace: The Role of Violence in the Politics of Reconstruction*. Athens: University of Georgia Press, 1984.

Raine, James W. *The Land of Saddlebags*. New York: Council of Women for Home Missions and Missionary Education Movement, 1924.

Rasmussen, Barbara. "Monroe County, W.Va.: Life and Work Where There Is No Coal." Paper presented at the Appalachian Studies Conference, West Virginia University, Mar. 1989.

Rice, Otis K. *The Hatfields and the McCoys*. Lexington: University Press of Kentucky, 1982.

Richardson, James D., comp. *Messages and Papers of the Presidents*. New York: Bureau of National Literature, [1917].

Schmeckebier, Laurence F., and Francis X. Eble. *The Bureau of Internal Revenue: Its History, Activities and Organization*. Baltimore: Johns Hopkins University Press, 1923.

Scomp, Henry D. *King Alcohol in the Realm of King Cotton: A History of the Liquor Traffic and of the Temperance Movement in Georgia from 1733 to 1887*. [Atlanta]: Blakely, 1888.

Sellers, James Benson. *The Prohibition Movement in Alabama, 1702 to 1943*. James Sprunt Studies in History and Political Science, vol. 26, no. 1. Chapel Hill: University of North Carolina Press, 1943.

Shadgett, Olive H. *The Republican Party in Georgia: From Reconstruction through 1900*. Athens: University of Georgia Press, 1964.

Shapiro, Henry D. *Appalachia on Our Mind: The Southern Mountains and Mountaineers in the American Consciousness, 1870–1920*. Chapel Hill: University of North Carolina Press, 1978.

Simpkins, Francis B. *Pitchfork Ben Tillman, South Carolinian*. Baton Rouge: Louisiana State University Press, 1944.

Skowronek, Stephen. *Building a New American State: The Expansion of National Administrative Capacities, 1877–1920.* New York: Cambridge University Press, 1982.

Trelease, Allen. *White Terror: The Ku Klux Klan Conspiracy and Southern Reconstruction.* New York: Harper Torchbooks, 1972.

Waller, Altina L. *Feud: Hatfields, McCoys, and Social Change in Appalachia, 1860–1900.* Chapel Hill: University of North Carolina Press, 1988.

Webb, Ross A. *Benjamin Helm Bristow, Border State Politician.* Lexington: University Press of Kentucky, 1969.

Wells, David A. *The Theory and Practice of Taxation.* New York: D. Appleton, 1900.

White, Leonard D. *The Republican Era: A Study in Administrative History.* New York: Macmillan, 1958.

Whitener, Daniel J. *Prohibition in North Carolina, 1715–1945.* James Sprunt Studies in History and Political Science, vol. 27, no. 1. Chapel Hill: University of North Carolina Press, 1946.

Williams, Cratis D. "The Southern Mountaineer in Fact and Fiction." Ph.D. dissertation, New York University, 1961.

Index